*Administrative Law
in a Global Era*

Administrative Law
in a Global Era

Alfred C. Aman, Jr.

CORNELL UNIVERSITY PRESS

Ithaca and London

First published 1992 by Cornell University Press.

International Standard Book Number 0-8014-2372-4
Library of Congress Catalog Card Number 91-33216

Printed in the United States of America

*Librarians: Library of Congress cataloging information
appears on the last page of the book.*

∞ The paper in this book meets the minimum requirements
of the American National Standard for Information Sciences—
Permanence of Paper for Printed Library Materials, ANSI Z39.48-1984.

TO MY PARENTS

Contents

Preface

The year 1935 was not a good one for the Roosevelt administration. The Supreme Court struck down as unconstitutional virtually all of the New Deal legislation that came before it.[1] May 27, 1935, was a particularly bad day: "the Court struck three times."[2]

In Louisville Joint Stock Land Bank v. Radford, the Court used the takings clause of the Fifth Amendment to declare unconstitutional certain amendments to bankruptcy law designed to help farm owners in distress.[3] Of even greater significance to the future of the New Deal was the Court's second decision in A.L.A. Schechter Poultry Corp. v. United States, a case declaring section 3 of the National Industrial Recovery Act to be an unconstitutional delegation of legislative power.[4] That act granted to the president broad authority to set fair codes of competition for various trades and industries with little or no congressional guidance. In striking down these provisions, the Court noted that "[e]xtraordinary conditions may call for extraordinary remedies,"[5] but "[e]xtraordinary conditions do not create or enlarge constitutional power."[6]

Schechter was a significant but not a wholly unexpected setback for the Roosevelt administration. The statute involved was experimental, and the record on which the Court decided the case was—from the government's point of view—weak. Moreover, the Court had only recently struck down another part of this same statute on the same grounds in Panama Refining Co. v. Ryan.

The third case decided that day was Humphrey's Executor v. United States.[7] The Court's decision was both surprising and significant. President Roosevelt was prevented from firing William E. Humphrey, a federal trade commissioner appointed by President Hoover, despite the clear suggestion by previous cases such as Myers v. United States[8] that the president had this power. But the Court's rationale was even more significant than the result it reached. Although at the time of the decision the case appeared to be a rebuke of President Roosevelt, it in fact helped establish a constitutional foundation for an approach to separation-of-powers issues, which enabled New Deal commissions to fit, albeit uneasily, within the tripartite structure of the Constitution.

In retrospect, May 27, 1935, was not nearly so bleak as it then seemed to New Deal supporters. The takings clause approach of Louisville Joint Stock Land Bank v. Radford never developed into a serious constitutional impediment to governmental regulation in general or the New Deal in particular.[9] The nondelegation doctrine, as it turned out, peaked on May 27, 1935. Although Panama and Schechter technically continue to be good law, the Court has yet to strike down another act of Congress on the grounds that it violates the nondelegation doctrine. The decision in Humphrey's Executor, ironically, became genuinely helpful through its bestowing of constitutional legitimacy on independent commissions.

The constitutional questions raised in these cases over fifty years ago were and remain fundamental. Yet, for nearly fifty years, such constitutional questions sparked little more than sporadic academic interest and had little practical effect at the federal level. They were not decided in so authoritative and clear a manner as to justify or explain why they eventually became, essentially, nonissues. Humphrey's Executor, in particular, was immune from serious judicial reexamination. Occasionally, a court might invoke the nondelegation doctrine ghosts of Panama or Schechter,[10] usually in dissent, and every now and then a significant takings-clause challenge would reappear.[11] In general, though, the expansive and expanding role that the New Deal charted for the federal government was eventually accepted, both legally and politically.

In the late 1970s and early 1980s the extent of this acceptance began to change. Constitutional issues relating to the structure and place of administrative agencies in our federal system were once again in the courts.[12] Even the delegation doctrine seemed to have new life.[13] More important, these constitutional challenges coincided with a general policy shift at the federal level toward deregulation and greater reliance on the market and market-based forms of regulation. The fundamental role of the federal government was once again at the center of our political debates. The Reagan administration's campaign rhetoric thus emphasized as one of its primary goals "getting government off of the backs of the people."

Along with this rhetoric, however, fundamental structural change also was envisioned. Speaking for the administration, then Attorney General Edwin Meese III, for example, saw deregulation at the federal level as an opportunity for state and local governments to reclaim some of the decision-making authority they had long ceded to the federal government. "By federalizing so many issues we have shifted the forum of dispute resolution away from our communities, away from our local governments and courts, to Washington. By creating an immense federal bureaucracy to regulate, promulgate—and, too often, obfuscate—with regard to federal legal matters, we have lost an ability to affix responsibility; and that is an ability central to the health and success of our democratic government."[14] To help accomplish this realignment or reallocation of governmental powers Attorney General Meese encouraged a return not only to federalism but to an interpretation of basic separation-of-powers principles he claimed were enunciated by the Founding Fathers:

> The men who wrote the Constitution were keenly concerned with accountability. They were too familiar with the dangers of despotic authority and the weaknesses of an unwritten constitution to leave the spelling out of authority and the accumulation of power to chance. The Founding Fathers could not anticipate all the problems with which government would eventually grapple, but they could do at least two things: they could count and they could divide. They created a federal government of *three* well-defined branches. And they carefully enumerated the powers and responsibilities of each. With a few exceptions, such as the veto and impeachment powers, they vested the legislative power *solely* in the Congress, the executive power *solely* in the President, and the judicial power *solely* in the courts.[15]

Such a constitutional approach had definite implications for both the structure and status of federal administrative agencies. It reopened many of the constitutional issues long thought settled since the New Deal, and it was also very much of a piece with the substantive deregulatory policies the Reagan administration sought to establish.

In this book I have addressed the question of why these particular constitutional and deregulatory issues reemerged in the late 1970s and 1980s with such force. To put it another way: What factors made relevant once again legal and policy arguments that had been essentially dormant for over fifty years? Certainly the commitment of the Reagan administration to deregulation was an important factor in the processes of change occurring in our public system of law. But at a deeper level, the need for regulatory reform corresponds to patterns of change that originate far beyond the politics of the Reagan administration. The return of many of the constitutional and policy issues so intensely debated during the early days of the New Deal is an indication of more than just the desire on the part of some to turn back the clock to a time when the federal government played a minimal role in the national economy. Rather, as I argue in this book, these issues reflect the emergence of a new era and the transition from a primarily national to a truly global economy typified by intense, worldwide competition in many key industries. Other signs of globalization are less tangible; they are to be found in the language, legal interpretations, and politics of legislators, executive officials, agency decision makers, and courts.

It is within this larger context of globalization and its effects on industry, language, politics, and law that I examine the processes of legal change during this new era. As with many of the regulatory reforms initiated and institutionalized during the New Deal, the president and the executive branch of the federal government do and have played a major role, especially when it comes to shaping the deregulatory reforms. A close look at the processes by which these reforms are institutionalized reveals, however, some important differences between the change in this era and change in other regulatory eras. Of primary importance now is the relative absence of sufficiently direct congressional involvement in shaping new regulatory and deregulatory structures. This relative absence of positive congressional response to change makes closer judicial scrutiny of executive deregulatory reforms both more understandable and necessary. More important, the role that the executive branch has played in initiating certain deregulatory reforms necessitates a different perspective on the relationship of the executive branch to administrative agencies, the legislature, and the courts. My primary focus therefore is on deregulatory contexts; within these contexts, I argue for the importance of judicial review as well as the limits of executive power to transform regulatory regimes in the absence of direct congressional involvement.

In analyzing these processes of deregulatory change, I take an approach to law that emphasizes its relation to the cultural, political, and economic contexts in which it is created. This book is not a cultural history of the regulatory eras it examines, but it does represent an attempt to understand law as only a part of larger societal forces and patterns of change. It is this broader perspective on law and its relationship to change that suggests the importance of transcending abstract debate over whether there should or should not be federal regulation. The contours of a new era—one shaped by global competition and the increasing importance of global-environmental issues, as well as by a growing awareness of the great disparities in wealth among the nations of the world—make clear that we need major regulatory reform in many areas, reform that goes beyond the regulation-deregulation debate. We must reassess our own domestic approaches to issues against a new global background. Ultimately, we will, as a global society, need new domestic and international regulatory structures and statutes for the era in which we now live.

This book has benefitted from the generous comments I have received from my colleagues over the years. I thank in particular Gregory Alexander, Don Brand, Paul Craig, Yvonne Cripps, Thomas Drennen, Cynthia Farina, Walter Gellhorn, Carol Greenhouse, Alfred E. Kahn, Peter Kountz, William Mayton, D. Marie Provine, E. F. Roberts, Victor Rosenblum, Peter Strauss, Robert Summers, and David A. Webster.

In addition, since a substantial portion of this book first appeared in a slightly different form in the *Cornell Law Review*, I also have had the benefit of the *Review*'s contribution to the editing and footnoting process. Eve Hill and Jennifer Carol of the class of 1983 were especially helpful throughout this project, as were all of their colleagues who worked on Volume 73. I also learned from the conversations I had with my administrative law students in and outside of class at the Cornell School of Law during the years the book was under way.

This book would not have been possible were it not for the careful, meticulous work of my secretary, Judy Oltz. Her good humor throughout this project and her high professional standards were invaluable to its successful completion. Leah Adams and Jan Turner also contributed as this manuscript was put into final form, and I am grateful for their help as well.

Finally, in the creation of any book there are always some people whose help means more than they will ever know. My wife, Carol

Greenhouse, was not only a careful reader of the manuscript but a source of encouragement and perspective as well. Most of all, her love and understanding throughout this project makes this a very special book for me.

The book is dedicated to my parents, who have supported all of my endeavors throughout my own eras of growth and discovery. The gifts of their love, encouragement, and faith have given me the strength, energy, and curiosity to create and pursue my goals.

ALFRED C. AMAN, JR.

Ithaca, New York

*Administrative Law
in a Global Era*

Introduction

When President Reagan took office in January 1981, one of his first official acts was to decontrol completely the price of domestic crude oil.[1] Because of the peculiarities of the Emergency Petroleum Allocation Act,[2] he had full authority to do so.[3] With a single stroke of the pen he brought to a close a complex, costly, presumably "temporary" governmental program that, in one form or another, had operated for more than eleven years.[4] The Reagan Revolution had begun.

Though the decontrol movement began earlier,[5] decontrol fever swept Washington during the Reagan administration. Washington law firms no longer appeared to be quite the growth industry they once were.[6] Pennsylvania Avenue was awash with resumes, particularly those of government lawyers made redundant in their respective regulatory agencies.[7] Government in the form of bureaucracy, command-control rules, and regulations was no longer viewed as an appropriate means of solving societal problems—and neither were the lawyers who had formerly promulgated, interpreted, and enforced these regulations. Government in and of itself was seen as the fundamental problem.[8] "Less government" became the prescribed solution for problems ranging from civil rights to the price of natural gas at the wellhead.[9] Most Reagan regulatory appointees adhered to this philosophy. Some publicly proclaimed that their primary goal was to close down the agencies they were chosen to head.[10]

But revolutions are not made in a day. The Reagan administration's

increased reliance on deregulation punctuated a long cultural, political, and legal process.[11] This book examines some of the continuities
and discontinuities of this process by differentiating among three distinct, yet overlapping, eras of administrative law: the New Deal–APA
era; the environmental era; and the global deregulatory era.[12] It argues
that, particularly in the global deregulatory era under President Reagan, not only did the substance of regulation change, but the processes
of change themselves began to change, giving rise to the doctrine of
presidential deference as well as to litigation attempting to redefine the
constitutional relationships among courts, agencies, the executive, and
Congress. These developments were often at odds with a deliberative
conception of administrative law, one that emphasizes incremental
legal change based on reasoned decision making that reflects regulatory policy goals enunciated or at least implied by Congress. The
conception of administrative law underlying deregulatory change often
differs, at least in degree, in three important ways from a more deliberative approach. It favors more abrupt change, initiated by the president and the executive branch rather than by Congress or the courts.
The new system also more easily rationalizes change in terms of political power and executive accountability rather than agency expertise or
reasoned agency deliberation.

Decontrol of a particular regulatory area—such as the decontrol of
petroleum in 1981—rarely results from just a stroke of the executive's
pen or from fiery speeches by agency heads. But clear-cut deregulatory
acts by the legislative branch also have been relatively rare,[13] in part,
perhaps, because of the increasingly persistent fragmentation of political views in Congress,[14] and its well-known penchant to muddle
along.[15] Reformers have thus had to work within the constraints of
statutory frameworks created during earlier regulatory eras, whose
prevailing premises regarding the role of government in general and
agencies in particular were very different. As a consequence, regulatory agencies themselves have accomplished much deregulatory law
reform. Paradoxically, agencies cast as villains in the political drama
that preceded deregulatory reforms became heroes in the actual process of decontrol.

Most decontrol at the agency level occurs within the very statutory
frameworks that gave rise to the offending regulations in the first place.
To survive judicial review of such reforms, agencies must often justify
the market values and results of deregulation as simply another form of
regulation.[16] Thus, the discourse of the regulatory past shapes the very

terms under which these reforms proceed. For this reason, I use the term *regulatory matrix* to refer to the form and substance of the regulatory context of agency deregulatory efforts. The matrix is not self-evident, but results from interpretations by agencies and courts in relation to specific deregulatory strategies. Whoever controls the interpretation of the matrix has a great deal of influence upon the future.

In this book I analyze the role that various interpreters of the regulatory matrix have played during the deregulatory process, focusing particularly on the courts and the president. I examine not only the context of administrative law within which these interpreters act but also the relation of constitutional law to administrative law. Constitutional law, as I will demonstrate, is a very important part of the context in which regulatory and deregulatory change occurs. The doctrines of constitutional law of an era influence the doctrines of administrative law, and both affect the relative ability of the three branches of government to influence agency change. I articulate some of the contextual and doctrinal links that exist between administrative and constitutional law. In so doing, I show how the overall structure of our public law is related to the relative power of courts, agencies, Congress, and the executive to interpret the regulatory matrix.

The increasing involvement of the executive branch in the day-to-day affairs of individual agencies—that is, the rise of the administrative presidency—has made the executive branch a particularly significant interpreter of the regulatory matrix in the global deregulatory era. The extent of the executive's involvement in deregulatory contexts in particular highlights the apparent unwillingness (or perhaps, inability) of Congress to effect significant legislative change on its own. This congressional inertia may be due to the fact that Congress and the president honestly differ on what regulatory reform strategies and approaches are appropriate. It also may be that the global era has not yet created the sense of urgency necessary to generate legislation as comprehensive as that of the New Deal and the environmental eras. It may simply be that Congress as an institution is naturally more local and regional than global in its outlook. For whatever reason, this lack of comprehensive congressional involvement has meant that the pressure for, and the initiation of, regulatory change—particularly deregulatory change—has come largely from the executive branch.

Article II of the Constitution provides broad authority for executive coordination of regulatory policy. Section 3 of Article II specifically requires the executive to "take care that the laws be faithfully executed." In many contexts, this provision justifies the executive branch's concern for efficiency and the minimization of regulatory costs, consistent with the goals of Congress. But in other contexts, particularly some deregulatory contexts, the substitution of market values for the regulatory values Congress once sought to further may very well go beyond the supervisory role that the executive branch is expected to play, inappropriately converting the "take care" clause of Article II into an unconstitutional source of executive legislation. Determining when the line between executive supervision and executive legislation is crossed is by no means easy, and it is not the purpose of this book to suggest that the executive branch does not or should not have considerable discretion in carrying out its duties. It is, however, important to attempt to differentiate between the use of regulatory and deregulatory approaches to further the goals of a regulatory framework created by Congress from those that seek to transform this structure into an essentially new set of legislative goals and directives. New eras require legislative definition as well as executive initiative and guidance.

As we shall see, the deregulatory dimensions of the global era have not been, to any great extent, defined by Congress, but rather by the agencies themselves. To understand the significance of the processes of deregulatory change instituted by these agencies in this era, we must compare them with the processes of change in earlier ones. I thus begin with the New Deal–APA era and the environmental era, examining in Chapter 1 their legal, regulatory, and political contexts by focusing on the role that courts played when reviewing agency and congressional change. Chapter 1 traces the development of the judicial review doctrines of *deference* and *hard look*. I argue that these doctrines were products of the very different conceptions of progress and change which typified these two eras. I also relate these doctrines of administrative law to the dominant doctrines of constitutional law of the times, and demonstrate how both Congress *and* the president played relatively important roles in defining the legal parameters of these two eras.[17]

Against this backdrop, in Chapter 2, I then examine deregulation, focusing primarily on judicial tendencies to apply New Deal deference when dealing with economic deregulation and, in some cases, the hard-look doctrine when facing health, safety, or environmental deregulation. This doctrinal choice has a significant impact on the degree to which courts can effect agency decontrol. For example, the application of the New Deal doctrine of deference to agency decisions in economic deregulatory contexts facilitates agency deregulation, but it also transforms the meaning of the relatively producer-oriented statutes of the 1930s by applying a consumer perspective that typifies the statutes (and the temper) of the 1970s.

In Chapter 3 I explore how judicial deference to agency deregulation in environmental, health, and safety contexts can, in effect, give distinctly consumer-oriented legislation a more production-oriented bias. Specifically, I examine the global era of administrative law by focusing on the emergence of the doctrine of presidential deference set forth in Chevron v. Natural Resources Defense Council, Inc.[18] This doctrine is placed within a global regulatory context and linked to the formalistic constitutional rhetoric that is also very much a part of the beginning of this era, with the implication that, particularly in the context of environmental deregulation, courts have a duty to supervise presidential policymaking far more closely than the Supreme Court's approach in *Chevron* suggests.

Chapter 4 concludes the book with a discussion of the relevance of emerging global environmental and developmental issues to domestic regulation and deregulation. The demands of this new era are likely to temper domestic regulatory discourses that emphasize only the issues of global competition and world trade. It is highly likely that a multidimensional global discourse is now developing that will shape both our international and domestic regulatory responses to a variety of concerns in the future and include the possibility of creating a new, *international* system of administrative law.

The heart of the book's approach to administrative law is its interpretive argument that specific changes in the conceptualization of regulatory problems and regulatory progress by courts, agencies, the executive and Congress, define important thresholds in the continuous development of administrative law. Thus the central arguments of this book focus on the role various interpreters of the regulatory matrix play in effecting change. The underlying premise of the book is that changes in the form of the belief in progress are embedded in historical context and consciousness, although an in-depth examination of these dimensions of cultural consciousness lies beyond this book's scope. The book relates changes in the overall structure of public law to changes in the substance of what agencies regulate. Each regulatory era is defined by the responsiveness of the regulatory matrix to its times, giving each era a certain coherence that transcends the legal system.

My goal in analyzing the doctrines of administrative and constitutional law as I do is to provide the seeds for a unitary theoretical approach to public law. As I hope to demonstrate, ultimately such an approach can account more fully for substantive differences and parallels among agencies and eras than can less contextualized approaches. It may also provide insight into the future of the politics of the reform of domestic and international regulatory law.

1

Agency Regulation and Judicial Review

In many ways, the best and the worst that can be said for substantive agency law is that it is disposable. An agency need not mobilize the legislature every time it wants to change its rules and regulations. It can experiment, and it can adapt to new circumstances in the industries with which it deals. This flexibility is particularly significant because the costs of the processes of agency change are usually much less than the cost of mobilizing 535 representatives to amend, pass, or repeal a law. This is particularly true in the absence of any dramatic crisis to place an issue on the legislative agenda and muster the necessary political support to pass it.

On the other hand, when agency law is too easily disposable, it breeds uncertainty and disrespect.[1] Law made by administrative agencies is born of politics and has political effects. To be legitimate, however, agency law must be reasonably stable and not immediately reflect every change in the political winds.[2] Major shifts in agency law or policy that appear to be at odds with an agency's enabling act can raise statutory and, on occasion, constitutional problems as well.[3] Our constitutional system assumes that major legal change should be costly. The nondelegation doctrine requires that Congress make fundamental policy decisions. If change is necessary and new legislative bargains must be struck, Congress, rather than an agency or any other single branch of government, should strike them.

These aspects of our legal system have profound implications for the processes by which change occurs and, more important for our purposes, for the willingness of courts either to facilitate, frustrate, or remain neutral in the face of change. In close cases, where the lines between policy and law often blur, or where the constitutional requirements of the nondelegation doctrine are virtually ignored, the spirit of an age and the concept of progress that it embodies have significant impact upon the way in which litigants and courts choose to understand and decide constitutional, statutory, and agency policy issues.

JUDICIAL DEFERENCE IN THE NEW DEAL–APA ERA

It has been argued that the costs of change during the New Deal–APA era were far too low.[4] Congress sidestepped difficult political issues by delegating broad legislative power to administrative agencies.[5] Those agencies, in turn, often were able to use and expand their power with relatively little scrutiny from the courts.[6] The Administrative Procedure Act (APA),[7] passed in 1946, provided the primary statutory basis for most judicial review of federal agency action well into the 1960s. In interpreting that act, particularly the provisions governing the scope of judicial review, courts usually read it in a way that resonated with the deferential judicial approaches they applied to constitutional questions involving essentially economic issues. In fact, agency interpretations of law rarely received the judicial scrutiny that the APA itself would allow.[8] The hands-off approach of the judiciary to the issues of constitutional delegation and statutory jurisdiction, coupled with the relatively deferential approach the APA required when reviewing agency fact-finding and policy decisions, facilitated agency change and the evolutionary growth of the administrative state.[9]

The consequences of these judicial approaches to agency action appear much clearer in retrospect. At the time, however, the judicial hands-off approach that typified this era was part of a much larger pattern of change, very much of a piece with the Court's willingness to let Congress decide how best to deal with the essentially economic issues spawned by the Great Depression.[10] It was all part of deferring to a Congress that had, in large part, passed the programs demanded by a strong and popular president. This was a marked departure from the Court's previous use of the doctrine of substantive due process, embodied in such early twentieth-century cases as Lochner v. New

York,[11] to declare unconstitutional economic legislation at the state and federal levels. With the demise of the doctrine of substantive due process still fresh in everyone's mind, judicial deference in the context of administrative law was an attempt to give the New Deal agencies created by Congress at least a chance to work.

The basis for this judicial deference is best understood by examining the larger political, regulatory, and constitutional context in which the courts were operating. That context included a supportive political consensus for an administrative state strengthened by at least four additional and interrelated factors: the constitutional doctrines of judicial restraint that had developed during and after the Roosevelt administration—doctrines which emphasized the primacy of the legislature and the need for judicial restraint; the perceived independence and expertise of the regulators involved and the relationship of that independence and expertise to the concept of representation that typified this era; the development of a regulatory discourse that was particularly conducive to agency expansion and judicial approval; and the essentially economic nature of the regulation involved and the implications of this for the relationship of the individual to the state, as articulated by the courts.

Constitutional and Administrative Law
in the New Deal–APA Era

The doctrine of judicial restraint, which typified the Supreme Court's approach to legislation after the decline of the doctrine of substantive due process set forth in *Lochner v. New York*,[12] facilitated social and economic experimentation. It had its intellectual beginnings in the depths of the Depression as a reaction to the substantive due-process approaches of the Supreme Court that had seriously obstructed New Deal experimental legislation. The context of these legislative experiments was perceived as extraordinary. As then Professor Felix Frankfurter wrote in 1933: "In this the fourth winter of our discontent it is no longer timorous or ignorant to believe that this depression has a significance very different from prior economic stresses in our national history. The more things change the more they remain the same is an epigram of comfortable cynicism. There are new periods in history and we are in the midst of one of them."[13] Frankfurter went on to comment that "in our scheme of government, readjustment to great social changes means juristic readjustment." This readjustment required, if not a sophisticated pluralistic conception of society, at least an understanding that, in the words of Justice Oliver Wendell Holmes, the Constitution "is made for people of fundamentally differing views, and the accident of our finding certain opinions natural and familiar or novel and even shocking ought not to conclude our judgment upon the question whether statutes embodying them conflict with the Constitution of the United States."[14] Yet Frankfurter did not see judicial restraint as reflecting a desire to have the Supreme Court play a weaker role than the other branches of government: "The Justices of the Supreme Court are arbiters of social policy because their duties make them so. For the words of the Constitution which invoke the legal judgment are usually so unrestrained by their intrinsic meaning or by their history or by prior decisions that they leave the individual Justice free, if indeed they do not compel him, to gather meaning not from reading the Constitution but from reading life."[15] But in "reading life" the Court "must have a seasoned understanding of affairs, the imagination to see the organic relations of society, [and] above all, the humility not to set up its own judgment against the conscientious efforts of those whose primary duty is to govern."[16] Indeed, Frankfurter was so convinced of the primacy of the legislature in its efforts to solve these societal problems that he went so far as to quote Ernst Freud for the proposition that " '[i]t is unlikely that a legislature will otherwise than through inadvertence violate the most obvious and cardinal dictates of justice; gross miscarriages of justice are probably less frequent in legislation than they are in the judicial determination of controversies.' "[17] If the profound problems of the Great Depression were to be solved, "the Supreme Court's attitude towards the most inclusive of all our problems, namely, how to subdue our anarchic competitive economy to reason" and "how to correct the disharmonies between production and consumption,"[18] needed to tolerate, and indeed encourage, experimentation in both federal and state legislatures.

Justice Harlan F. Stone's famous opinion in United States v. Carolene Products Co.[19] epitomized the Supreme Court's recognition of the primacy of legislative solutions for economic problems and the appropriateness of a restrained judicial role when reviewing such legislation. In that case, the Court rejected a substantive-due-process challenge to a federal statute that prohibited the shipment in interstate commerce of "filled milk" (a mixture of skimmed milk and non-milk fats). In so doing, it set forth guidelines defining essentially a rational-basis test for judging the constitutional validity of this kind of economic legislation.[20] The Court did not conclude that Congress was required to assert that "filled milk" might be injurious to public health in order to assure the constitutionality of the statute. Even if Congress did not directly address the reasons for its actions, "the existence of facts supporting the legislative judgment is to be presumed, for regulatory legislation affecting ordinary commercial transactions is not to be pronounced unconstitutional unless in the light of the facts made known or generally assumed it is of such a character as to preclude the assumption that it rests upon some rational basis within the knowledge and experience of the legislators."[21] In a footnote, however, the Court recognized that not all legislation should be treated in the same way. It established, in effect, a two-tiered approach to judicial review.[22] Under this approach a more stringent standard of judicial review was appropriate "when legislation appears on its face to be within a specific prohibition of the Constitution, such as those of the first ten amendments."[23]

In retrospect, one could easily interpret this two-tiered review as requiring closer judicial scrutiny when individual rights were at stake and less judicial scrutiny for economic concerns. In the context of the Great Depression, however, severe and widespread economic concerns were the most important issues of the day. Such collective problems were seen as demanding collective solutions. The perspective of the time was that of the group, not of individuals, that of the nation, not of individual states. Judicial restraint was encouraged because no more significant issue existed than the economic well-being of a nation characterized as one-third "ill-housed, ill-clad, ill-nourished."[24]

Conceptually speaking, the problem of the Depression resembled Justice Holmes's reasoning in Bi-Metallic Investment Co. v. State Board of Equalization.[25] In that case, property owners complained that certain changes in their tax assessments violated their due-process right to a hearing. Justice Holmes rejected their claim. The large number of people involved and the commonality of their plight made this an issue appropriate for resolution by the legislative branch. To the extent that economic rights common to many individuals were trampled by the majority, their recourse was to seek redress at the ballot box rather than in the courts.[26]

Underlying this constitutional approach was a pluralistic conception of the political marketplace that justified a kind of judicial laissez-faire. Though the economic market may have been moribund, the political market reacting to it was still vital. For similar conceptual reasons the courts refused to formulate issues in terms of individual economic rights. As Roosevelt's famous "court-packing speech" emphasized, the courts' earlier willingness to intervene to protect individual economic rights had "cast doubts on the ability of the elected Congress to protect us against catastrophe by meeting squarely our modern social and economic conditions."[27] The interventionist spirit of the courts had stood in the way of progress, now defined as economic prosperity for all, rather than the economic rights of individuals.

The doctrine of judicial restraint that emerged during this period was, therefore, very much a sympathetic part of a larger pattern of change—one that viewed the economic legislation produced through legislative experimentation as a form of progress necessary to extricate a substantial portion of the nation from the grips of poverty and despair. In this sense, judicial deference to the legislature was really a kind of judicial activism.

In most political movements, and this was particularly true of the New Deal, distinctions among various kinds of legislative action and among the constitutional provisions that apply to these actions often are blurred and distorted. Courts do not compartmentalize as much as the analytical frameworks implied by certain statutory provisions or clauses of the Constitution might or should imply. The spirit of an age has a way of working its way into all the cases with which a court deals. Thus, the liberal, expansive interpretation the New Deal Court began to give the commerce clause and the legislative power it authorized was reflected in its approach to other clauses of the Constitution as well. It is perhaps no surprise that the judicial use of the delegation doctrine as a means of checking legislative power reached its high point on May 27, 1935, when the Court decided Schechter Poultry Corp. v. United States.[28] Similarly, neither the takings clause,[29] the Tenth Amendment,[30] nor the contracts clause[31] ever seriously impeded the regulatory approaches advocated after the New Deal. The courts no longer perceived economic rights as individual constitutional rights, but with an entire nation battling to free itself from the grips of the Depression, rather as collective, group rights.[32] The issues could be formulated in a way that did not pit individuals against the government so as to raise close constitutional scrutiny, but rather pitted the government against the chaos of the market.

Economic legislation occupied a central place in the New Deal.[33] Statutes to help infant industries such as airlines and communications, to correct the problems caused by natural monopolies such as interstate natural gas pipelines, and to ensure fairness in securities markets and equal bargaining power in labor markets all aimed at creating a market economy that worked.[34] These statutes, and the reforms they embodied, were fundamentally capitalist in their orientation and design.[35] They did not seek to nationalize industries; nor did they, on the other hand, permit a voluntary, corporatist approach to regulation.[36] Rather, the New Deal sought to forge a partnership between government and business on a middle regulatory ground. Given that reviving the economy was one of the New Deal's main goals, the importance of reviving old businesses and enabling new businesses and industries to succeed cannot be overestimated.[37]

The Nature of the Agencies

Many of the agencies established to address social issues were executive in nature.[38] Most of those dealing with economic matters, however, were set up as independent commissions.[39] In so doing, New Deal reformers looked to business and the corporate structure, rather than to government, for organizational models for a constitutional approach to separation-of-powers issues that would facilitate their vision of governance and the implementation of their economic regulatory reforms.[40] James Landis, an important New Deal architect, explained this position as follows: "[W]hen government concerns itself with the stability of an industry it is only intelligent realism for it to follow the industrial rather than the political analogue. It vests the necessary powers with the administrative authority it creates, not too greatly concerned with the extent to which such action does violence to the traditional tripartite theory of governmental organization."[41]

Thus, in stark contrast to Attorney General Meese, who fifty years later advocated a formalistic separation-of-powers approach to such issues, Landis formulated a more pragmatic constitutional approach conducive to the creation of the relatively independent and efficient administrative agencies he envisioned. In Landis's view, Congress was to be the engine of change and the font of new ideas, and the administrative agencies were to be its primary front-line agents, organized in a manner that maximized their flexibility and minimized the cost of change.

The Supreme Court perhaps inadvertently established the constitutional basis for this more fluid approach to separation-of-powers issues with Justice George Sutherland's opinion in Humphrey's Executor v.

United States.[42] That case was, ironically, a setback to the Roosevelt administration initially, because it refused to grant the president the power to remove William E. Humphrey from the Federal Trade Commission on the basis of serious policy differences between Humphrey and the chief executive.[43] In rejecting Roosevelt's bid to remove Humphrey for essentially political reasons, the Court took an analytical approach that distinguished purely executive officers from federal trade commissioners such as Humphrey who occupied "no place in the executive department" and did not exercise any "part of the executive power vested by the Constitution in the President."[44] Though federal trade commissioners did investigate and report antitrust violations, the Court, however, concluded that to the extent the commissioner "exercises any executive function—as distinguished from executive power in the constitutional sense—[the officer] does so in the discharge and effectuation of . . . quasi-legislative or quasi-judicial powers, as [an officer of] an agency of the legislative or judicial departments of the government."[45]

This opinion came as a shock to the Roosevelt administration. Precedents such as Myers v. United States[46] implied strongly that the president's duty to "faithfully execute the laws" gave him the power to remove such officials at will. Commenting on this case many years later, Justice Robert H. Jackson aptly summarized its impact at the time it was decided:

> [W]hat the court had before declared to be a constitutional duty of the President had become in Mr. Roosevelt a constitutional offense. Small wonder that the decision became a political instrument. Those who saw executive dictatorship just around the corner had their fears confirmed: the President could be restrained only by the Court. Those who thought the ghost of dictatorship wore judicial robes had their fears, too, confirmed: the Court was applying to President Roosevelt rules different from those it had applied to his predecessors.[47]

In retrospect, one could now add that *Humphrey's Executor* justified the fears of those who foresaw a dramatic expansion of the administrative state. Justice Sutherland's opinion set forth an approach to separation-of-powers issues that made the "headless fourth branch" constitutionally possible. The distinction between executive power and executive functions, enabled federal trade commissioners to retain a certain amount of political independence while assuring the constitutional integrity of an agency that combined executive, legislative, and judicial functions.

What James Landis referred to as the "intelligent realism" of such an administrative structure now had a constitutional foundation.[48] The congressional use of broad delegation clauses and the creation of agency structures that combined executive, legislative, and judicial powers significantly lowered the cost of change. Agencies did not have to obtain congressional approval before adapting their policies to novel factual situations. They could solve problems as they arose, in the process often extending their powers to fulfill their regulatory missions. By delegating such combined powers, Congress intended to foster regulatory experimentation. The agencies were not just to carry out specific duties, but also to act as overall regulators, responding to new situations with presumably creative expert decisions. The relative independence from direct political control that the Supreme Court authorized in *Humphrey's Executor*, coupled with the presumed expertise of agency personnel, ultimately became important sources of legitimacy for agency power, particularly as the crisis mentality of the Great Depression gave way to relative complacency engendered by the prosperity of the period after World War II.

Just as it would be wrong to overemphasize the radical nature of New Deal regulatory approaches, it would also be wrong to underestimate the importance of the relationship of agency independence and expertise to the underlying conceptions of legislative representation and democratic theory. New Deal regulatory agencies are sometimes characterized in a way that juxtaposes their independence with political control and their expertise with political judgments.[49] Yet, underlying the willingness to view employees of agencies as independent experts is the fact that they are the agents of elected representatives. According to one theory of democracy, elected representatives themselves can be viewed as experts, wiser and more knowledgeable about social and economic affairs than the average voter.[50] When legislative representatives themselves are seen as experts, their expertise conventionally is associated with their agents. Judicial development of the doctrine of legislative primacy was thus quite sympathetic to a view that emphasized the legislature's need to designate its own independent agents. The emphasis on the expertise and independence of agency personnel is thus but an extension of a larger conception of representation.

This approach was of a piece with the underlying political theory of the New Deal and the view of democracy that favored the primacy of legislative experimentation and presidential power. It willingly delegated enormous political power to groups of experts, both elected and unelected,[51] representing what B. R. Barber has labeled "thin democracy."[52] Thin democracy is democracy based on large delegations of power to representatives with only limited political participation in the day-to-day operations of government by the citizenry at large. Indeed, in a thin democracy, the foremost, and virtually only, kind of participation is the vote. Furthermore, in a thin democracy it is a short step from congressional representation to agency expertise. Under this approach, agencies were the agents of Congress and if Congress delegated their tasks to them, courts assumed it was for a good reason: Congress believed, in its expert judgement, that such delegation was the best way to get a very important job done.[53]

This willingness to defer to "experts" after the Great Depression was an understandable, very American approach to complex problems.[54] The thin democracy of expertise represented a pragmatic attempt to find workable solutions. Although New Deal legislation never represented a coherent, integrated means of achieving the era's common goals,[55] deference to the legislature and its agents contributed to a common search for effective governance. In this sense, the New Deal conception of the Constitution was, particularly as seen by reviewing courts, intensely political. It emphasized the primacy of legislative political processes, of which the agencies, at least when they were first created, were obvious extensions. It was but an incremental step from Congress making law to agencies implementing the details of Congress's legislative vision.

The New Deal, however, did not squelch the desire for individual economic rights. The fear and dislike of government intervention in general, and agencies in particular, persisted. These different philosophical views of government colored the debates over the Administrative Procedure Act.[56] From its inception the act represented, as Justice Jackson observed, "a long period of study and strife," and ultimately, upon its passage, "a formula upon which opposing social and political forces have come to rest."[57] The act provided elaborate administrative procedures for formal adjudication and formal rulemaking proceedings. While its provisions for informal rulemaking were simple, direct, and straightforward, most of the important issues of the day, including policy questions, were decided in adjudicatory proceedings. Agency ratemaking and licensing functions, for example, were almost always exercised in an adjudicatory manner, and agency policy was more often than not also formulated in adjudicatory contexts.[58]

The impact of this penchant for deference to legislative solutions had an impact on the resolution of various nonconstitutional issues as well.

This was apparent in the courts' approach to the scope of judicial review of agency action, and most particularly, the treatment of questions of law. Although section 706 of the APA would allow a *de novo* judicial role when dealing with questions of law, the courts developed elaborate doctrines of deference not only to agency policy decisions, but also to agency law making and interpretation that they continued to apply after passage of the APA.[59] This did not mean that courts would always defer to any and all agency interpretations of law.[60] Courts, however, generally used the language of deference, particularly when upholding or extending agency jurisdiction.[61] When it came to carrying out the will of Congress, courts equated progress with agency experimentation, change, and, ultimately, growth.[62] The legal discourse used to justify such extensions of agency power relied upon broad notions of congressional intent and was usually cast in a legal rhetoric particularly familiar to the common-law minded judges who wrote these opinions.[63]

Regulatory Discourse and Regulatory Growth

As New Deal agencies dealt with regulatory issues, they inevitably faced questions that legislators did not, and often could not, foresee. In many instances, their proposed solutions extended their substantive jurisdictional mandates and thus, their substantive regulatory powers. When the actions of the various agencies were challenged in court, the cases generated a legal discourse that made it relatively easy for essentially common-law minded judges to defer to agency decisions.

Agencies typically argued that Congress had authorized them to regulate X and Y, but it was impossible to do that effectively unless they also regulated Z. Given the broad language of most New Deal statutes,[64] the phrase in question in a case often was not decisive. Legislative histories were similarly inconclusive.[65] Courts tended to resolve all doubts in favor of extended agency jurisdiction.[66]

Traditional judicial discourse, with its penchant for precedent, reasoning by analogy, and reliance upon the past, is essentially conservative.[67] It proceeds "backwards from a receding past into an unknown future."[68] The legal arguments most likely to secure judicial approval of agency change, therefore, referred to the past and advocated the kind of gradualism that common-law judges understand best. Such arguments usually result in incremental, rather than radical, change that adapts easily to a preexisting regulatory scheme. As applied during the

New Deal–APA era, this kind of reasoning not only reinforced a sense of regulatory progress, but it also encouraged an essentially monolithic regulatory approach to the resolution of new problems. For example, if competition from trucks undermined the Interstate Commerce Commission rates for railroads, the solution was to extend the commission's power to regulate trucking, rather than to consider seriously what role, if any, competition should play.[69] Given that the market often undercuts the explicit and implicit regulatory goals of the statutes involved, courts, not surprisingly, concluded that congressional intent required solutions involving regulatory expansion.

Perhaps the best example of this logic, the regulatory discourse that it generated, and the agency power that the court ultimately created and extended to the Federal Power Commission can be found in Phillips Petroleum Co. v. Wisconsin. Phillips Petroleum Company was a large, integrated oil company that produced, gathered, and sold natural gas. It did not sell gas in interstate commerce nor was it affiliated with any interstate natural gas pipeline company. Rather, Phillips sold natural gas to interstate pipeline companies, which resold the gas to consumers and local distributing companies. The Federal Power Commission investigated Phillips to determine whether Phillips was a "natural gas company" within the commission's jurisdiction under the Natural Gas Act,[70] and if so, whether its rates were reasonable and just.[71] It concluded that Phillips was not such a company and ceased its inquiry at that point. The United States Court of Appeals for the District of Columbia Circuit, however, reversed the commission's decision,[72] and the Supreme Court affirmed.[73]

The specific provisions of the Natural Gas Act that concerned the Court were a jurisdictional provision[74] and a provision defining a natural gas company.[75] The jurisdictional provision contained an exemption clause excluding from the Federal Power Commission's authority the production and gathering of natural gas. The definitional provision limited the FPC's authority to those companies transporting gas in interstate commerce or selling gas in interstate commerce for resale.[76]

The majority of the Supreme Court disagreed with the commission's conclusion that it had no jurisdiction and would not defer to the agency's interpretation of its own statute. It would, however, defer to the proposition that the agency should have the power necessary to carry out the tasks that Congress had delegated. Thus the Court reasoned that because production and gathering end before sales begin and because the congressional intent behind the Natural Gas Act was to give the commission jurisdiction over all wholesale transfers of natural gas in interstate commerce, Phillips was a natural gas company as defined by the act.[77] Thus, the commission had jurisdiction to regulate its rates.[78] As the Court pointed out, "[p]rotection of consumers against exploitation at the hands of natural-gas companies was the primary aim of the Natural Gas Act."[79] The Court believed an extension of commission power was necessary to help ensure that ultimate goal: "Regulation of the sales in interstate commerce for resale made by a so-called independent natural-gas producer is not essentially different from regulation of such sales when made by an affiliate of an interstate pipeline company. In both cases, the rates charged may have a direct and substantial effect on the price paid by the ultimate consumers."[80] By this reasoning, the Court refused to weaken this protection for consumers by engaging in what it felt would be "a strained interpretation of the existing statutory language."[81]

The Court's opinion in *Phillips* is indicative not only of the impact of a deferential, pro-regulatory substantive approach, but also of the regulatory momentum that builds up when one aspect of an industry is regulated and another is not. The Natural Gas Act clearly authorized regulation of the monopolistic and monopsonistic practices of interstate natural gas pipeline owners.[82] This, however, did not necessarily solve all natural gas pricing problems. It had become increasingly difficult to regulate those pipelines which also produced their own natural gas because such owners could simply charge themselves a higher price and then pass that price on to consumers.

In Interstate Natural Gas Co. v. FPC,[83] decided seven years before *Phillips*, the Supreme Court had authorized the Federal Power Commission to regulate the production price of such producers, holding that the commission's rate-making jurisdiction extended to natural gas producers affiliated with interstate pipelines. The Court then carefully distinguished this case from one involving wholly independent producers. Yet the Court in *Phillips* took that next step and extended jurisdiction to independent producers.[84] In so doing, it read the Natural Gas Act broadly: "[W]e believe that the legislative history indicates a congressional intent to give the Commission jurisdiction over the rates of all wholesales of natural gas in interstate commerce, whether by a pipeline company or not and whether occurring before, during, or after transmission by an interstate pipeline company."[85] The Court thus resolved ambiguous legislative language in favor of increased agency power, with a result that Congress probably could not have effected politically. In fact, nearly forty years passed before Congress could even partially undo the Court's decision.[86]

This is not to imply that the deferential, pro-regulatory approach of the courts resulted in affirmance when there was, in fact, no legal basis for the agency decision under review. Rather, in close cases, courts were more often than not, very receptive to arguments that extended agency power and jurisdiction, particularly when such extension was clearly necessary to carry out the will of Congress, *broadly construed.* And courts usually read agency enabling statutes broadly—as if they were remedial in nature. These jurisdictional cases allowed the evolution of the regulatory process to continue without frequent resort to Congress, for as the courts viewed it, enabling statutes implied congressional intent to give the agencies whatever authority necessary to get the job done. As long as the steps the agencies sought to take were gradual and incremental and reasonably tied to the fundamental goals prescribed in the statutes, thus falling within the common-law form of discourse, courts were generally very willing to approve specific agency actions or extensions of agency authority.

A Producer Perspective

The extension of substantive agency power benefitted not only from the common-law discourse to which it was amenable, but also from the economic substance of the problems with which many New Deal enabling statutes dealt.[87] These independent agencies and bureaus were affirmative, comprehensive attempts to correct the flaws of a chaotic market[88] and were established by Congress in an attempt to lift the country out of the Great Depression.[89]

Although consumers were expected to benefit from New Deal legislation,[90] New Deal statutes and the regulatory regimes they established were largely producer or production-oriented. The National Industrial Recovery Act[91] ambitiously sought to achieve comprehensive industrial planning. The Agricultural Adjustment Act[92] provided substantial subsidies to farmers. The Federal Power Commission,[93] the Federal Communications Commission,[94] and the Civil Aeronautics Board[95] were designed to regulate conflicts among producers, broadcasters, and members of the industry in general as well as their inherent tendencies to compete destructively. The Federal Power Commission, for example, dealt with conflicts among producers, transporters, and consumers of natural gas.[96] Such legislation did not disregard consumers, *per se*, but rather by focusing on producers sought to create and maintain an orderly market, from which both producers *and* consumers would benefit.

Regulatory regimes generated and were generated by issues that usually arose in the economic conflicts among the various regulated entities.[97] In resolving the reasonableness of rates for natural gas sold in interstate commerce or the appropriate routes and fares for a particular airline, agencies usually applied an economic perspective common to all of the regulated entities. The wealth-distribution issues at stake could be accommodated within that common regulatory perspective. A primary statutory goal, in many instances, was the mitigation of the conflict among various segments of the business community. It is little wonder then that a common perspective would arise between agencies and the regulated.[98]

Agencies themselves were thought to represent the public interest and, thus, the general citizenry as well as the regulated. More important, the overall thrust of the legislation and regulation involved was not consumer oriented as we understand that concept today.[99] The regulatory initiatives of the New Deal conceived of the industries to be regulated less as potential perpetrators of harm than as potential victims of the chaotic market forces that the legislation sought to control. Ensuring the continued existence and viability of these industries was an important goal of much of the New Deal's economic regulatory legislation. If the market could be made to work, if unnecessary labor strife could be eliminated, if rates truly approximated what they would be in a smoothly functioning market, producers, consumers, and, indeed, society itself would be better off. This view generated a group perspective on economic problems that maintained traditional conceptions of the individual but held administrative law and administrative agencies to be the means to protect that individual from the market.

Individualism and administrative law were thus related in the broad New Deal regulatory goals. In the pre–New Deal, laissez-faire era, the primary function of administrative law was to protect the individual from the government.[100] Administrative law thus developed along the guidelines of what some commentators have called "red light" theories of how to limit the role of government.[101] The New Deal, however, sought to protect individuals and firms from the faltering markets of the Great Depression and from market failures such as natural monopolies, which prevented individuals from acting freely. Since governmental correction of these market failures was seen as enabling individuals to act more freely in their own self-interest, the role of administrative law shifted from protection of the individual from the government to protection of the individual from the market. This role required "green light" theories of administrative law, theories of how to enable government to carry out its statutory tasks.[102] The shift in the role of administrative law generated a corresponding shift in the judiciary. Judicial deference to agency decision making in economic matters was one such green light approach to the New Deal.

The clear need for governmental action in the face of devastating market failure did not, however, result in clear-cut, unambiguous statutes. There were no "solutions" to such enormous economic problems. Experimentation by Congress and agencies offered the most promising approach to the resolution of the economic disaster of the Great Depression. Legislative experimentation resulted in open-ended, discretionary grants of legislative power to agencies, which were expected to develop new approaches to new issues on a day-to-day basis.[103] And perhaps because of the experimental nature of the New Deal, those doing this day-to-day administrative work were regarded as experts who were, for the most part, above the political fray.[104]

One of the basic linchpins of the New Deal was the independent regulatory commission, with its ability to legitimize congressional agents of reform with the imprimatur of independence.[105] Because of this independence, courts viewed the results of agency efforts not as the self-serving output of political appointees, but as the considered opinion of experts. Indeed, they were Congress's experts and what they produced was a regulatory process whose rationality courts simply assumed.[106] Inherent in the very breadth and scope of the statutes passed by Congress was the belief that wide discretion was necessary and justified. Thus, courts viewed deference to the agencies as, in effect, deference to Congress.

The judicial-review provisions of the Administrative Procedure Act[107] do not mandate such a deferential approach. Yet judicial interpretation of these provisions resembled the deference doctrines then developing in constitutional law.[108] On matters of policy, the courts equated administrators with legislators.[109] On matters pertaining to the application of law, courts allowed administrators the interpretive discretion normally reserved to judges.[110] Hand in hand with the deferential approach to most administrative decision making was an equally deferential attitude to legislation typified by the resolution of the constitutional questions raised by such cases as Railway Express Agency v. New York, Day-Brite Lighting v. Missouri, and Williamson v. Lee Optical. These cases applied a rational-basis approach to the judicial review of legislation, which made judicial approval virtually automatic. As Edward Shils has argued, persons are accorded deference corresponding to the degree to which they serve the central value systems of the society.[111] The same could be said of agencies in the New Deal–APA era. Therefore, at least while the effects of the Depression were foremost in the collective political consciousness, courts were usually very willing to defer to the various agencies as they attempted to deal with the manifestations of those effects.

The political winners of an era inevitably attempt to institutionalize, if not constitutionalize, their view of progress. But as the New Deal approach to economic problems became institutionalized and the relative prosperity of the postwar years became a reality, the administrative agencies created in the New Deal era dealt less and less directly with the burning issues of the day. As they became less visible, they became their own centers of power rather than the agents of elected representatives.[112] The more remote they grew, the less flexible and responsive they became. Soon, these agencies were the trapped by their reliance on precedent, their penchant for incremental change, and their need to adhere to a certain type of legal logic. Choices made in the past limited options in the future. As these agencies matured, they became more easily neutralized if not captured by the interests they were supposed to regulate.[113]

New Deal agencies also became increasingly more judicialized in their approaches to issues and less capable of significant innovation. Agencies and their law-making processes tended to become ends in themselves rather than the means of solving pressing societal problems. Congress's failure to assert itself in the face of anything less than total crisis empowered the agencies to pursue their own goals with relative impunity. The accretions of agency law that developed made change difficult, but also insulated agencies from any pressures to change. Their respective regulatory matrices became increasingly entrenched.

Administrative agencies thus institutionalized the New Deal and its regulatory approach to problem solving. They did not, however, constitutionalize this approach, in the sense that they became legally permanent. Theoretically, agency mandates can be changed or revoked overnight by new legislation. They were and remain the creatures of the legislature and the courts' expansive approach to such constitutional issues as delegation, the scope of the commerce clause, and the demise of substantive due process. Judicial review of agency decisions including agency fact-finding, policymaking, and even lawmaking functions reflected this type of judicial deference to legislative regulatory solutions. The doctrines of judicial deference that developed in constitutional law in the aftermath of the Great Depression and World War II, along with the legal and political theories that justified them, provided an influential backdrop for judicial interpretations of the Administrative Procedure Act[114] for at least the next fifteen to twenty years.

THE HARD-LOOK APPROACH AND JUDICIAL ACTIVISM

Just as judicial deference to agency decision making was the hallmark of the New Deal–APA era, more overt judicial activism characterized the environmental era that followed. If Congress's powers had been stretched to the constitutional breaking point by the broad delegation clauses that characterized New Deal legislation, the power used by federal courts to ensure that the various agencies conformed to environmental values raised new institutional concerns. Judicial review of agency environmental decisions highlighted the differences between the absolutist legal requirements of environmental legislation and the costs of economic growth. Indeed, the environmental constraints on economic growth moved to the center of legislative and judicial attention during the environmental era. The definition of progress had changed. Growth now had to accord with an emerging set of environmental values and a more collective approach to risk and risk assessment. As one court put it, "[s]everal recently enacted statutes attest to the commitment of the Government to control, at long last, the destructive engine of material 'progress.'"[115]

The new environmental statutes often took an absolutist approach to such problems as air and water pollution. These statutes also applied across industry lines and often dealt with issues of great scientific complexity.[116] Moreover, these issues were interdisciplinary in character and raised a variety of related legal, social, economic, and ethical questions. Proposed solutions to such questions, more often than not, demanded interdisciplinary and often intergovernmental approaches, for the substantive problems that characterized the environmental era spilled over state and national boundaries. The "common-pool" aspects of the market failure that underlie the need for environmental regulation encouraged a concept of the relation of the individual to society that I will refer to as interdependent individualism. An interdependent concept of individuals recognized more fully that society's overall interest in clean air or clean water cannot be equated with the aggregate of individuals pursuing their own atomistic self-interests. Indeed, it was an atomistic conception of individual freedom that had created many environmental problems in the first place. An interdependent concept of individualism resonated with and was reinforced by the interdependent and interdisciplinary conceptions of both the problems and the solutions that characterize the environmental era. Accordingly, a new understanding of progress was needed to deal with such new levels of interconnectedness.

The new environmental legislation also reflected a distinct consumer perspective.[117] The statutes interjected environmental values into the relationships between the regulated and the regulators. More often than not, producers of goods were now seen in a new light—as producers of harm.[118] Those who sought to benefit from these environmental statutes had an even more compelling interest in the outcome than in the economic benefits of a properly functioning market. They were likely to be the personal victims of pollution or toxic substances. Economic conflicts of interest among the regulated gave way to more fundamental conflicts of value that did not translate as easily into a common economic discourse. Unlike a determination of the cost of capital in a rate proceeding, economic approaches to the calculation of the value of a human life met with not only technical concerns, but with concerns based on radically different value systems. It was, thus, not at all obvious how a legislature or an agency could calculate the cost of a human life or of irrevocable damage to the environment. The administrative process thus became more complex and contentious as it sought to accommodate a number of new, broadly defined, and often conflicting environmental interests, values, and groups.[119]

Given the interdependent perspectives involved in the nature of the regulatory problems presented and in the congressional and administrative solutions suggested, agency rationalizations for policy change inevitably became more complicated.[120] Because environmental, health, and safety questions now cut across industry lines, single-mission and single-industry commissions waned, as did regulatory issues with reasonably specific economic answers. Setting rates was relatively easy compared with assessing the overall health, safety, and environmental effects of various manufacturing processes. The scientific uncertainty that accompanied these assessments often triggered a more holistic judicial conception of the regulatory problems involved. This is not to say that courts abandoned New Deal deference in all environmental cases. But the nature of these issues did require more explanation of more interrelated factors even when courts took a deferential rational basis approach.[121] Furthermore, the life-and-death nature of the issues at stake often encouraged courts to supervise agency policymaking much more closely than did the economic questions involved in the New Deal Era. More important, statutes such as the National Environmental Policy Act as well as the more complicated hybrid-rulemaking procedures set forth in most of the health, safety, and environmental statutes passed during this era provided the legal basis for more exacting judicial scrutiny of agency explanations of whether and how they chose to incorporate environmental values into their decision making. Judicial control grew. Initially, at least, some courts played this role most willingly. Judge J. Skelly Wright wrote in his opinion in Calvert Cliffs' Coordinating Comm. v. Atomic Energy Comm'n: "[I]t remains to be seen whether the promise of this legislation will become a reality. Therein lies the judicial role."[122]

The courts had much new legislative and agency material with which to work. Between 1966 and 1981, the administrative bureaucracy grew considerably, both in terms of the numbers of new laws and agencies involved[123] and the amount of new regulation these agencies produced.[124] Both aspects of this growth created a need for greater supervision of the bureaucracy. The constitutional context in which this new regulation was being created, its nature as well as the kinds of market failures with which it dealt, the value issues it raised, and the more interdependent conceptualization of the individual's relationship to the state and to other individuals that it encouraged all combined to create a new value-laden regulatory discourse. Within this context the courts developed more activist doctrines of administrative law to use when reviewing substantive agency action. These innovations in the doctrine of administrative law tended to have distinct constitutional overtones.

Constitutional and Administrative Law in the Environmental Era

The primacy of the legislature and the rational-basis test of the New Deal era helped shape the constitutional context within which the doctrines of deference to pro-regulatory administrative law developed. Similarly, the civil rights cases following Brown v. Board of Education[125] helped create the climate of judicial activism that encouraged courts to scrutinize agency decisions closely in the environmental era. When governmental action was taken that conflicted with fundamental constitutional rights of individuals or significantly and adversely affected a discrete and insular minority, such as a racial minority, the courts now required compelling reasons to justify such action.[126] In short, the constitutional law that developed and flourished during the environmental era had courts playing a major role as the guardians of individual rights. Rather than economic legislation, the more stringent standards of judicial review referred to in Justice Stone's footnote to United States v. Carolene Products Co. became the focus of constitutional law.[127]

This constitutional hard-look approach was reflected in the doctrines of administrative law developing in this period. It is ironic that, in a regulatory era characterized largely by its interdependence and complexity, a constitutional focus on individual rights would emerge in administrative law; yet, the most significant aspect of the relationship between administrative and constitutional law during this period was the increasing use in administrative law of an approach to the supervision of agency rationality that, at times, resembled the judicial strict scrutiny prevalent in constitutional contexts. This may be due to the similarities between certain constitutional rights and the legislature's and courts' conceptualization of environmental, health, and safety issues. Or it may be that the courts tended to look more closely at certain environmental decisions and this compelled them to seek judicial justifications that, perhaps, emphasized these similarities.

The Nature of the Issues—Absolutism

Many of the new administrative statutes and agencies that came into being in the early 1970s treated health, safety, and environmental issues in absolutist terms.[128] Air was clean or dirty; water clean or polluted. Questions of degree were not entertained. Evil had been identified, and Congress quickly passed statutes to eradicate it.[129] This approach may have been necessary to generate the political support required to mobilize Congress, but absolutism often resulted in legislation that ignored the importance of economics in general and the cost of regulation in particular.[130] Even statutes that mandated the regulation of only "unreasonable risks" often generated an agency approach that was far more rigorous than a cost-benefit calculation might suggest.[131] As in cases in which constitutional rights were at stake,[132] cost was not viewed as a serious factor mitigating the duty of polluters to conform to the environmental goals outlined in the statutes. Nor was cost seen as a serious factor in limiting the promulgation of agency rules designed to carry out Congress's goals.[133]

This absolutism translated into a demand for quick solutions to the complicated social and economic problems spawned by an industrialized society. Statutes such as the Clean Water Act,[134] for example, were designed to eliminate pollution quickly. Unlike the Supreme Court's approach to eliminating racial discrimination with all "due deliberate speed,"[135] this statute in particular set definite, unrealistic dates for the complete elimination of pollution.[136]

The absolutist nature of such statutes also reduced agency discretion and transformed the regulatory discourse. The burden of proof that certain environmental values had, in fact, been adequately considered was on the agency.[137] The deference the courts had shown Congress and its agents during the New Deal era was revoked. The courts would usually not presume environmental rationality on the part of the agencies involved.

Particularly in the early days of the environmental era, the courts often interpreted statutes in a manner that furthered or, on occasion, introduced absolutist imperatives. The expansionary regulatory discourse that typified the Court's approach in *Phillips Petroleum* was replaced with a cost-benefit logic, but one that emphasized environmental, rather than economic, benefits and costs. Citizens to Preserve Overton Park, Inc. v. Volpe[138] set the judicial tone for the new, emerging era of environmental law. In that particular case the Court turned an otherwise discretionary environmental statute into an absolutist one.[139] The Court demanded that the secretary of transportation show that he had, in fact, engaged in a serious environmental discourse such that he could convincingly justify his decision to build a highway through a park in Memphis, Tennessee.[140] As the Court put it:

> Congress clearly did not intend that cost and disruption of the community were to be ignored by the Secretary. But the very existence of the statutes indicates that protection of parkland was to be given paramount importance. The few green havens that are public parks were not to be lost unless there were truly unusual factors present in a particular case or the cost or community disruption resulting from alternative routes

reached extraordinary magnitudes. If the statutes are to have any meaning, the Secretary cannot approve the destruction of parkland unless he
finds that alternative routes present unique problems.[141]

This kind of discourse, common in environmental litigation,[142] dealt
with burden-of-proof questions in a manner not unlike constitutional
litigation. It put the burden on the party seeking to disrupt the environment, whether that party was the government or a private
firm.[143] Constitutional rights such as those guaranteed by the First
Amendment, for example, speech, could be curtailed or prohibited
only if there were a compelling reason for taking such action and only if
there were no realistic alternative to the action proposed. This heavy
burden of proof rested on the person seeking to prohibit or curtail
speech.[144] In a variety of environmental cases, courts similarly put a
heavy burden on the party seeking to disrupt the environment.[145]

Yet another similarity to constitutional law followed from casting
environmental issues in absolutist terms. A decision to curtail or prohibit speech is likely to be irrevocable, just as environmental damage is
likely to be irreversible. Once a road is built through parklands or a
dam is placed on a scenic river, the environmental damage is not easily
repaired.[146] Damage to the health and safety of individuals, especially
if the damage is life-threatening, is likewise conceived as irrevocable.
This raises the stakes considerably and lessens judicial tolerance for
reasonable guesses and regulatory discourses involving probabilities
rather than certainties, particularly if those guesses suggest to the
courts that the agencies involved had not given the environmental
issues at stake serious consideration. For certain agencies, such as the
U.S. Army Corps of Engineers, this often was the case.[147]

Statutory environmental rights thus took on constitutional weight.
The techniques of judicial review that courts applied to constitutional
issues were extended to environmental policy issues as well. The
absolutist nature of the statutes and the perceived irrevocability of the
harm generated a legal discourse that often sounded more constitutional than statutory or regulatory.[148]

The Nature of the Regulation—
A Consumer Perspective

Environmental statutes combined an absolutist character with an
essentially consumer-oriented perspective. The acts reflected

new desires associated with the advanced consumer economy that came
into being after World War II. Some of these services pertain[ed] to
outdoor recreation and the allocation of air, land, and water to natural
environment management and use; others pertain[ed] to new objectives
concerning health and well-being and to the adverse effects of pollution
on both biological life and human beings; still others deal[t] with matters
such as "least cost" technologies in energy, smaller-scale production, and
population—resource balance.[149]

These quality-of-life concerns generated certain environmental values
that Congress sought to impose on decision-making processes. These
values were those of individual consumers. Indeed, the statutes themselves sought to eliminate specific harms by preventing specific producers from inflicting these harms on the environment in general and
individuals in particular. Unlike the New Deal's more abstract concern
with an adequately functioning market from which all might benefit,
the environmental era sought the direct benefit of individual consumers. Though a conception of individuals as interdependent may
underlie the basic need for environmental regulation, a conception of
rights as individual energized the enforcement of these statutes.

The conception of the problems involved and the focus on the particular causes of harm made it easier for courts to consider environmental, health, and safety issues in terms of individual rights. The beneficiaries of the statutes were already distinct from the regulated.
Producers were the producers of harm, and environmental consumers
were, in fact, victims. The courts were accustomed to protecting individuals from harm, and the judicial techniques developed in civil-
rights contexts were easily transferred to this new arena.[150] The nature
of the market failure that environmental statutes sought to correct was
also distinctive. The common-pool or tragedy-of-the-commons form of
market failure that typified the environmental era came about because
individuals sought to maximize their own self-interest.[151] Because
there were no enforceable property rights in the environment, "rational" self-interest could lead to disaster. Unlike regulation of natural
monopolies, which sought to protect the individual from monopolistic
enterprises, regulation of common pools sought to protect individuals
from themselves. This conception of market failure not only generated
statutes that sought to resolve fundamental conflicts of value, but often
gave rise to a values discourse and value conflicts not unlike those
regularly confronted in constitutional litigation.[152]

Environmental, health, and safety problems were also marked by their complexity and by the collective nature of many of the risks they presented. In an increasingly complex and technocratic society, the information needed to act rationally was difficult to acquire and to understand. Sensible risk assessment of potential environmental harm required collective information gathering. Questions such as whether to utilize nuclear power or where and how to build a safe nuclear plant did not lend themselves to individual risk calculations. Nuclear accidents could have ramifications and effects reaching far beyond those living near the plant.

In short, the complexity of these issues, the common-pool nature of the market failure to which environmental regulation was a response, the sense of interdependent individualism that this conception of the problem spawned, and, most important, the judicial individual rights discourse that the consumer perspective inherent in many environmental health and safety statutes encourages are all important aspects of the nature of the regulation of this era.

The Nature of the Agencies— Conflicts of Interest

Not only did the nature of the issues and the nature of the regulation involved affect the way courts in the environmental era conceptualized the cases before them, but the nature of the agencies themselves also influenced the character of judicial review. Generic statutes, such as the National Environmental Policy Act,[153] were binding on all governmental agencies.[154] Many of these, however, had interests at odds with the public-interest goals of the statutes. Many early "environmental" agencies were actually very development oriented.[155] The Army Corps of Engineers, the Bureau of Reclamation, and the Federal Power Commission, for example, often found environmental values antithetical to their own basic missions.[156] Thus, such a governmental entity charged with applying environmental values often disregarded them completely in favor of its own statutory duties and goals. It was, therefore, just as likely as any private entity to violate environmental law.[157] In such cases, courts sometimes acted as if they were super-agencies, ultimate guardians of the true public interest. In so doing, courts often reversed agency action by taking a hard—as opposed to a deferential— look at the reasons agencies gave for their actions and finding those reasons inadequate.[158]

In Calvert Cliffs' Coordinating Committee, Inc. v. Atomic Energy Commission,[159] for example, the United States Court of Appeals for the District of Columbia Circuit reviewed, for the first time, the application of the National Environmental Policy Act[160] to the Atomic Energy Commission. At that time, the commission had a built-in conflict of interest, for its mandate required that it regulate the safety aspects of nuclear power *and* promote its use.[161] As in many other cases involving development-oriented agencies, the court recognized that the agency's own goals undercut its ability to take environmental values into serious consideration.[162] Protecting the environment, and Congress's desires regarding the environment, therefore, became the province of the courts. In dramatic fashion, Judge Skelly Wright threw down the judicial gauntlet:

> These cases are only the beginning of what promises to become a flood of new litigation—seeking judicial assistance in protecting our natural environment. . . . In these cases, we must for the first time interpret the broadest and perhaps most important of the recent statutes: the National Environmental Policy Act (NEPA). . . . We must assess claims that one of the agencies charged with its administration has failed to live up to the congressional mandate. *Our duty, in short, is to see that important legislative purposes, heralded in the halls of Congress, are not lost or misdirected in the vast hallways of the federal bureaucracy.*[163]

This approach is radically different in tone and stance from the deference doctrine of the New Deal era. The courts recognized that government agencies could be just as indifferent to the public interest as private industry. This was particularly the case when the primary mission or goal of the agency conflicted with the environmental values mandated by Congress.

Thus, the courts thus took it upon themselves to ensure that the government itself live up to the mandates of the National Environmental Policy Act. They chose to play the role of protector of the values and goals expressed by Congress, a role akin to the executive's constitutional duty "to take care that the laws be faithfully executed." Carried too far, such a judicial stance arguably could raise concerns regarding the limits of the judiciary's legitimate supervisory role.[164] Courts clearly had the power and the duty to ensure that congressional mandates were not violated. In practice, though, the intensity of their scrutiny of the performance of government agencies blurred the constitutionally mandated differences among judicial review, legislative amendments to statutes, and executive administration and coordination of agency policy.[165]

Active judicial involvement during the environmental era nevertheless became an important means by which progress in this new era was defined and advanced. Courts, especially the Circuit Court of Appeals for the District of Columbia, which heard the bulk of administrative law litigation, now became much more explicit interpreters of the new regulatory matrices established by Congress in the 1970s. The judicial tools and techniques they used, however, were not fashioned out of whole cloth. The hard-look doctrine involved close judicial scrutiny of the reasoning and the procedures agencies used to make their decisions. These approaches to judicial review had distinct continuities with the past. New Deal deference was by no means discarded, but it was now often enhanced by a blend of common-law logic that came naturally to essentially generalist, common-law judges and the constitutional-law doctrines that had been applied in civil rights contexts throughout the 1960s and 1970s.

COMMON-LAW ASPECTS OF THE HARD-LOOK DOCTRINE

Though the hard-look doctrine came into its own during the environmental era, it began much earlier when the New Deal minimal-rationality approach was still very much in vogue. Expressing his disagreement with the Second Circuit's penchant for almost always deferring to agency decisions, Judge Jerome Frank inadvertently set forth the underlying basis of the hard-look doctrine—the use of reason to secure and enhance an agency's legitimacy. Commenting on the Interstate Commerce Commission's use of discretion in determining the accuracy of a railroad's property valuations, he advocate rejection of what he called the doctrine of "woosh-woosh":

> If, however, the Commission is sustained in this case, and, accordingly, behaves similarly in future cases, then its conduct will indeed be a mystery. Its so-called valuations will then be acceptable, no matter how contrived. In that event, it would be desirable to abandon the word "valuation"—since that word misleadingly connotes some moderately rational judgment—and to substitute some neutral term, devoid of misleading associations, such as "aluation," or, perhaps better still, "woosh-woosh." The pertinent doctrine would then be this: "When the I.C.C. has ceremonially woosh-wooshed, judicial scrutiny is barred."[166]

Judge Frank, however, was quick to observe that his desire to over-turn this administrative decision was *not* based on any antiagency bias. Indeed, he was a friend of administrative agencies, but "[t]o condone the Commission's conduct here is to give aid and comfort to the en-emies of the administrative process, by sanctioning administrative irresponsibility; the friends of that process should be the first to de-nounce its abuses. If the courts declare themselves powerless to rem-edy those abuses, judicial review will become a sham."[167]

A similar desire to protect the administrative process and to empha-size the distinctive role of agencies was the basis for the Supreme Court's decision in SEC v. Chenery Corp. In that case the Court refused to give its reasons for a particular result until the agency first set forth its views. Indeed, the Court noted that "a reviewing court, in dealing with a determination or judgment which an administrative agency alone is authorized to make, must judge the propriety of such action solely by the grounds invoked by the agency."[168]

Because notions of expertise were founded upon faith in the reason-ing behind agency decisions, the ability of an agency to engage in this process was an important source of its legitimacy and a demonstration that it was, indeed, a responsible agent of Congress. This procedural aspect to the role of reason in agency decision making was at the center of the hard-look doctrine first set forth in Greater Boston Television Corp. v. FCC.[169]

The underlying premise of this purely procedural version of the hard-look doctrine was that the process of agency reasoning produced good results, which not only enhanced the legitimacy of the agency itself, but also increased the likelihood of wise policies that furthered statutory goals.[170] This emphasis on the agency's need to display a reasoned approach to its tasks, particularly when significant changes in policy were contemplated, had strong overtones of an evolutionary common-law methodology.

Like changes in common law, changes in agency law were expected to occur gradually, to fit into preexisting legal frameworks, and to represent a form of regulatory progress.[171] Change was more likely to occur in this way if it was in fact the product of reasoned analysis and not merely the result of a new set of political forces. The hard-look doctrine thus assumed a high degree of rationality and, along with it, a highly developed doctrine of administrative *stare decisis*. In its most procedural form, it did not seek to have courts substitute their own substantive views for those of the agencies, but rather to have the courts determine whether the agencies had engaged in the process of reasoning in order to ensure that a reasonable approach, if not necessarily the best approach, would, in fact, be taken. Thus, courts could test substantive rationality by requiring that agencies explain the links between the congressionally expressed belief in progress and the reasonableness of the regulation being reviewed. The courts required that reasonableness be articulated, not assumed. The more substantive the courts' demands for articulation became, however, the more power courts had to alter or stop completely the changes proposed by agencies. This kind of exacting review is the essence of the judicial approach and it is a court's primary tool for organizing and ordering reality.

A Common-Law Approach to
Agency Changes

The common-law flavor of this doctrine is fully evident in Greater Boston Television Corp. v. FCC. In that case, the Federal Communications Commission, during proceedings regarding renewal of a television station's operating license, had conducted complete comparative licensing proceedings contrary to its usual policy of renewing licenses without such comparative proceedings.[172] The television industry protested that this change in commission policy would place current license holders on equal footing with new applicants every time their licenses came up for renewal. The industry began organizing to seek legislative reversal of the commission decision.[173] In response, the commission added a paragraph to its opinion to clarify that this was an unusual case.[174] On appeal, the court elaborated the need for the agency to take a "'hard look' at the salient problems."[175] In so doing, the court set forth the circumstances under which a hard look would be required and explained just what the hard-look approach entailed.[176] The court then concluded that the commission in this case had taken the necessary hard look at the issues and had adequately explained its reasoning to the court.[177]

The court would apply the hard-look approach when certain danger signals were present. Foremost among these was what the court perceived as a reversal in agency policy. Specifically, Judge Harold Leventhal noted:

> Judicial vigilance to enforce the Rule of Law in the administrative process is particularly called upon where . . . the area under consideration is one

wherein the Commission's policies are in flux. An agency's view of what is in the public interest may change, either with or without a change in circumstances. But an agency changing its course must supply a reasoned analysis indicating that prior policies and standards are being deliberately changed, not casually ignored, and if an agency glosses over or swerves from prior precedents without discussion it may cross the line from the tolerably terse to the intolerably mute.[178]

Hard-look doctrine thus reflected common-law doctrine by putting a premium on the past and by demanding continuity in agency policy.

The call for a "reasoned analysis" inevitably implied a substantive component to the doctrine. While it was not entirely clear from this case just how good a reason an agency must give if it does decide to change course, the opinion strongly implied that not just any reason would do. Indeed, the court apparently anticipated reasoning that "promotes results in the public interest by requiring the agency to focus on the values served by its decision, and hence releasing the clutch of unconscious preference and irrelevant prejudice. It furthers the broad public interest of enabling the public to repose confidence *in the process* as well as the judgments of its decision-makers."[179] It was expected that the process of decision making would yield substantive reasons that the public (through the courts) would recognize as good reasons, though not necessarily reasons with which all might agree. By requiring agencies to articulate their rationales explicitly, courts encouraged results worthy of judicial deference and public approval. The reasoning process was thus a means to a more acceptable end. The reasoning process could not, however, be divorced completely from its products.

How good an agency's reasons had to be and how much deference a court would give to those reasons were matters of degree. If the court had a procedural cast of mind, it would, in the face of a reason it might not agree with, reluctantly conclude that Congress had intended that the agency make the substantive decision. Such a court would require only that the decision be made in a manner capable of explanation to a court. A court that preferred a process-oriented approach would allow virtually any reason as long as the agency's action was within its statutory powers. At the other end of the spectrum, a court that favored substantive approaches would mandate that the agency choose not just a good reason, but the best reason. Of necessity, "best" would be defined according to what the court believed Congress had intended when it passed the legislation.[180]

The more demanding a court became in assessing agency reasoning, the more substantive its review would become. Indeed, a court's analysis of the reasonableness of an agency policy decision would often begin to resemble a determination of whether the agency action was *ultra vires*. If the action were outside the agency's legal powers, no one would object when courts intervened; however, when the policy advocated by an agency was technically within its powers, but philosophically beyond what Congress presumably intended, problems could arise. A substantive hard-look approach would make the courts the ultimate arbiters of *wise* policy choices, that being defined as what a court thought Congress would have wanted at the time it passed the legislation involved. This approach could easily slip into a decision about what Congress might do today if it were willing to expend the political capital necessary to change the law.

Recognizing that there are degrees of judicial deference to agency reasoning processes and judgments does not negate the fact that the net result of the hard-look approach was an increase in judicial power. This was true of even its most "procedural" decisions. This increase in power gave courts a greater role in determining the direction and pace of agency change. The common-law basis of this doctrine puts a premium on the past, demanding continuity in agency policy. Moreover, the less predictable it becomes whether and how vigorously the hard-look approach is to be applied, the greater the ultimate shift of power from the agency to the court. Judge Leventhal, in Greater Boston Television Corp. v. FCC, however, did not see this doctrine solely in terms of power. Nor did he see the courts as separate from the administrative process. Like Judge Frank and other New Deal judges who supported the regulatory experiment, Judge Leventhal considered judicial involvement necessary for the good of the administrative process in general and agencies in particular. For Judge Leventhal "agencies and courts together constitute a 'partnership' in furtherance of the public interest, and are 'collaborative instrumentalities of justice.'"[181] Given this view, it is not surprising that courts would, on occasion, engage in an examination of not only an agency's reasoning process but the substantive legal framework within which the reasoning process occurred.

Process and substance were inextricably intertwined, even when courts reviewed only the reasoning process in which an agency may or may not have engaged. The implicit or explicit requirement that not just any reasons but good reasons or even the *best* reasons be provided usually arose in cases involving health, safety, and environmental issues, which triggered absolutist approaches.[182] Even within the procedural approach, the degree of judicial scrutiny afforded often corresponded to the substance of the case.[183] There are, however, even more direct substantive approaches to judicial review that coincide directly with the change in substantive regulation that occurred largely in the 1970s. The more substantive approaches precipitated a discourse that, at times, began to sound more like constitutional than common law. The result, however, was the same: judicial power over agency discretion grew.

A Constitutional Approach to Judicial Review of Agency Action

Judicial review of agency action approached the stringency of constitutional law when the substantive regulation involved value questions in the context of health, safety, and the environment. As we have seen, the type of market failure involved usually differed from the traditional New Deal concerns with natural monopoly or mutually destructive competition. It was more likely to be based on a lack of the information necessary for informed individual and collective choice (about worker safety or the placement of a nuclear plant) or on a common-pool type of market failure where the blind pursuit of individual self-interest would only exacerbate the problem. Because such questions involved life-and-death trade-offs or irrevocable damage,[184] seemed to require calculation of the value of human life,[185] and were compounded by scientific uncertainty, the judgments being made seemed less the result of expertise and more the result of essentially political value judgments. This sense of the substance involved suggests what Chief Judge David Bazelon had in mind when he noted, in a case dealing with pesticide safety, that "courts are increasingly asked to review administrative action that touches on fundamental personal interests in life, health, and liberty. These interests have always had a special claim to judicial protection, in comparison with the economic interests at stake in a ratemaking or licensing proceeding."[186]

This basis for close judicial scrutiny of agency decision making encouraged a judicial methodology that was directly analogous to the substantive constitutional approaches taken on decisions involving questions of fundamental rights or suspect classifications. Thus, the initiator of action affecting "fundamental personal interests in life, health, and liberty"[187] had to carry a heavier burden than an actor who affected only economic interests.[188] Under Judge Leventhal's process rationale, the economic issues and the apparent change in agency policy involved in Greater Boston Television Corp. v. FCC demonstrated a combination of danger signals that justified close judicial scrutiny. More substantive versions of the hard-look doctrine, however, do not necessarily require such danger signals and may authorize judicial intervention in the absence of any clear change in policy direction, presumably, even when reasons are given.[189] Moreover, in cases involving health, safety, and environmental issues, complex issues of law and policy often were blurred to the extent of being seen as issues of law alone, thus authorizing more extensive judicial review.[190] This was particularly true when courts felt justified in relying on their interpretation of a statute that presumably either justified or prohibited certain agency actions.

The Court in Citizens to Preserve Overton Park, Inc. v. Volpe, for example, had to decide whether the secretary of transportation had adequately considered environmental values before making his decision to permit the building of a highway through Memphis parklands. The Court treated this question as an issue of law. It interpreted the relevant statute as requiring the secretary of transportation to give greatest weight to environmental values when making route selections. The characterization of the issue as a question of law, rather than policy, allowed the Court to apply a standard of review higher than the deferential "arbitrary and capricious" standard of the Administrative Procedure Act.[191] The Court could thus use process demands to insist that the secretary pursue the substantive environmental goals.

When all of the circumstances militating in favor of the hard-look doctrine coincided—namely, a change in agency policy, life-and-death issues, and what were perceived as flimsy or incomplete agency reasons—in the context of an issue that could be characterized as a violation of substantive law leading to faulty policy, courts were very likely indeed either to take a hard look themselves at agency action or remand the matter to the agency for a hard look.[192] By insisting that better reasons be given than those initially offered, or that alternatives be considered for which further new reasons would be required, or that the agency explain what appeared to the court to be an *ultra vires* act, courts, in effect, were taking a hard look at much more than the process of agency decision making.[193]

The more substantive hard-look approach to issues of policy was tied to the "arbitrary and capricious" clause of the Administrative Procedure Act.[194] The substantive approach, however, was usually buttressed by provisions in agency enabling acts that gave courts an opportunity to claim that Congress intended to insert a sliding-scale approach into the Administrative Procedure Act.[195] Most statutes passed in the 1970s provided their own rulemaking procedures[196] rather than relying on the APA's relatively uncomplicated informal procedures in section 553.[197] These hybrid rulemaking statutes called for the application of a substantial evidence test to policymaking determinations. Courts often used these standards to authorize a closer look at agency policies.[198] This reliance on enabling act provisions avoided the problems that arose when appellate courts explicitly glossed the Administrative Procedure Act in ways that Congress arguably did not intend when it passed the act in 1946.[199] The result, however, was the same: the "arbitrary and capricious" clause of the Administrative Procedure Act[200] could and, on occasion, did take on various meanings depending on the circumstances of the case, much like the equal-protection or due-process clauses of the Constitution.[201] More importantly, the hard-look discourse tended to demand *right* answers, not just examples of agency reasoning, and granted the courts more discretion to decide what the right answers were than they exercised when applying traditional New Deal doctrines of deference.

In short, the hard-look discourse opened the judicial door for more intense discussions of the rationality of agency decisions. During the environmental era, unlike the New Deal era, rationality was not always presumed and could not always be established by minimal adherence to the Administrative Procedure Act's requirement of a "concise general statement of . . . basis and purpose."[202] The questions raised, the value conflicts inherent in those questions, the human stakes involved, and agency inability, often because of conflicts of regulatory interests, to inspire judicial confidence in agency expertise all led to an era of greater judicial involvement in defining what constituted progress in the environmental era. Interdependence and the relationships among individuals, agencies, and the law spawned a much more complex sense of progress that often raised philosophical issues similar to those that courts often confronted in the constitutional realm.

This is not to argue that New Deal deference was obsolete or that the hard-look approach and the environmental era had supplanted the New Deal. Rather, a new mode of legal discourse was added to law that already existed. New interpretive possibilities, especially for courts, were created by the hard-look approaches that coincided with a new set of wide-reaching statutes. Legal discourse became more complex and new regulatory dialogue, especially between Courts and agencies, more likely.

2

Agency Deregulation
and Judicial Review

Chapter 1 examined various aspects of the regulatory matrices created during the New Deal and environmental eras. The most fundamental changes in these eras were accomplished by legislation. New Deal statutes created the basic regulatory framework within which mostly independent commissions sought to regulate markets, save established and encourage infant industries, and provide an equitable safety net for the aged and unemployed. The regulatory discourse was economic in nature, but not free-market. It was a regulatory economic discourse shaped by the perception of failing markets and significant concerns over equity. The statutes of the environmental era were a new type of legislation. More detailed than New Deal statutes, they sought to regulate polluters, increase safety on the road and in the workplace, and lower the risk of diseases such as cancer. They often sought to force technological breakthroughs. Their regulatory discourse spoke more in terms of science, probabilities, and risk assessments. Their relationship to the market was at best, indirect, and they established a number of executive agencies that relied heavily on their rulemaking capabilities to create new law.

Coming into being is a deregulatory, global era that is not characterized by any coherent set of legislative initiatives. Yet, important changes are taking place in the global economy, and they are reflected in our domestic regulatory structure, usually in the form of agency deregulatory action. The primary path to regulatory or deregulatory change in this new era, however, is through statutory interpretation, not new legislation. The primary agent of change is the executive, not the Congress. The primary forum in which interpretive change is either meshed with or rejected as incompatible with the regulatory matrices of preexisting eras is the courts. Deregulatory change at the agency level and how it is presented to, and accepted or rejected by the courts is the primary focus of this chapter. Given the administrative strategy that the Reagan administration chose to pursue to effect its deregulatory policies, an examination of the role played by courts and the regulatory discourse that this created is fundamental to our understanding of the processes of regulatory and deregulatory change at this time in the global era.

Legislation, of course, is the most direct way of achieving major adjustment to our public system of law. It is the appropriate institutional response to major structural changes in industry and to any fundamental revision in the reality or perception of regulatory problems. But change can also occur without a major overhaul of the regulatory structure. Agencies can change their own rules, repealing some and revising others. This kind of change requires a reassessment of agency policy and often a reinterpretation of an agency's own enabling legislation. Such change can be initiated by the executive, particularly when it is carried out by executive agencies, and it usually invites both congressional and judicial review. Interpretive change is, thus, an important source of new law. In this regard, the executive branch plays a major interpretive role in pursuit of its constitutional responsibility to "take care" that the laws are "faithfully" executed. Presumably, by deferring to these interpretations or by legislating their overturn, Congress can, at least theoretically, also play a major role. When these interpretations are challenged in court, the judiciary is also involved.

These statutory structures and the legal, political, and economic contexts in which these interpretations occur thus generate various legal discourses within the executive, legislative, and judicial branches. As factual contexts change and particularly as the underlying structure of old regulatory regimes begins to change, new interpretations of old doctrines or what appear to be obsolete statutes can often generate new legal discourses. These new discourses, however, seldom fully replace those that preceded them. Rather they draw upon the past and create a new layer of discourse on top of what was already there. The legal discourse developed in one regulatory era usually builds upon, uses, and changes the law developed in the era that preceded it. It is in this way that legal discourses tend to change and multiply. The regulatory dialogues that they make possible inevitably become more complex. They are new, yet very much rooted in the past.

Legal change through interpretation is a source of enormous flexibility in any legal system. No system of law can possibly be born anew for every new factual situation. But fresh interpretations of old law made against a background of new circumstances that derive from fundamental changes in society usually are just the precursors of much more dramatic changes in our legal system. Changing technologies or changing political economies that create a new cast of global competitors are the kinds of contextual factors that can give the act of interpretation a transformative effect well beyond the usual incremental effects of interpretive change that occurs when statutes are applied to new facts within essentially the same political and economic structure.

In the 1980s, courts were increasingly asked to review agency deregulation. The judiciary now had its choice of at least three different review approaches: New Deal deference, procedural hard look, or substantive hard look. The approach a court selects when reviewing agency deregulatory action often has a substantial effect on the action's likelihood of success, and, more important, this doctrinal choice can also have a transforming effect on the body of judicial doctrine itself as well as on the statute under review.

When a variety of major factors mandating change converge, the interpretive problems and possibilities that these new circumstances present usually go well beyond the incremental, common-law processes of applying old doctrines to new facts. The kinds of structural changes in the basic political and economic frameworks brought about by global competition require the kind of fundamental change that only legislatures can effect. This, however, did not happen to any great extent in the 1980s. Thus, the administrative strategy pursued under President Reagan highlights the importance of the interpretive role played by the executive branch and especially the willingness of courts to accept these new interpretations. To understand how these issues were presented in court, it is necessary, first, to examine the discourse of deregulation.

THE DISCOURSE OF DEREGULATION

The political rhetoric that surrounds deregulation often implies that "deregulation" has a clear definition. To those who favor deregulation,

regulation often stands for the heavy, inefficient, all-too-visible hand of the federal government, while deregulation represents individual liberty and a free marketplace. Those advocating deregulation often approach reform as if regulation and deregulation were opposites and as if the debate were truly dialectical.[1]

This, however, is an oversimplification. Deregulation, particularly that occurring at the agency level, is not simply the antithesis of regulation. Rather, deregulation can and does implement a variety of policy goals and aspirations and may be advocated for theoretical, normative, or pragmatic reasons, or for combinations of all three.

Microeconomic theory forms the basis for deregulation.[2] The following is a typical deregulatory argument from microeconomic theory: Government intervention is unnecessary where markets can or do exist and where they can function reasonably freely. Markets can best allocate society's scarce resources to their highest and best use. Law is only necessary to bolster or help create a market. No law should try to undo, change, or modify the results produced by a free market. Thus, according to this view, there is no need to control the price of a commodity, such as (for example) natural gas or oil, because competition exists at the production level and the law of supply and demand will reach an equilibrium by means of the pricing mechanism.[3] Those who cannot afford to pay will simply fall off the demand curve.[4]

Closely related to the theoretical justifications for deregulation are the normative or philosophical reasons favoring deregulation. A market approach not only furthers efficiency, but arguably furthers such values as liberty, creativity, decentralized government, and the excellence that comes with maximum individual freedom of choice. Thus, for example, Milton Friedman writes: "The preservation of freedom is the protective reason for limiting and decentralizing governmental power. But there is also a constructive reason. The great advances of civilization, whether in architecture or painting, in science or literature, in industry or agriculture have never come from centralized government."[5] Friedman goes on to note that, while some governmental regulation might improve the standard of living of many individuals, "in the process, government would replace progress with stagnation . . . [and] substitute uniform mediocrity for the variety essential for that experimentation which can bring tomorrow's laggards above today's mean."[6] In short, the market is intrinsically good. The market leads to efficiency, and this, in turn, enables other positive values and individual economic rights to flourish.[7]

Viewed in these theoretical and normative ways, the regulation-deregulation debate is dialectical. Government intervention stands as the antithesis of the free market. Whether to advocate the *process* of deregulation, however, is a political question, and the political reasons for advocating a market regime over a regulatory approach are usually based on pragmatic, often short-term, policy goals. The market, like the law, is viewed and used instrumentally. Advocating and adopting market approaches to problems is not a return to nature, but the use of an impersonal regulatory tool, particularly appropriate, for example, for the allocation of scarce energy supplies, which can be decisions for which no politician particularly wants to take responsibility publicly. Likewise, when the market reaches or promises politically popular results, deregulation is embraced.[8] When the market's results are not politically popular, the market is rejected, regardless of the underlying theoretical or normative views of regulation.[9]

At the congressional level deregulation tends to be presented as a kind of consumer legislation. Airline deregulation, for example, was presented as being aimed at lowering air fares and increasing services for consumers.[10] Advocates of oil decontrol pitched it as a conservation measure and coupled the initiative with a stiff windfall profits tax to redistribute wealth in a politically acceptable manner. Such goals are similar to the policy aspirations and goals of traditional New Deal statutes. Though the means for achieving these ends is the market, the implementation is the same as that of any other government program. Bills must be introduced, speeches given, positions established, votes taken, and laws passed. And legislators use the process from beginning to end to sharpen their images. Deregulation is, in short, political and what it promises has much to do with whether or not it will be implemented.

Viewed in this manner, it is impossible to see the regulation-deregulation issue simply in either/or terms. Control and decontrol, regulation and deregulation are the same side of the same coin.[11] To decontrol, one must first control. To deregulate, one must first regulate. Both actions require affirmative governmental proceedings. Much of the decontrol that has occurred to date continues to focus attention on the federal government; yet, in some cases, decontrol may actually increase federal power, particularly if the area decontrolled cannot, under the Constitution, be regulated by the states.[12] In short, even if one thinks of decontrol in normative and theoretical terms, it is nonetheless, ironically, another kind of government program as well, albeit one that does not necessarily require any expenditure of federal funds.

Decontrol, therefore, need not be, and seldom is, the antithesis of control. It is, rather, a continuation of the same kind of political, regulatory processes as before. This is particularly the case for deregulation that occurs at the agency level.

DEREGULATION AT THE AGENCY LEVEL

The president can advocate deregulatory change on philosophical and theoretical grounds. Similarly, Congress can pass new market-oriented laws and repeal command-and-control types of regulation for theoretical or normative reasons alone. Agencies, however, usually cannot, if such are its only purposes. Created by Congress with the mandate to achieve certain statutory goals, an agency must justify market-oriented rules and approaches in pragmatic terms that satisfy those goals. For deregulation to occur at the agency level, it must be characterized as a form of progress within a regulatory scheme whose legislative history may be incompatible with deregulatory change. Nevertheless, in the absence of congressional action, agencies play the most significant role in the deregulatory process. Agency deregulatory action takes a variety of forms.

The Forms of Deregulation

An agency may seek to repeal or rescind existing rules[13] or postpone indefinitely the effective date of rules already promulgated.[14] Such actions are retrospective in nature and usually are supported on the grounds of changing circumstances and/or the ineffectiveness of the prior regime. Similarly, an agency may refuse to take action concerning problems that it has the power to regulate.[15] The agency may be unsure what to do or it may feel that the market will achieve results that are as good as or better than any attainable through a regulatory approach. Such prospective market action is not necessarily decontrol, but it has obvious deregulatory effects. This type of regulatory forbearance relies on the market as its primary regulatory tool and assumes that the market will do at least as good a job as a new regulation.

Most regulatory forbearance is essentially unreviewable and, thus, permits normative or ideological reasoning even at the agency level.[16] Similarly, decisions to enforce or not to enforce existing agency rules can also have significant deregulatory effects, and, though rationalized in terms of prosecutorial discretion and the allocation of resources, may nonetheless be quite consistent with certain ideological views as well. These decisions too are, practically speaking, immune from effective judicial review. [17]

Most agency deregulation that has provoked litigation, however, has been the retroactive kind—that which seeks to rescind old rules and replace them either with new, market-oriented rules or with nothing at all. [18] Because retroactive change requires that the agency explain itself, this process has given rise to a number of legal issues, most of which have involved the legal power of the agency either to formulate new market-oriented rules against an essentially New Deal legislative backdrop or to, in effect, appear to "refuse to regulate." Before examining some of these cases in detail, it is useful to consider whether one can or should think of agency deregulation from a theoretical or normative point of view, rather than a pragmatic one. Can the rescission of rules be justified legally on theoretical or normative grounds alone? Specifically, what assumptions should underlie judicial review of this kind of action? As we shall see, the narrower the scope of judicial review of such questions, the greater the discretion of the agency and, presumably, the opportunity to act primarily for ideological reasons.

Agency Deregulation from a
Normative Perspective

Significantly, the Administrative Procedure Act does not distinguish between the promulgation and the repeal of a rule. [19] The same procedures and, presumably, the same standards of judicial review apply to both. [20] But does it follow that the scope of judicial review for deregulatory action should be the same as it is for regulatory? One way to narrow the scope of review for deregulatory action is to, in effect, differentiate sharply between substance and procedure.

Professor, now Justice, Antonin Scalia argued some time ago that "parity of process does not necessarily entail parity of substance." [21] Logically then, courts should not necessarily equate the scope of review of regulatory action with that of deregulation. They should give deregulation the greater deference because "the substantive inertia of our laws . . . favors not the status quo but private autonomy, whether or not [private autonomy] is what the status quo prescribes." [22] The burden of proof should thus always be on the party seeking to retain regulation, not on the party seeking the freedom of the marketplace by the rescission of a present rule. Moreover, "an agency's elimination of burdens upon private parties—like an agency's failure to impose burdens in the first place—must fall within that portion of the [sliding scale of review] giving the administrator the broadest leeway, and the courts the narrowest scope of review."[23] Though the courts ultimately rejected this argument,[24] it is worth exploring for its implications concerning change in general and the administrative process in particular. More important, it shows how an ideological point of view can improperly color what should be a purely regulatory approach.

To view deregulation as "the elimination of burdens on private parties" is to see this process solely in terms of the regulated, to the exclusion of the purported beneficiaries of the regulations the agency seeks to rescind.[25] The statutes passed by Congress and the agency rules promulgated under to those statutes are presumed to be in the public interest. They impose costs on some for the benefit of many. While one may quarrel with the efficacy or wisdom of the regulation involved, it is difficult to equate the purported beneficiaries of these laws with the regulated and, from there, to argue that deregulation is better for everyone.[26]

Nor is it correct to contend that the removal of regulatory burdens can be equated with failing to regulate in the first place. From the point of view of at least some beneficiaries of the rescinded rules, there is likely to have been a loss—be it an economic benefit of some kind or a modicum of protection for one's environment, health, or safety. A decision to remove a benefit once conferred cannot be treated as if the rule in question had never existed.[27] Such a perspective would be an appropriate way to view a congressional decision to repeal legislation, but it is not appropriate when an agency rescinds a rule in the context of the same statute that generated the rule as part of the agency's attempt to carry out its regulatory obligations. Rescission requires the agency at least to consider the regulatory significance of this action in terms of its obligation to act on behalf of a certain class of beneficiaries. Under these circumstances, change is not impossible, but it should be justified in ways consistent with the goals of the statute involved.

In addition, it is not possible to separate substance and procedure in order to analyze an agency rescission without considering what substantive action the agency has proposed to take after the rescission. An agency may decide to promulgate a new, arguably better rule or, for a variety of reasons, it may choose not to regulate further for the time being. In assessing the validity of an agency rescission, one cannot fully separate these two decisions. A philosophical preference for private autonomy rather than the regulatory status quo cannot be the legal basis of a rescission unless it is reflected in the agency's enabling act or is susceptible to public-interest discourse triggered by the statute itself. Given the fact that the regulatory framework within which agency decontrol must occur usually seeks to replace or substantially alter the market, a preference for private autonomy is not likely to be stated in regulatory terms. A rescission followed, for example, by a decision against regulation, in order to allow the market to work more freely, would thus have to be justified in terms of the goals of the regulatory statute involved. If the market is likely to yield results that advance the public-interest goals of that statute, courts, as we shall see, are usually willing to defer to such an agency decision. Though the end result may be an increase in private autonomy, that possibility alone can constitute neither the statutory justification for an agency rescission nor a judicial basis for deferring to that action.

Similarly, certain premises inherent in a philosophical approach to agency decontrol that place a premium on private autonomy arguably are fundamentally at odds with what administrative law is, or should be, particularly given the substantive goals of most statutes. A preference for private autonomy implies a view of administrative law that has, as its primary purpose, the protection of the individual from governmental intrusion. [28] The New Deal statutes were, of course, a legislative reaction against precisely that kind of thinking. Though they often reflected a clear producer perspective, their goal was market correction, not private autonomy. To achieve that goal, the autonomy of many firms and industries was necessarily compromised. Administrative law seeks to implement the goals of the statutes involved. Justifications for agency action (or inaction) that focus solely on the issue of private autonomy are necessarily incomplete, for it is impossible to view a return to the market (especially at the agency level) as anything but a regulatory act, requiring affirmative governmental action. Thus, the question is not whether a rescission will further private autonomy, but whether it will further the public-interest goals of the statutes under which the rule was promulgated. The market cannot be equated with a state of nature. [29] In the context of an existing regulatory statute, resort to the market is the substitution of just another kind of complex, *regulatory* approach.

Regulatory cases concerning health, safety, and environmental protection tend to involve questions that are complex, irrevocable, and often final; therefore, it is not surprising that agency deregulation might more easily be accomplished within the matrix of traditional New Deal regulation dealing with economic matters, for it is easier, in economic contexts, to justify recourse to the market as a regulatory tool since the goals of the statutes themselves are fundamentally economic in nature. If competition between natural monopolies offers the prospect of fairer rates for consumers,[30] or if the market may produce reasonable diversity in radio programming to comport with the broad "public interest" goals of the statute involved,[31] the use of the market need not be defended on ideological grounds, but rather as an essentially pragmatic response to new circumstances. Theoretical, philosophical, and pragmatic reasons for decontrol thus can converge in a decision whose justification is expressed in regulatory, public-interest terms.

The decontrol that results can satisfy all three levels of analysis. It may be both theoretically and normatively pure and, most important of all, capable of explanation in pragmatic, regulatory terms. Such explanations enable courts to view deregulation as a kind of regulation and to defer to the new deregulatory bargains negotiated among the agency, the regulated, and the beneficiaries.[32] This kind of discourse is more likely when the regulation involved is economic in nature and the conflicts that arise are more in the nature of conflicts of economic interest, rather than fundamental conflicts of value.[33]

Judicial deference to market approaches applied in the context of health, safety, or environmental issues is much more problematic. As we have seen, the statutes involved usually provide less flexibility than the broad public-interest statutes of the New Deal. More important, decisions to rescind rules in this context are not easy to defend when they are based either on the use of the market as a regulatory tool or on notions of individual, private autonomy. This is particularly true when granting an individual complete autonomy in nineteenth-century or classical-economic terms might jeopardize the health, safety, and economic interests of the community at large. The stakes are different in such cases. First, these cases often deal with trade-offs difficult to express in monetary terms that are reasonably consistent with a legislature's intent. Monetary values cannot begin to capture or express all of the various points of view that underlie these statutes and few regulatory statutes ever attempt to be so specific. In fact, most of them speak primarily in absolute terms of preserving life and avoiding injury. Second, administrative law's traditional function of protecting the individual from unfair governmental intrusion or from unfair market effects must be viewed in relation to the paramount interest of protecting a community of individuals from the excesses of individualism. Cases such as these raise more fundamental conflicts of value, the resolution of which is more likely to be viewed as fundamentally political and less amenable to resolution in quantifiable terms.[34]

These tensions and shifts of emphasis from an individualist approach to a more collective approach are evident in some judicial responses to agency attempts to deregulate. If the statutes involved allow the issues of a case to be expressed primarily in terms of conflicts of economic interest, courts are usually willing to approve an agency's use of an economic regulatory discourse and apply what looks like the traditional deferential model of judicial review. If, however, courts perceive the issues in the case to involve fundamental conflicts of value, economic discourse alone is unlikely to withstand judicial scrutiny, and the courts will likely apply, in both substance and effect, a procedural or substantive hard-look approach. In other words, when it is clear that a market discourse alone cannot fully capture the regulatory values and conflicts that the relevant statutes embody, courts usually require a fuller explanation of agency deregulation.

The doctrines of judicial review devised for regulation are thus fully applicable to deregulation as well, but their application in deregulatory contexts can have transforming statutory effects. Judicial deference to deregulatory action in an economic context facilitates the use of a market perspective on issues that arise within statutory frameworks designed long ago to combat market failure. This occurs, in large part, because of the court's willingness to adopt a consumer-oriented beneficiary perspective when interpreting statutes that usually never considered the needs of consumers or beneficiaries *per se*. An even more significant statutory transformation occurs when courts choose to defer to rather than examine closely agency deregulation in environmental, health, and safety contexts.

Deference to agency deregulation of health, safety, and the environmental issues transforms consumer-oriented statutes into producer-oriented legislation. Interpretation of a statute inevitably produces an evolutionary change of its meaning, but that change is much more extensive when the interpretation leads to deregulation rather than to new regulation. Market means can easily become regulatory ends. While that may arguably be a wise policy approach for the global era in which we now live, this kind of transformation through interpretation can raise important institutional concerns. These concerns are, perhaps, less apparent in the deregulatory reforms instituted by New Deal agencies, in part because it is easier to fuse the language of economics and regulation and, in part, because of the post-*Lochner* cases, courts continue to treat economic regulation largely as a matter best left to political processes.

JUDICIAL APPROVAL OF
AGENCY DEREGULATION

The reasons for traditional, judicial deference to the economic regulatory decisions of New Deal agencies are equally applicable to economic deregulation.[35] When deregulation is presented as a form of public-interest regulation that uses the market as a regulatory tool to achieve agency goals, the likelihood of judicial deference is greatly increased. The case for deregulation can be put in the same rhetorical form as the case for regulation. The common-law discourse of incremental change with its reliance on fitting new approaches into a preexisting regulatory structure coupled with an expression of belief in regulatory progress thus becomes the means by which agencies dismantle the regulatory regime previously created through the same rhetoric. An agency's ability to explain its decision in pragmatic economic terms is, thus, crucial to its deregulatory success. Essentially, this depends on three key factors: the nature of the regulation involved; the statute under which the agency operates; and, most important, the regulatory rhetoric that statute makes possible, which will ultimately determine the reasons an agency is able to use to explain its deregulatory actions.

Economic regulation under the provisions of open-ended New Deal statutes facilitates agency rationalizations for deregulation. In this context the agency, the regulated, the beneficiaries, and the court can frame and resolve conflicts by resort to a common rhetorical discourse that arguably satisfies the statute involved. The ability of market rhetoric to fit within a regulatory framework means that agencies can substitute market approaches for regulatory approaches as if the market were as simply another kind of pragmatic, regulatory tool. Thus, deregulation at the agency level cannot be seen as a way of rescinding old rules for ideological, philosophical, or political reasons. Deregulation must be viewed in the courts as the replacement of old rules with a new, hopefully more effective *regulatory* approach. Courts are usually willing to assume the effectiveness of these newer, more market-oriented approaches because the agency predictions of benefits to be derived from the market are accepted on the presumption of agency expertise. Since agency action under the relevant statute is held to be for the benefit of society at large, it is from that point of view that the court analyzes each case.

Perhaps the most successful agency decontrol to take place over a sustained period of time has occurred at the Federal Communications Commission. The open-ended nature of the Federal Communications Act (like most New Deal statutes), the broad economic goals of the regulation involved, and the extensive technological changes that have occurred in this industry have made it relatively easy for courts to view agency recourse to the market as a new regulatory tool designed to advance "the public interest."

FCC v. WNCN Listeners' Guild[36] is a prime example of the Court reviewing agency deregulation from a consumer or beneficiary point of view and the agency explaining its use of the market in pragmatic, as opposed to ideological or theoretical terms. In so doing, the agency was able to promote deregulation with the same sort of discourse that it had used to justify earlier regulation. The FCC was not shirking its duty to regulate; it was pursuing a new kind of regulatory progress, and all that had changed, presumably, was the character of the regulation involved. The agency was thus asking the Court to evaluate this change in terms of the public interest and to take note of the fact that, in the agency's view at least, the intended beneficiaries of the regulation would most likely be better off if the market were allowed to work more freely than it had in the past.

WNCN Listeners' Guild involved the FCC renewal of a broadcast license. The FCC renews or transfers broadcast licenses if the "public interest, convenience and necessity [is] served thereby."[37] Pursuant to this broad, discretionary mandate, the FCC issued a policy statement that said that it would no longer examine changes in entertainment programming (called "format changes") when ruling on applications for license renewal or transfer.[38] The FCC concluded that by letting market forces dictate station format, the public interest, as measured in terms of public satisfaction would be better served than in the past.[39] According to the FCC, relying on market forces would and, indeed, at the time of this litigation, already had led to significant inter-station as well as intra-station diversity in large markets.[40] Moreover, the agency maintained that such an approach was more flexible and more responsive to the public than traditional regulation.[41] In short, by arguing that reliance on the market would, in fact, more fully satisfy its duty to regulate in the public interest, the agency presented its deregulatory action as an alternative kind of regulation.

Various citizens' groups supporting radio formats not common in modern commercial markets challenged this change in regulatory approach.[42] These groups included those in favor of classical music formats, educational radio, and bilingual education. They all considered themselves to be legitimate, direct beneficiaries of the FCC's traditional regulatory practices. Without format regulation, they feared that the kind of programming they favored would not survive in a fully competitive market place. This was a chance they did not wish to take. They were, in effect, winners under the former regulatory approach, and they saw themselves as distinct regulatory beneficiaries of the act that the market would not favor. They thus argued that resorting to the market could not be equated with a form of regulation and that in reality, by leaving format decisions wholly to the market,[43] the FCC was simply failing to carry out its statutory duties.

The Supreme Court disagreed with this group of purported beneficiaries, holding, in effect, that a decision to use the market as a regulatory tool was fully within the agency's expertise and powers. As the Court noted, the commission had argued that:

> [I]n large markets, competition among broadcasters had already produced "an almost bewildering array of diversity" in entertainment formats. Second, format allocation by market forces accommodates listeners' desires for diversity within a given format and also produces a variety of formats. Third, the market is far more flexible than governmental regulation and responds more quickly to changing public tastes. Therefore, the Commission concluded that "the market is the allocation mechanism of preference for entertainment formats, and . . . Commission supervision in this area will not be conducive either to producing program diversity [or] satisfied radio listeners."[44]

Justice Byron White was therefore able to state that "[t]he Commission has provided *a rational explanation* for its conclusion that reliance on the market is the best method of promoting diversity in entertainment formats."[45]

The majority went on to approve the commission's judgment that the benefits of such an approach appeared to outweigh the harm. The new policy need not achieve perfection to be upheld:

> In making these judgments, the Commission has not forsaken its obligation to pursue the public interest. On the contrary, it has assessed *the benefits and the harm* likely to flow from Government review of entertainment programming, and on balance has concluded that its statutory duties are best fulfilled by not attempting to oversee format changes. . . .
> It did not assert that reliance on the marketplace would achieve a perfect correlation between listener preference and available entertainment programming. Rather, it recognized that a perfect correlation would never be achieved, and it concluded that the marketplace alone could best accommodate the varied and changing tastes of the listening public. These predictions are within the institutional competence of the Commission.[46]

Several aspects of this case merit special emphasis. First, Justice White found the agency's explanation of its decision to deregulate to be a rational one.[47] From this, one may presume that not just any explanation would have been accepted as rational. Here, the language of the market easily fit within the regulatory framework. The market regulatory approach promised to be at least as effective as the rules that preceded it. The statute sought diversity, and it was reasonable to assume that the market could do that as well or better than agency regulation.[48] Second, the Court found no reason to disagree with the agency's conclusion that the benefits of this new regulatory approach outweighed the costs of regulation.[49] The Court was quite willing to defer to the agency's conclusion on this largely untested question. The agency prediction was taken as based on agency expertise and thus was held worthy of judicial deference. Finally, and perhaps most important, this was a case that called for the rational-basis approach. This was precisely the kind of agency regulation that courts had always deferred to.

It is, of course, difficult to argue that this case involved only economic conflicts of interest among the agency, the regulated, and the regulatory beneficiaries. The petitioner-beneficiaries probably had strong value interests in the kinds of programming they favored that arguably transcended mere monetary considerations. Nevertheless, the basic issues in this case and the values they implied were capable of expression and resolution within a regulatory framework that sought diversity and easily accommodated the rhetoric of the market. Though the ultimate outcome in terms of the number and kinds of stations the market would in fact produce may not have been at all consistent with the petitioners' goals in this case, both the conflict in this case and its resolution were capable of being expressed in a common rhetoric—a rhetoric of diversity that satisfied the statute, the court, and deregulatory reformers. The agency was thus able to show that resort to the market was not a rejection of its regulatory framework, but simply another way to deal with the problems Congress had authorized it to solve. Under these circumstances, the court easily deferred to the agency's deregulatory actions.

The United States Court of Appeals for the District of Columbia Circuit took an even more deferential view of the FCC's decontrolling actions in NAACP v. FCC.[50] In that case, the commission had decided to repeal its "Top-Fifty Policy" on television ownership.[51] This policy required that, absent a compelling demonstration that a proposed acquisition would be in the public interest, applications on behalf of those seeking to acquire a third station in one of the fifty largest television markets would not be granted.[52] The FCC concluded that no problem of concentration of ownership had, in fact, developed and that this rule was no longer necessary. The court noted that it was reviewing "a reversal of a prior position," but it nevertheless upheld the agency's judgment.[53] The FCC had a duty to promote, on behalf of "all the people of the United States, a rapid, efficient, nationwide, and worldwide wire and radio communication service" and a duty to regulate as the "public interest, convenience, and necessity" requires.[54] The court commented on the flexibility this standard gives the FCC, and deferred to the FCC's judgment concerning the ineffectiveness of the rescinded rule and to its predictions concerning the concentration of ownership in the future.[55]

The petitioners in this case, arguably the beneficiaries of the regulation, were really only secondary beneficiaries. One effect of the ownership rule was that it increased the chances for minority black ownership of radio and television stations.[56] Once again, the petitioners fared better under the prior regime and were not at all sanguine about their chances under a free market. But these regulatory beneficiaries presented a less sympathetic case than had the petitioners in *WNCN Listeners' Guild*. Ensuring a certain racial diversity in ownership, while arguably an excellent side effect of the rule, was not the rule's primary, or even secondary, goal. Though the petitioners in this case raised more wide ranging objections, their actual concern appeared to be their vested interest in maintaining the present regime because of unintended consequences of the rule.[57] Still, although their economic interests were adversely affected by the agency decision, they could not present a true conflict of value within the existing statutory framework. An economic discourse fully in tune with the main goals of the rule and the Federal Communications Act itself easily resolved the conflicts that did exist. Neither the act nor the rule was intended to increase minority black ownership of stations;[58] it was intended to decrease concentration of ownership and in the FCC's judgment, this was not necessary.

Petitioners, however, argued that, on the contrary, no concentration of ownership problem had arisen because the rules now being rescinded had worked. They contended that the agency had the burden of proving that this was not the case. The commission, on the other hand, argued that since waivers to this rule were granted quite liberally, it had not, in reality, ever been in existence at all. Whether or not this was true, the court was unwilling to shift the burden of proof onto the agency: "We conclude that . . . [a]n agency need not seek out all available information on the subject before it but must attempt to have all viewpoints represented. Petitioner's views were directly represented. . . . They could have submitted testimony of experts on the impact of the Policy."[59] The Court substituted procedure and the chance to participate for any substantive requirement that the agency submit evidence of a certain kind. According to the Court, the agency had supplied a reason for its action, and it was not necessary for the agency to meet all conceivable objections by all conceivable beneficiaries.[60]

The court was willing to trust the commission's judgment in this matter, noting that the agency had been quite aware of its change in policy, that the agency was not required by statute to have a Top-Fifty policy, and that "[w]hile it may be that the Commission would have defined more precisely what level of concentration it considers harmful, we have to agree that it was certainly within its discretion and area of expertise to find these potential levels not so threatening that the Top-Fifty Policy should be retained."[61]

The Court's willingness in these cases to defer to agency deregulation and then resort to a market as opposed to a regulatory discourse is understandable. In the context of a New Deal statute the agency's action can be perceived in "public interest" rather than solely ideological terms. In rescinding its rules, the agency was not just dismantling what had gone before. It had a positive, *regulatory* replacement for its actions. The market was able to achieve what its rules did not or substitute for rules no longer deemed necessary. The clauses in the governing statutes that authorized a broad delegation of power in the public interest proved to be capable of facilitating both regulation and deregulation, provided the deregulatory discourse went beyond ideology and advocated the benefits of the market as a form of "public interest" regulation.[62] Progress thus remained defined as the furthering of the public interest, albeit a public interest that was served by regulatory contraction rather than growth, and by market rather than regulatory values. These market values, however, were defended by a regulatory, public-interest discourse that retained the same rhetorical form and triggered the same kind of judicial deference that had facilitated regulatory growth in the first place. It was very important to the courts that the discourse of deregulation sound like the discourse of regulation.

Judicial deference to an agency's ability to express its deregulatory preferences in pragmatic, regulatory terms can, however, often imperceptibly blend with and be reinforced by a reviewing court's own ideological preferences for deregulatory change. To the extent that ideological forces are driving the agency to rescind certain rules, a court's willingness to defer to the agency's pragmatic deregulatory rationalizations of its goals may nevertheless seriously transform the regulatory goals of the statutes involved. At some point, the flexible public-interest language of the statutes involved can become a source of new, deregulatory legislation that bears little relationship to Congress's original statutory goals.

This is precisely what the court feared in International Ladies' Garment Workers' Union v. Donovan,[63] when it refused to sanction the Labor Department's attempt to rescind long-standing restrictions on the employment of homeworkers in the knitted outerwear industry. The Labor Department saw this simply as a market-oriented regulatory approach that would produce widespread benefits for workers in the home.[64] The court, however, was struck by how drastic a change this approach represented from the original intent of the Fair Labor Standards Act. The court recounted the long history of regulation of homework, noting that it had always been difficult to ensure that these workers were appropriately identified, their hours of work ascertained, and their minimum wages, consequently, guaranteed.[65] Moreover, it did not appear that any of these problems had, to any substantial degree, been solved. Thus, the agency's creative approach to the implementation of the Fair Labor Standards Act appeared to the court to be an executive attempt to amend the legislation involved:

> We recognize that a new administration may try to effectuate new philosophies that have been implicitly endorsed by the democratic process. Nonetheless, it is axiomatic that the leaders of every administration are required to adhere to the dictates of statutes that are also products of democratic decision making. Unless officials of the executive branch can convince Congress to change the statutes they find objectionable, their duty is to implement the statutory mandates in a rational manner.[66]

In closer cases like *WNCN Listeners' Guild*, however, where the agency's deregulatory discourse fits easily within the applicable regulatory framework, judicial deference to agency deregulation is not the same as deference to New Deal statutes and goals. Not only does deregulatory deference result in a very different kind of regulation, but it is also usually accompanied by an agency explanation that takes a consumer or beneficiary perspective on the deregulation the agency seeks to achieve. Program diversity will increase for consumers or more employment will be possible if in-house worker restrictions are eased. Such an approach to the implementation of legislation may have a number of salutary effects. It can undercut considerably any cartel-like aspects of the regulation involved by giving competition and the entry into the market of new licensees or new workers a greater chance to occur. This could also help reverse any agency capture that might have occurred by those whom regulation has helped.[67] The New Deal Congress, however, designed the cartel-like aspects of the regulation of airlines and communications, in large part, with industry in mind. Congress was trying to mitigate the destructive effects of competition on the industry itself, thereby making it possible for such infant industries to survive in a most uncertain world. Indeed, much New Deal legislation sought to police relationships among producers to the point that "a common perspective seemed to arise between the regulation and the regulated."[68] Consumers were, of course, expected to benefit indirectly from a smoothly functioning market, but this was not the primary purpose of these statutes. In fact, consumers initially had very little influence on the regulatory compromises reached by agencies in the New Deal regulatory era and beyond. Judicial deference to agency decisions usually meant deference to agency expertise and the extension of agency power for the benefit of the diverse interests of various segments of the industry. Consumers of the products these industries produced were benefitted, but usually much less directly than the consumer perspective the deregulatory cases now suggested.

The end results of deference to deregulation under these statutes are not the same as the deference given to regulatory applications or extensions of these statutes in the New Deal era. Nor are the results of deregulatory deference always clear. Deregulatory deference may actually benefit some of the regulatory beneficiaries of the statute involved or those benefits might be speculative at best, as in deregulation of program formats to encourage greater diversity. Sometimes, the resort to the market is more of a boon to the regulated, since it usually reduces their costs and widens their discretion to act in new ways. What is clearer, however, is that deregulatory deference in economic contexts in particular is sympathetic to and resonates with the view of agencies and regulation reflected in the work of such economic theorists as George Stigler and Richard Posner,[69] as well as such consumer-oriented deregulators as Mark Green and Ralph Nader.[70]

These theorists generally argue that agencies implementing economic regulation generally do so in a manner that aids the regulated, usually at the expense of consumers. Such agencies, they contend, are often captured by the very groups they are created to regulate. Their substantive output is thus often at odds with the interests of consumers. That it is these very agencies that accomplish the deregulation they propose would seem to contradict such theories of capture,[71] but arguably the appointment of commissioners during the Carter and Reagan administrations who approached their regulatory work primarily with the analytical tools of microeconomic theory and a preference for market rather than regulatory results has led to considerable agency deregulation, particularly at agencies like the ICC, the FCC, and, before Congress acted, the CAB.

The interest of the regulated in a stable, relatively competition-free environment has given way to a new era emphasizing competition whenever possible.[72] Producer-oriented statutes passed at a time when the ability of the market to avoid chaos was viewed with great skepticism are now glossed with the economic point of view of the consumer or regulatory beneficiary in mind, not necessarily the industry. Deregulatory deference thus does more than simply facilitate the disman-

tling of the New Deal regulatory framework. It helps to transform the
statutes from cartel-like, producer-oriented legislation to legislation
with a consumer orientation that uses the market both as a standard and
as a regulatory tool.

The broad public-interest language of the New Deal statutes involved is, indeed, a two-way street.[73] But the return trip does not
necessarily take us back to where we started fifty years ago. There is a
difference between conceiving of the market as a regulatory tool and
actually returning to a laissez-faire era in which federal regulation plays
a minimal role. The New Deal agency structure is still largely intact,
though its staff and responsibilities are reduced.[74] More important, the
federal government's role of imposing the market as an alternative
regulatory approach is as pragmatic a judgment as the creation and
implementation of the New Deal. Agency deregulation is still a federal
activity with preemptive power vis-à-vis the states.

Moreover, the market approaches to regulation now employed are
more the result of global economic forces and major changes in technology and markets than an ideological preference for a simpler, less-
complicated age. Deregulation in the 1980s can be understood as a
regulatory response to global competition and part of a federal policy
designed to enhance the competitiveness of U.S. industry.

Given the nature of New Deal statutes, the discourse they generate,
and the broad "public-interest" delegation clauses those statutes contain, the Reagan administrative agency strategy for achieving deregulatory reforms worked reasonably well in agencies like the FCC. It fared
less well in the courts when applied to the regulations of the 1970s.
Indeed, one of the major deregulatory battles fought in the courts
involved the Reagan administration's attempt to rescind a federal rule
mandating airbags in cars by 1982. We shall examine that case—Motor
Vehicles Manufacturers Association v. State Farm Mutual[75]—in detail.
Like *Phillips Petroleum* in the 1950s, *Overton Park* in the early 1970s,
and Chevron v. NRDC in the 1980s, it is a paradigm for our purposes.
The legal issues arise in a context that highlights some of the major
regulatory debates of its time. The case epitomizes various perspectives on these issues and, in particular, various judicial approaches that
belie certain fundamental assumptions about the administrative process. Finally, *State Farm Mutual* can be an important precedent. It
infuses the deregulatory context with a judicial discourse that allows
courts, on occasion, to play a major supervisory role concerning both
the source and the means of regulatory and deregulatory change.

Judicial Rejection of
Agency Deregulation

The more modern, specifically consumer-oriented statutes of the 1970s have been more resistant to agency deregulatory transformations than their New Deal counterparts. The environmental, health, and safety statutes of the 1970s created a new regulatory discourse that focused directly on the needs of consumers and could trigger more careful judicial scrutiny. Deregulating under these statutes can evoke similar judicial scrutiny, thus making deregulatory change much more difficult to achieve at the agency level. Such statutes involve perspectives different from those of the essentially economic regulatory statutes of the New Deal. Market approaches to health, safety, and environmental regulation often introduce a view of regulatory problems that can raise serious value conflicts and more directly involve statutory meaning and legislative history. It is not as easy for a pragmatic economic discourse to justify deregulation when the regulatory goals involved are often the lives, health, and well-being of individuals. When deregulation is attempted in this context, it often appears much more ideological, transforming the very clear consumer perspective of the statute itself into the kind of producer or economic perspective that many of these statutes unequivocally reject. There was, perhaps, no clearer example of this than the attempts of the Reagan administration to deregulate the auto industry. Shortly after Reagan took office, he announced a major program for regulatory relief of the auto industry called "Actions to Help the U.S. Auto Industry." Unemployment and intense, unprecedented foreign competition, especially from Japan, made regulatory reform in this industry a top priority for the Reagan White House.[76] Lowering costs through deregulation was an important part of this strategy. One phase of this program met with considerable judicial opposition.

In Motor Vehicles Manufacturers Association v. State Farm Mutual, the Supreme Court reviewed the Department of Transportation's rescission of a rule mandating airbags or passive restraints in various model cars by 1982. An economic discourse grounded in the imperatives of global competition might have explained why the administration was trying to lower the costs of a domestic industry, but it could not have begun to capture the complexity and philosophical depth of the substantive issues involved in this case, nor could one have argued that regulatory progress within the context of the controlling statutes could be achieved by greater emphasis on increased industry productivity and efficiency. Agency attempts to argue in terms of efficiency were not only unsuccessful but, to some judges suggested both a conflict of interest on the part of the agency and a course of action that seemed openly to elevate ideology or a new global competitive strategy above the congressionally mandated goal of safety.[77] Indeed, the confluence of factors in this case militating in favor of close judicial scrutiny made the decision almost inevitable. The nature of the social regulation involved raised conflicts of value not at all susceptible to an economic discourse.[78] The statute itself arguably required more than the usual judicial scrutiny in that it called for hybrid rulemaking,[79] and the agency's weak reasons for its rescission strongly suggested an ideological basis for its decision rather than a good faith attempt to propose new regulatory solutions to congressionally recognized problems.[80] Though the judicial result in this case may have been preordained, the importance of the case lies in the range of judicial approaches it elicited to deregulatory actions taken by agencies pursuant to statutes like the National Traffic and Motor Vehicle Safety Act of 1966.[81]

This act was one of the first statutes passed by Congress that forced technological improvement in a product. Its primary goal was to reduce the carnage on our highways by forcing manufacturers to design and build safer cars.[82] Its premise was that the market would not create enough demand to justify construction of safer automobiles for all consumers. Indeed, all consumers were not necessarily free to choose safe or safer cars, nor were they adequately informed to make a correct choice. Congress thus rejected arguments that the market alone would provide the level of automobile safety that Congress now sought to ensure.[83]

The technology-forcing aspects of the Motor Vehicle Safety Act were relatively novel in 1966.[84] Compared to the more traditional forms of New Deal economic regulation, it represented a much more direct assault on private corporate autonomy,[85] threatening to interfere with automobile manufacturers in what had always been one of their most important concerns—automobile design.[86] Though the statute sailed through Congress, its implementation has produced years of experimentation, delay, and litigation.[87]

The airbag controversy outlasted five presidents, seven heads of the Department of Transportation, and at least six heads of the National Highway Traffic Safety Administration (NHTSA).[88] Each president, each secretary of transportation, and each head of the NHTSA has had his or her own peculiar view of the act in general and of passive restraints in particular.[89] Shortly after passage of the act, for example, the National Highway Safety Traffic Administrator, the secretary's delegate in these matters, promulgated a rule called Standard 208. It required all automobile manufacturers to install manual seatbelts on all vehicles.[90] This rule, however, did little more than formalize a practice already in existence. Virtually all automobile companies provided manual seatbelts as standard equipment.[91] The problem was that a significant percentage of drivers did not wear them. Manual seatbelts thus did little to lower the injury and death rate due to highway accidents and further action seemed necessary to fulfill the Safety Act's objectives.[92]

NHTSA thus began to consider more effective measures. In 1969, the Transportation Department formally proposed a standard requiring the installation of passive restraints, that is, automatic seatbelts of one kind or another.[93] To this end, the agency revised Standard 208 to include passive protection requirements, and in 1972, the agency amended the standard to require full passive protection for all front-seat occupants of vehicles manufactured after August 15, 1975.[94] In the interim, vehicles built between August 1973 and August 1975 were to carry either passive restraints or lap and shoulder belts coupled with an ignition interlock that would prevent starting the vehicle if the belts were not connected.[95] Most car manufacturers chose the ignition interlock option, but the public outcry over this decision led Congress to amend the act specifically to prohibit a motor vehicle safety standard from requiring or permitting compliance by means either of an ignition interlock or a continuous buzzer system.[96] The 1974 amendments also provided that any safety standard that could be satisfied by a system other than seatbelts would have to be submitted to Congress where it would be subject to a veto by concurrent resolution of both houses.[97]

The agency extended the effective date for mandatory passive-restraint systems to August 31, 1976.[98] But in June 1976, President Ford, the third president to deal with this act, initiated, through Secretary of Transportation William Coleman, a new rulemaking proceeding on the issue.[99] Their regulatory approach was to be less intrusive.[100] Although Secretary Coleman found passive restraints technologically and economically feasible, he suspended the passive-restraint requirement because he feared that, as with the ignition interlock buzzer, there might be widespread public dissatisfaction and resistance to such a new system.[101] Secretary Coleman proposed, instead, a voluntary demonstration project to smooth the way for public acceptance of passive restraints at a later date. [102]

This gradualist approach, however, was rejected by President Carter's secretary of transportation, Brock Adams. His delegate, Joan Claybrook, took a more activist regulatory approach and issued a mandatory passive-restraint standard known as Modified Standard 208. [103] It required the phasing in of passive restraints beginning with large cars in model year 1982 and extending to all cars by model year 1984. The two principal systems that would satisfy Modified Standard 208 were airbags and passive belts. Auto manufacturers could choose which system to install. [104] Both systems, however, were fully automatic and required no action on the part of the drivers. Congress did not veto the rule, and the United States Court of Appeals for the District of Columbia Circuit subsequently upheld its legality. [105]

When President Reagan took office in 1981, however, one of his stated general objectives was to get government "off of the backs of the people." [106] More specifically, regulatory relief for the auto industry was a high priority item for the new administration. [107] In line with a more market oriented, deregulatory approach to government, one of the first acts of President Reagan's secretary of transportation, Drew Lewis, was to delay the effective date of the Carter passive-restraint rule by one year. [108] He then reopened the entire rulemaking record and, after a seven-month proceeding, decided to rescind Modified Standard 208. [109]

In rescinding this rule, the Department of Transportation reasoned as follows: In 1977 when the rule was first issued, it had been assumed that airbags would be installed in 60 percent of all new cars and automatic seatbelts in 40 percent. [110] By 1981, however, it became apparent that automobile manufacturers planned to install automatic seatbelts in approximately 99 percent of new cars. [111] The agency, however, assumed that the overwhelming majority of such seatbelts could, and presumably would, be easily and permanently detached. [112] If this did occur—and Drew Lewis's Department of Transportation thought this highly likely—the life-saving potential of the automatic seatbelt would be completely undercut. [113] The result would be similar to that which occurs when only manual seatbelts are installed. Thus, the Department of Transportation concluded that no basis existed for reliably predicting that a rule, which could be satisfied by installing automatic seatbelts that might be detached, could lead to any significant increase in safety. [114] Given the great expense of implementing the passive-restraint rule and the minimal benefits anticipated, the agency feared that the public would regard this rule as yet another instance of ineffective regulation—in other words, unnecessary, wasteful government on the backs of the people.[115] The rule was rescinded and the rescission was promptly challenged in the courts.[116]

This particular rescission was not an isolated incident. It was part of an across-the-board move by the Reagan administration to put an end to what it considered unnecessary federal intrusion into the private sector.[117] For philosophical and symbolic reasons, the administration ordered a general regulatory freeze. Regulations were rescinded or suspended at EPA, OSHA, NLRB, NHTSA, and other agencies.[118] Rescission of the airbags rule was but one part of a broader bureaucratic offensive.

For various reasons, however, the airbags case turned out to be relatively easy to decide against the agency. Not a single judge on the United States Court of Appeals for the District of Columbia Circuit, nor a single justice in the Supreme Court voted to uphold the agency's decision. While all found fault with its reasoning, or the lack thereof, a variety of judicial approaches and scopes of review emerged. Underlying these approaches are very different judicial conceptualizations of the administrative process and the role of courts in that process. Each approach has very different implications for the impact courts can have on agency deregulatory decisions. We begin with the lower court's analysis. It represents an interpretive approach that emphasizes the court's duty to ensure that the will of Congress is truly carried out.

The Judge as Agency Critic

In Judge Abner Mikva's majority opinion for the United States Court of Appeals for the District of Columbia Circuit the procedural and substantive strands of the hard-look doctrine converged. This convergence highlighted both the common-law assumptions behind the procedural hard look and the constitutional assumptions inherent in the more substantive approach. It also indicated, implicitly, Judge Mikva's conception of the administrative process and his apparent working conception that what was at stake here was nothing less than judicial protection of Congress from an overly intrusive executive.[119] That Judge Mikva would be particularly protective of Congress is not surprising. As a former congressman, he was acutely aware of the impact that agency action (or inaction) could have on the substance of the legislation involved. Judge Mikva's sense of the need to protect Congress was reflected in his opinion and in his emphasis on the importance of recognizing the legal significance of the outcome of an agency battle.

Implicit in Judge Mikva's opinion was a view of the administrative process as an ongoing struggle towards rational solutions to significant problems.[120] His careful and thorough recounting of the administrative and judicial skirmishes that preceded the promulgation of Modified Standard 208 demonstrated his assumption that these administrative proceedings matter.[121] They were not random political spasms, but rational attempts to resolve complex problems.[122] As such, the results of these proceedings, especially those at the agency level, ought not to be regarded lightly. As in the common law, there is an assumption of progress here. A change in agency policymaking direction should not signify simply a new set of policymakers with a new political outlook, but a judgment that real progress toward solving the problem with which Congress was concerned will be achieved through the change. This view of the process and this respect for its ultimate product led Mikva to apply "thorough probing, in-depth review,"[123] to the issues presented in the airbags case. This review required that the court determine "whether the agency has engaged in reasoned decisionmaking, making actual judgments concerning the significance of the evidence in the record and supporting its decision with 'reasoned analysis.'"[124]

Mikva explicitly based this decision to take this kind of a hard look on two reasons. First, he noted that the rescission meant a "sharp change in policy" and that this was, itself, a "danger signal."[125] He went on, however, to note that, while Judge Leventhal's hard-look approach was developed in the context of an adjudicatory proceeding, this case involved rulemaking. Judge Mikva noted, "Agency departure from precedent raises obvious problems, but why should courts have similar concerns about erratic agency policymaking or reversals in the course of rulemaking?"[126] To bridge the gap between the adjudicatory version of the hard-look doctrine and the legislative context in which he now sought to apply it, Judge Mikva noted an important separation-of-powers concern: "The answer to this question lies in the fact that an agency is not a legislature. Congress delegates rulemaking power in the anticipation that agencies will perform particular tasks. . . . Even when there is no claim that the agency has exceeded its jurisdiction, as there is not in this case, sudden and profound alterations in an agency's policy constitute 'danger signals' that the will of Congress is being ig-nored."[127] Thus, it was his sense of executive interference with Con-gress that justified application of the essentially common-law hard-look approach in the legislative context now presented.

Indeed, here the procedural and substantive strands of the hard-look doctrine began to blend. Judge Mikva read the regulatory statute as a kind of regulatory constitution governing the agencies involved. De-viations from that constitution justified the court's scrutiny. The court treated the statute as a constitution because, as Judge Mikva recog-nized, no statutory violation had occurred here.[128] The agency clearly was not compelled to issue a rule mandating a passive restraint system in the first place. Having done so, there was nothing in the law compel-ling the agency to continue that particular approach. For Judge Mikva, however, the rescission jeopardized the will of Congress, viewed as if the court were interpreting the spirit and ultimate intent of the Found-ing Fathers of a constitution. His reasoning proceeded as follows: Everyone knows that Congress intended the agency to do something to reduce the carnage on our highways and, after years of debate and struggle, the agency decided to mandate passive restraints. Congress has *not* interfered or expressed dissatisfaction with that decision. To now revoke it and put nothing in its place undermines the basic safety goals of those "Founding Fathers." In short, Judge Mikva's concern that Congress and its substantive goals were being ignored by this rescis-sion ultimately provided the primary basis for his decision to take a hard look.[129]

Judge Mikva did not credit his fears to intuition or speculation. The rule being rescinded had been the cause of intense congressional debate, though ultimately Congress chose to do nothing about it.[130] Congress failed to veto the passive-restraint rule under the legislative-veto provision, and though it had chances to amend or repeal the rule, it chose not to do so.[131] Though congressional inaction of this sort can speak many ways,[132] Judge Mikva interpreted it as a kind of congressio-nal approval for the passive-restraint rule, an implicit expression of the will of Congress.[133] With this view of the legislative process surround-ing the administrative process, Judge Mikva went on to reiterate Judge Leventhal's view on the relationship of courts to agencies: "[C]ourts, administrative agencies, and Congress are partners, not adversaries. . . . Courts do not substitute judgment for that of the agency, but ensure that agencies exercise their judgment only in accordance with the will of Congress."[134] Although Congress had not acted affirmatively

here, neither had it acted negatively. Against this backdrop of legislative history, Judge Mikva demanded that any proposed rescission be
accompanied by "clear and convincing reasons."[135]

Though the weak rationale provided by the agency might have failed
a lesser standard of review, Judge Mikva saw this as a case of first
impression, as well, perhaps, as the first of a series of actions taken by
the new executive in seeming disregard of the legislative branch.[136]
Moreover, for Judge Mikva, agency processes and the results they
produced were not only entitled to respect, but a kind of administrative
stare decisis.[137] Agency law was not written in stone, but neither was it
so easily disposable, especially when the agency seemed to be ignoring
the underlying spirit of the statute and the will of Congress.[138]

Judge Mikva's approach to judicial review in this case was both
procedural and substantive from an agency and legislative point of
view. From an agency perspective, there had been a 180 degree change
in direction. That alone justified close judicial attention. The change
not only undercut Congress's substantive statutory goals, but did so in a
way that jeopardized the validity of the legislative process. In this
regard, Judge Mikva added a novel dimension to his analysis. By
focusing on congressional inaction, he not only emphasized the substantive side of what the agency was doing, but introduced a separation-of-powers consideration as well. He feared executive legislation.
Put another way, he feared an administrative presidency so powerful
and effective that the natural development of congressional statutes
and agency law would be not only stopped, but ultimately turned on its
head. This was a separation-of-powers case for Judge Mikva, even
though only the reasonableness of an agency policy question was technically at issue.

The level of scrutiny he applied to this case was that usually reserved
for cases in which a fundamental constitutional right or discrimination
against a suspect class is involved. When this approach is taken, the
end result is usually preordained, but Judge Mikva's underlying theoretical justification for this level of scrutiny was not simply the application of the statutory command that agency action not be "arbitrary and
capricious." It was judicial protection of the legislative process itself
and a Vermont Yankee–like warning to the executive.[139]

Combined with this more constitutional or substantive mode of
analysis was the traditional common-law methodological approach,
which is perhaps the most formidable judicial tool for controlling
agency discretion. Inherent in this use of the hard-look doctrine were

several biases deeply embedded in western culture.[140] Indeed, what particularly enabled Judge Mikva to apply strict scrutiny to the agency's action was not only the fact that the agency's action raised fundamental questions of value, but also the fact that the agency's proposed method of implementing its changes ran counter to three crucial assumptions about the administrative process.

First, the Mikva opinion displayed a deep belief in a sense of progress in administrative law proceedings. All of the sixty or so administrative hearings that preceded the issuance of Modified Standard 208 and the give and take that they entailed *must* mean something.[141] To Judge Mikva they represented an evolutionary political approach toward a reasonable reconciliation of the conflicting desires of the participants, one that is not easily put aside simply because of a change in administrations or economic climate.[142] Battles were fought, issues were thrashed out, but once the rule was finally agreed upon, the issues no longer remained open.

Second, any new administrative policy or approach should be adaptable. It should fit within a preexisting decisional framework. Thus, unless a deregulatory act reversing a previous agency policy can be adapted to the decisional framework of the agency and easily explained within that agency's own regulatory framework, it is suspect.[143] This is particularly true when a rescission is proposed, and nothing affirmative is proposed to replace the rescinded rule.

Third, and closely related to adaptability, is the expectation that change be gradual. Change at the agency level should be incremental. A policy reversal is the antithesis of gradualism and therefore deserves a very close judicial look.[144] All of these judicial biases of how change should occur, particularly at the agency level, were sounded in the airbags case, and Mikva responded with a very hard look indeed.[145]

The upshot of this approach is an ironic kind of judicial activism. Courts could invoke their most conservative, change-resistant doctrines to block agency deregulation that either cut against the courts' perception of the substantive will of Congress or that raised concerns about executive interference with the legislative process. This approach clearly has implications for the ease with which agency change can occur and it counters, somewhat, the increasingly powerful administrative role played by the president. It does this not only in the name of congressional will, but also in the name of rationality, deliberation, and a view of the administrative process as a kind of civilized politics that matters. When the executive uses its administrative power to exercise not just supervisory control but legislative initiative as well, such a hard-look approach may be particularly appropriate; however, the Supreme Court itself specifically disavowed any such recognition that strict scrutiny under the arbitrary and capricious clause is either possible or necessary.

The Supreme Court Majority—A Hard Look without the Rhetoric

The Supreme Court majority of five, speaking through Justice White, also found the agency's action arbitrary and capricious. In so doing, however, it rejected the lower court's approach to the scope of judicial review as well as its attempt to intensify that scope based on a reading of legislative events. [146] If anything, the Supreme Court found that precisely the opposite conclusion regarding congressional support for airbags could be drawn from the congressional debates relied upon so heavily by Judge Mikva, [147] and in any event, the Court decided that such inaction was irrelevant. [148] The Supreme Court, nevertheless, agreed that "[a]n agency changing its course by rescinding a rule is obligated to supply a reasoned analysis for the change beyond that which may be required when an agency does not act in the first instance." [149] But just how reasoned this analysis must be remains subject to the arbitrary and capricious test. [150] For the majority, the arbitrary and capricious standard was, theoretically, no stronger than usual, even if this case happened to involve decontrol. In the words of the Court, "the direction in which an agency chooses to move does not alter the judicial standard of judicial review established by law." [151] "We will," said the Court, "uphold a decision of less than ideal clarity if the agency's path may reasonably be discerned." [152] The Court even went so far as to suggest that "the removal of a regulation may not entail the monetary expenditure and other costs of enacting a new standard, and accordingly, it may be easier for an agency to justify a deregulatory action." [153]

This was hardly the case here, however, as the majority application of its reasonableness test to the rulemaking record before it ultimately resembled in its intensity the analysis made by the court of appeals. Moreover, like Judge Mikva, Justice White also saw agencies as something less than legislatures. [154] The reasonableness test he applied was not the reasonableness test normally applied to judicial scrutiny of economic legislation. Because the agency gave no reason for its abandonment of the airbag option, the Supreme Court did not put its degree of scrutiny to the test. But the majority went on to assess the agency's reasons for concluding that detachable, automatic seatbelts would not work[155] and went even further to conclude that the agency should have given reasons why another alternative was not mentioned at all: nondetachable seatbelts.[156] In effect, the majority took a substantive hard look at the agency's evidence and found it wanting.[157] Given the perceptual glasses through which the Court reviewed the immense record, it, unlike the agency, resolved all evidentiary doubts in favor of long-term safety, rather than the short-term market.[158]

In so doing, the majority implicitly recognized the validity of cost as a factor in the agency's calculations; but rather than defer to the agency's views on this matter, it rejected the agency's interpretation of its own cost-benefit data as applied to the use of detachable passive seatbelts.[159] The Reagan NHTSA had been quick to conclude that the use of detachable passive belts could not reliably predict "even a 5 percentage point increase as the minimum level of expected usage increase."[160] Given the overwhelming evidence of the benefits of increased usage of seatbelts, however, the majority of the Court resolved all doubts in favor of usage, noting that "the safety benefits of wearing seatbelts are not in doubt, and it is not challenged that were those benefits to accrue, the monetary costs of implementing the Standard would be easily justified."[161]

The Court thus also rejected the agency's view of the evidence of the likely usage of automatic belts, finding that, at best, "the agency's view of the field tests on passive restraints indicates only that there is no reliable real-world experience that usage rates will substantially increase."[162] On the other hand, as the Court pointed out, "inertia—a factor which the agency's own studies have found significant in explaining the current low usage rates for [manual] seatbelts—works in *favor* of, not *against*, use of the [automatic] protective device."[163] The Court did not denigrate the agency's concern over the costs of passive restraints, but directed that "NHTSA should bear in mind that Congress intended safety to be the preeminent factor under the Motor Vehicle Safety Act."[164] This analysis represents an essentially substantive approach to judicial review that brings to bear the values of safety implicit in the statute.

These very different approaches to the evidence in this case resulted from the very different sets of perceptual glasses through which the agency and the majority of the Court viewed this case. The agency, at bottom, was looking at Modified Standard 208 and the record that supported it through philosophical, economic lenses.[165] It resolved all doubts in favor of individual private autonomy—the autonomy of individual consumers, but also, and more significantly, the private autonomy of the industry involved.[166] The agency at one point had emphasized the dire straits of the auto industry.[167] Indeed, the economic climate in which the agency acted seems to have been almost as important a consideration for the agency as the statute. The Court sought to uphold not just the strict letter of the statute, but also the values inherent in that statute. For good or ill, Congress had essentially rejected a market approach to these safety problems and had decided to force the agency to remain true to the particular political compromise reached in 1966.

In resolving all doubts in favor of increased safety, the Court took its values from the 1966 statute, not from the free-market norms that characterize the political climate of the 1980s. But in going beyond the merely procedural aspects of the hard-look doctrine and disagreeing with the agency's interpretation of its own evidence, the majority triggered Justice William Rehnquist's dissent. While the dissent focused on the majority's willingness to base its decision on additional substantive grounds, beyond the purely procedural fact that the agency gave no reason at all for rejecting the airbag alternative, Justice Rehnquist also began to spell out a very different deferential doctrine with very different implications for the supervisory roles to be performed by courts and the executive.

Presidential Deference and a New Discourse of Change

In analyzing the Department of Transportation's decision to rescind Modified Standard 208, then Justice, now Chief Justice, Rehnquist set forth a rationale for deference that emphasized politics and the electoral accountability of the executive. In arguing on behalf of facilitation of deregulatory change, he stated:

> The agency's changed view of the standard seems to be related to the election of a new president of a different political party. It is readily apparent that the responsible members of one administration may consider public resistance and uncertainties to be more important than do their counterparts in a previous administration. A change in administra-

tion brought about by the people casting their votes is a perfectly reasonable basis for an executive agency's reappraisal of the costs and benefits of its programs and regulations. As long as the agency remains within the bounds established by Congress, it is entitled to assess administrative records and evaluate priorities in light of the philosophy of the administration.[168]

While such an approach may resemble the traditional deferential model, both its underlying basis and the ultimate deregulatory effects it facilitates significantly differ from New Deal deference.

The Rehnquist model mixed politics with expertise more directly. While not completely denying the validity of expertise in general, it suggested that it is no longer possible to have an expert for all seasons. The essentially political nature of the valuative tasks agency experts undertake was emphasized by a deference that explicitly recognized that experts wear the philosophical perceptual glasses of the administration in power. Thus, it followed that agencies would, and courts should expect them to, interpret the facts and figures in a record developed under different circumstances by *different people* in a different administration in a new way.

What lends legitimacy to agency judgments is the fact that these judgments derive directly from an accountable official—the president. While Judge Mikva's approach, and to some extent the Supreme Court majority's approach, recognized a gray area where arguably "legal policy actions" could nevertheless have illegal substantive results, the Rehnquist approach would effectively put huge areas of agency discretion beyond judicial scrutiny with the admonition that there has been the "election of a new president of a different political party."[169] But even with this heightened deference, the agency's decision in the airbags case could not pass muster. Because the agency gave *no* reasons for dismissing the use of mandatory airbags, even the dissenting justices had to agree that there quite literally was no rational basis for the decision. In the dissent's view, however, the majority was wrong to go further. The agency's reasons regarding detachable automatic seatbelts were fully acceptable and the fact that the agency never considered the obvious alternative of non-detachability was irrelevant. New administrators could legitimately read the record with new philosophical glasses and reach different conclusions.[170]

Though the majority rejected much of the rhetoric of Judge Mikva's opinion, as well as his explicit recognition of a sliding-scale approach to judicial review under the arbitrary and capricious standard, this case seemed to establish a precedent for courts willing to play an active role in the agency decontrol movement, even when only policy issues were involved. It applied a middle-tier hard-look approach. The majority recognized that there had been a reversal in agency policy, that regulation and deregulation were, for review purposes, the same thing,[171] and that the Motor Vehicle Safety Act itself required a substantial-evidence test applied to a rulemaking record.[172] Accordingly, the Court justified an approach that enabled it to dismiss the agency's substantive reasons for rescission as inadequate.[173]

While Judge Mikva's approach, once activated, almost ensures agency reversal and Justice Rehnquist's approach usually ensures agency affirmance, there is little certainty or predictability in the majority's approach. The Court recited standard boiler-plate language and suggested that nothing new was going on, but its analysis of the agency's reasoning process was exacting. Like cases involving middle-level equal-protection analysis, where courts employ a standard of review more demanding than rational-basis approaches, but less intense than strict scrutiny,[174] you may win or you may lose, but since the reviewing court will engage in more than a perfunctory review of the issues, an appeal will almost always be worth pursuing.

It remains, however, not only unclear what result a court may reach if it engages in this kind of hard look, but also increasingly uncertain whether the airbags case was merely a sport. Though the presidential-deference approach outlined by Justice Rehnquist's dissent was narrowly rejected in *State Farm*, there are strong indications that it is, indeed, the doctrine of the future.[175] Chevron v. NRDC[176] promises to supplant the hard-look approach with a new form of deference, not unlike that suggested by Justice Rehnquist's dissent in *State Farm Mutual*.

As we shall see, underlying this approach is yet another sense of regulatory progress, one that equates progress with efficiency. The forces that are pushing in this direction are economic and global in nature. They are based primarily on one aspect—global competition—of a new multifaceted global regulatory discourse. This kind of global perspective gives great force to the use of economic discourse in regulatory matters across the board, whether or not they involve health, safety, and environmental concerns or traditional economic issues.

State Farm Mutual is a prime example of judicially imposed limits on both the processes and the substance of a certain kind of change.

Specifically, it addresses deregulatory change resulting from the incorporation of a dominant economic perspective into a safety regulatory structure without congressional action. This case invokes the hard-look mode of analysis that was so prevalent in the environmental era. This analysis helps create the doctrinal space necessary for courts to intervene in deregulatory cases like *State Farm Mutual*. That case, in effect, allows the Court to be the prime interpreter of the will of Congress. In so doing, it highlights the potential limits of an administrative strategy for deregulatory reform, at least for issues that are eligible for judicial review. As we shall see, however, the executive branch is able to exert considerable deregulatory influence in ways that never reach a court of law. In cases that do reach the courts, textualist judicial approaches to constitutional and statutory issues increasingly seem to prevail. The result is the predominance of the executive branch over the judicial as the prime interpreter of the will of Congress and the current regulatory matrix. The difference in judicial approaches between *State Farm* and *Chevron* involves more than just a difference in judicial tone or mood. What is at stake are the processes of change themselves and a determination of which branch—the judicial or the executive—should have the final say in matters such as these. What are the limits to the executive's power to create regulatory regimes for the global era *without* congressional involvement? Who shall articulate and enforce them?

3

The Administrative Presidency
and Global Competition

Deregulatory reform is fueled by major changes in technology, such as the revolution in communications technology,[1] and in economics, such as the creation of global capital markets and the imposition of a variety of new demands made by an increasingly global economy on virtually all competitive corporations.[2] Changes in technology can increase competition in industries where competition was once limited, obviating both market failure and the need for regulation.[3] Deregulation is thus more likely if real competition is possible. The arguments favoring deregulation become doubly powerful when a market is working and reaching politically acceptable results.

Global competition drives deregulatory forces more vigorously than regional or national markets can. It places the costs of domestic regulation in stark relief, whether or not new technologies encouraging competition are involved or true market failure, in fact, persists. A global perspective on domestic regulation encourages a more cost-conscious regulatory perspective[4] and often reinforces the increasingly global, market-oriented perspective of the regulated. Moreover, whether a regulation raises issues more easily defined as economic conflicts of interest rather than fundamental conflicts of value is of less importance when a global perspective is involved. The inability of regulators to impose regulation on producers worldwide emphasizes the impact of domestic regulatory costs. Though a variety of factors may account for the decisions of some industries to shift the production phase of their operations abroad, regulatory costs often are a significant component for many of these industries, raising the domestic costs of production relative to parts of the world that choose largely to ignore such concerns.[5] Environmental and worker-safety costs, for example, have had a significant effect on the copper, silver, and automobile industries.[6] Such costs increase when the statutes involved provide little economic flexibility and the agencies that implement them resist market approaches.[7]

Global competition creates pressure for a least-common-denominator approach to regulation similar to the political forces that affected state and local regulation before the New Deal. National regulation came about, in part, because certain problems were beyond the jurisdiction of individual states.[8] In addition, states often had significant incentives to avoid regulation that would increase manufacturing costs and put local industry at a competitive disadvantage.[9] Moreover, it was perhaps easier for opponents to block regulatory attempts at the state or local level than at the national level.[10] Global pressures favoring a more economical, cost-conscious form of regulation or no regulation at all need not necessarily translate into a return to laissez-faire, but they can encourage an identification of deregulation with "the public interest."[11] This is particularly true of global perspectives on domestic regulation based, essentially, on free trade rather than protectionist premises.[12]

Deregulation and regulatory forebearance are the hallmarks of the global era in which we now live. Just as Felix Frankfurter saw the Great Depression as the beginning of a new historic era, then Judge Antonin Scalia saw a new era taking shape in the deregulation movement fifty years later: "There are vast tides in human history: the Age of the Industrial Revolution, the Age of Enlightenment. Ours will doubtless go down as the Age of Deregulation in the history books of the future."[13] While it is, perhaps, hyperbole to compare deregulation to either the Industrial Revolution or the Age of Enlightenment, the "Age of Deregulation" to which Scalia refers undoubtedly constitutes a definitive moment.

A GLOBAL PERSPECTIVE

Whereas James Landis and the New Dealers may have looked to industry for inspiration concerning the regulatory structure they were creating, globally conscious regulators increasingly look to industry for the actual substance of the regulation they propose. Global realities can substantially reinforce deregulatory incentives, making a domestic deregulatory perspective appear very attractive indeed.[14]

A global perspective also underscores the complexity of regulatory tasks that involve international issues. No agency can be truly effective when dealing with such concerns, no matter what domestic regulatory powers it possesses. The problems caused by acid rain, for example, require that the United States and Canada develop a coordinated, international regulatory scheme.[15] Similarly, oil price controls imposed by Congress on domestic crude oil in the wake of the 1973 OPEC embargo may have mitigated, somewhat, the inflationary impact of OPEC's price increases. Still, nearly fifty percent of the oil used domestically came from abroad. Without the power to regulate the entire oil market, these controls were both inefficient and ineffective in their long-term effects on domestic production. In stark contrast to the relatively complete regulatory control exercised by the Federal Power Commission over natural gas prices in the wake of the Supreme Court's decision in Phillips Petroleum Co. v. Wisconsin,[16] regulators of the price of oil could not reliably deliver a regulated price to any of their constituents. The reality of *global* prices undercut considerably their ability to provide politically acceptable *national* prices.

While such shifts in focus might seem to be a natural function of a global perspective, they can, nonetheless, meet with resistance among domestic constituencies. An agency's inability to deliver regulatory benefits can adversely affect domestic perception of the usefulness of the agency. The price of oil, for example, may not have been high relative to what it might have been without regulation; nevertheless, consumer constituents saw absolutely higher average domestic prices as the unpleasant bottom line of the agency action. Such results provided an additional incentive for energy regulators to turn higher market prices into a regulatory, pro-conservation policy. Rather than appear to be ineffective or unable to control a situation for which they have been given regulatory responsibility, domestic regulators tried to use the market and claim success by explaining their approach in terms of pragmatic conservation-oriented policy goals.[17]

Agencies also worry about the industries they regulate. The usual political debate over whether an agency is being too easy or too hard on a particular industry or whether it is "captured" takes a very different tone when the industry being regulated is truly in danger of going under.[18] Administrative equity[19] is built into most regulatory schemes, either implicitly or explicitly. Exceptions processes often temper the dominant values of a regulatory regime with at least a modicum of economic reality,[20] but a global perspective that emphasizes the cost of regulation, the intensity of competition within the industry, and the likelihood that the accusing political finger may be pointed at a particular agency if jobs are lost and plants are closed often forcefully militates in favor of regulatory moderation and increased reliance on market forces.

The cumulative effects of a global regulatory perspective have fostered a new brand of regulatory politics—a politics of efficiency. In the canon of the politics of efficiency, regulatory ends often celebrate cost-efficiency as a central value.[21] Indeed, cost consciousness pervades the implementation of most current regulatory programs, particularly those administered by the president and subject to review by the Office of Management and Budget (OMB).[22] While cost consciousness is not an entirely new policy, the intensity and cost consciousness of OMB review has increased steadily in recent years. Cost-conscious executive review began in earnest during the Nixon administration,[23] continued with more persistence during the Ford and Carter administrations,[24] and was extended and considerably intensified by President Reagan's Executive Order No. 12,291.[25] The imposition of cost-benefit analysis can, of course, be a healthy development for the administrative process,[26] but it also creates significant risks.[27] This is particularly true in deregulatory contexts where the executive attempts to "take care" that the laws are not only "faithfully," but also "efficiently," executed.

Deregulation is closely related to regulatory cost cutting and is an end product of the politics of efficiency. Abolishing existing regulation in specific areas and avoiding the introduction of regulation to new areas constitute the ultimate cost cutting. Still, attempting to achieve regulatory goals as efficiently as possible differs from the wholesale substitution of a set of market goals and market values arguably at odds with a regulatory regime already in place, but the momentum generated by deregulatory change can blur these differences. Given a politics of efficiency focusing on competition with foreign corporations and foreign states who play by very different regulatory rules, deregulation's success as a cost-cutting device increases the likelihood that deregulation will be extended. It also risks the possibility that it will be illegally overextended.

During the Reagan years, for example, the OMB participated in regulatory reviews of proposed agency rules that sometimes resulted in considerable delay in the issuance of those rules, particularly the controversial ones.[28] On the other hand, OMB used categorical waivers when it came to the review of such deregulatory actions as the relaxation of pesticide tolerances and deletions from the list of toxic water pollutants.[29] It is, of course, appropriate to engage in deregulatory activity when the rules in place do not effectively carry out a regulatory program. It is another matter, however, to do so because the executive branch fundamentally disagrees with the regulatory framework devised by Congress. Thus, despite the importance and necessity of executive management of the bureaucracy, a matter to which we shall now turn, there can be a significant conflict of interest built into presidential administration of an agency. An executive agency's desire to transform noneconomic domestic statutes into cost-efficient global legislation may make sense from a policy point of view, but it also may risk converting the "take care" clause of the Constitution into an independent and unconstitutional source of executive legislation. This possibility militates in favor of keeping the president's supervisory role over the administrative process in perspective. As we shall see in the discussion of Chevron v. NRDC,[30] it is particularly in a deregulatory context that the following questions emerge: Who is the appropriate and ultimate interpreter of the regulatory matrix? How should this question be answered? More specifically, how should this interpretive authority be distributed among the courts, Congress, and the executive and its agencies?

Executive Management of the Federal Bureaucracy

Executive power in general has increased significantly since the founding of the Republic. The nature of the presidency, coupled with the magnitude and increasing significance of global events inevitably leads to the placement of more and more responsibility in that office.[31]

Executive influence over, if not control of, the federal bureaucracy has also grown considerably, particularly over the past twenty years. The Constitution provides a broad basis for executive management of the bureaucracy. It vests executive power generally in the presidency[32] and also speaks directly to issues that affect executive control of administrative agencies in three sections. The Constitution requires "the

Opinion, in writing" of heads of departments at the president's request, gives the president the power to appoint "Officers of the United States" with the advice and consent of the Senate, and most significantly, requires that the president "shall take care that the laws be faithfully executed."

It is likely that the "take care" clause was initially understood largely as "a ministerial function to enforce the laws and a prohibition against their suspension,"[33] but this clause has taken on new meaning of late. This change is due, in part, to an increasing need since the 1970s to coordinate the diverse policies of a burgeoning federal bureaucracy that has increasingly adopted rulemaking as its primary form of law making. As Theodore Lowi has noted: "Between 1969 and 1979, Congress enacted and Presidents Nixon, Ford, and Carter signed into law over 120 regulatory programs (by conservative count). . . . In 1960, there were 28 major federal regulatory agencies; in 1980 there were 56, and all but one of those were created after 1969. [The exception was the National Highway Traffic Safety Administration, established in 1966.] Between 1970 and 1980, the budgets for the federal regulatory agencies increased by 300% measured in real dollars."[34] Moreover, these new agencies were much more policy oriented than the New Deal agencies that preceded them. Rather than rely on case-by-case adjudication, which has long been the hallmark of such agencies as the NLRB or the Federal Power Commission (now the Federal Energy Regulatory Commission), agencies such as the Environmental Protection Agency, the Occupational Safety and Health Administration, or the Consumer Products Safety Commission relied heavily on the rule-making process. This, in part, accounts for another indicia of growth noted by Lowi: "[A]lthough many kinds of announcements are printed in the *Federal Register*, it is nevertheless indicative of the growth of regulation that the number of pages in the *Federal Register* increased from 14,479 in 1960 to just 20,000 in the whole decade of the 1960s, and then jumped by 300% to 60,000 pages in 1975. By the end of 1970, the number of pages had increased to 86,000."[35]

The sheer growth of regulation in the 1970s made even more complex than before the task of coordinating and controlling the actions of these disparate agencies. Moreover, given the tendency of an agency to view the world only from its own vantage point, coordination was also necessary to further a broader, perhaps more realistic view of what constituted the public interest. It was made somewhat easier for the executive branch to assume this leadership role by the fact that Congress had created some new regulatory structures that departed significantly from the independent-commission model that typified the New Deal. The Environmental Protection Agency, for example, is headed by a single administrator (now a member of the Cabinet) appointed by the president, with the advice and consent of the Senate. Moreover, Congress has delegated much of the substantive regulation dealing with health and safety issues to other cabinet officials such as the secretary of labor. Such governmental bodies are naturally more accountable to the president and more easily influenced by presidential views on policy. In addition, the executive branch itself has tried to institutionalize its influence and control through greater use of executive orders and, in particular, a strengthening of its own Office of Management and Budget.

The OMB had its beginnings in the Budget and Accounting Act passed by Congress in 1921.[36] That act created what Congress called the Bureau of the Budget. Its primary job was to help with the technical side of formulating a national budget. In 1970, President Nixon renamed the Bureau the Office of Management and Budget and added to its technical budgetary responsibilities the coordination of administrative policies and priorities. The OMB was also to examine agency policies to determine whether they were consistent with one another.[37] To do this, the OMB began to examine the spending priorities of administrative agencies through centralized budget reviews aimed at controlling agency spending and, inevitably, agency policy as well.[38]

Congress eventually reacted to the increased power OMB was acquiring. In 1976, it passed legislation making the appointments of the director and deputy director of the OMB subject to Senate confirmation.[39] Congress also created a central budget evaluator of its own, the Congressional Budget Office, to undercut the OMB's monopoly on agency budgeting processes.[40] The OMB, nevertheless, retained substantial policymaking responsibilities, responsibilities that grew through the increased use of executive orders.

President Nixon instituted "Quality of Life" reviews pursuant to an OMB circular.[41] Under its provisions, the EPA was required to circulate proposed regulations among other agencies and to respond to their comments. Presidents Ford and Carter issued their own executive orders that built upon and expanded the approach begun by President Nixon. President Ford required agencies to prepare "inflation-impact statements" for all major regulations,[42] and President Carter sought to control agency policy even more directly. He required agencies to set forth their rulemaking agenda in semiannual regulatory calendars and that they reevaluate old rules and conduct analyses of rules likely to have an economic impact of $100 million a year or more. He also established the Regulatory Analysis Review Group (RARG), composed of representatives of thirty-six executive and independent agencies. This group was to review and comment upon an agency's analysis of its own major rules.[43]

These attempts to coordinate and influence federal policy at the bureaucratic level by Presidents Nixon, Ford, and Carter were by no means insignificant. They provided the foundation for the much more extensive controls that President Reagan sought and, to a large extent, achieved with his Executive Order No. 12,291. Not unlike the orders that preceded it, Executive Order No. 12,291 requires that agencies justify so-called major rules with a Regulatory Impact Analysis (RIA).[44] This RIA must be forwarded to the OMB and describe the potential costs and benefits of the proposed rule, as well as any alternative approaches that might achieve the same goals at a lower cost. But this order is not limited to seeking information or advising agencies. Section 2 of the order imposes certain substantive requirements on agencies as they go about their tasks. Specifically, all agencies except "independent agencies" are required, "to the extent permitted by law," to include in their analysis a cost-benefit statement that certifies that "the potential benefits to society from the regulation outweigh the potential costs to society"[45] and a cost-effectiveness requirement that mandates that the regulatory alternative "involving the least net cost to society shall be chosen."[46] Thus, these cost-benefit analyses are not simply suggested as a guide. They are required. "Regulatory action *shall* not be undertaken"[47] unless these cost-benefit requirements are met.

In addition to these substantive requirements, the order gives OMB an active enforcement role. The order does not define just what a cost or a benefit is, nor how an agency should measure costs and benefits. By preparing standards for the development of RIAs, the OMB makes itself the sole judge of an agency's attempt to define and measure costs and benefits. More important, Executive Order No. 12,291 requires that both proposed rules and even final rules be submitted to OMB before they are published. OMB can, in effect, veto proposed rules before they ever see the light of day. This effectively insulates much of OMB's action from judicial review.

To strengthen the executive role in the agency planning process, the Reagan administration issued Executive Order No. 12,498 in 1985.[48]

The specific purpose of that order was "to provide for better planning earlier in the rulemaking process." To this end, the head of each agency is to submit to the director of the OMB an overview of the agency's regulatory policies, goals, and objectives for the program year. In addition, the director may request "any such information concerning significant regulatory actions, planned or underway, including actions to consider whether to initiate rulemaking as he deems necessary to develop the Administration's Regulatory Program."[49] This order, thus, provides an "early warning" system for OMB concerning new agency programs.

No one can doubt the need for regulatory management. Duplication of effort, unnecessary costs, and fragmented and contradictory policy initiatives have few supporters. Moreover, the Constitution grants the president broad, supervisory role in the conduct of government. As Judge Patricia Wald has noted:

> [T]he authority of the president to control and supervise executive policymaking is derived from the Constitution; the desirability of such control is demonstrable from the practical realities of administrative rulemaking. Regulations such as those involved here demand a careful weighing of cost, environmental, and energy considerations. They also have implications for national economic policy. Our form of government simply could not function effectively or rationally if key executive policymakers were isolated from each other and from the chief executive. Single mission agencies do not always have the answer to complex regulatory problems. An overworked administrator exposed on a twenty-four-hour basis to a dedicated but overzealous staff needs to know the arguments and ideas of policymakers in other agencies as well as in the White House.[50]

Though there is a need for this kind of coordination, there must be limits as well. Executive coordination can easily become aggressive management, and aggressive management can result in executive legislation, when the executive begins to interpret the regulatory matrix in a way that substantially transforms the regulatory statute involved. In the cost-cutting fervor of the global era the executive branch has on occasion, encroached on the prerogatives of Congress and the legislative frameworks within which agencies must operate. Overzealousness or abuse is, of course, bound to occur from time to time. But it is important in examining these abuses in a deregulatory context to recognize both the possibility and the realities of such abuse in relationship to other legal doctrines. Along with the increasingly demanding oversight role that the OMB now plays, one must also assess such doctrines as presidential deference and a constitutional theory of executive power that "envisions a unified and hierarchical branch with the president at the top and all administrative agencies arrayed below him."[51]

Executive Order No. 12,291 was carefully drafted to avoid direct conflicts with statutes that rejected cost-benefit analyses. It applies only "to the extent permitted by law."[52] Yet, the OMB has, on occasion, exercised its reviewing powers in such a way that seriously hindered agencies in the execution of their legislatively mandated tasks.

When the OMB attempts to impose its view of cost and its view of benefit on an agency engaged in rulemaking, any disagreements that result are usually not subjected to judicial review. The agency involved can quietly drop its proposed rule, or OMB can agree with the agency or a compromise can be reached. If the rule is then proposed for comments, it starts with these negotiations having already occurred.[53] If a proposed regulation never sees the light of day because of OMB opposition, a kind of executive veto has occurred based on an executive interpretation of the regulatory matrix that is out of public view. A few cases did come to light during the Reagan administration because the delays that OMB review caused violated statutory or judicially imposed deadlines. The delay was usually based on a clear conflict between the way OMB and the agency involved chose to interpret the agency's statutory mission.

In Environmental Defense Fund v. Thomas,[54] for example, the district court held that the OMB had "no authority to use its regulatory review under EO 12291 to delay promulgation of EPA regulations arising from the 1984 amendments of the RCRA [Resource Conservation and Recovery Act] beyond the date of a statutory deadline." The statute had required the EPA to promulgate final permitting standards for underground storage tanks that could not be entered for inspection by March 1, 1985.[55] The OMB commenced its review of the proposed regulations on March 4, 1985.[56] Differences of opinion between the EPA, which hoped to contain all leaks of waste disposals, and the OMB, which wanted to prevent only waste leaks that could be demonstrated by risk analysis to be harmful to human health, delayed OMB clearance of the regulations until June 12, 1985.[57] The court ordered that the final regulations be promulgated by June 30, 1986, noting that this was already sixteen months after the congressional deadline.[58] In its discussion, the court recognized that a certain degree of deference should be given to the president's authority to control and supervise executive policymaking, but that there are limits as well:

> [T]he use of EO 12291 to create delays and to impose substantive changes raises some constitutional concerns. Congress enacts environmental legislation after years of study and deliberation, and then delegates to the expert judgement of the EPA Administrator the authority to issue regulations carrying out the aims of the law. Under EO 12291, if used improperly, OMB could withhold approval until the acceptance of certain content in the promulgation of any new EPA regulation, thereby encroaching upon the independence and expertise of the EPA. Further, unsuccessful executive lobbying on Capitol Hill can still be pursued administratively by delaying the enactment of regulations beyond the date of a statutory deadline. This is incompatible with the will of Congress and cannot be sustained as a valid exercise of the President's Article II powers.[59]

The history of the Occupational Safety and Health Administration's (OSHA) attempts to regulate ethylene oxide (ETO), a highly toxic chemical used to sterilize hospital instruments, is another example of when OMB review not only created judicially cognizable delays, but also crossed the line between permissible executive supervision of a regulatory agency and interference of an order that raised significant statutory and constitutional concerns.[60] In 1982, prompted by evidence of ETO's toxicity, OSHA embarked on a regulatory campaign.[61] For a variety of reasons, however, no rule was forthcoming from the agency, and a public-interest litigant, the Public Citizen Health Research Group, sued OSHA. Petitioners maintained that OSHA had a duty to regulate and that failure to do so was in violation of its mandate. The D.C. Court of Appeals agreed and found OSHA's repeated delays to be unjustifiable. It ordered OSHA to promulgate a final rule within the year.[62] In response to the court order, OSHA proposed a rule that included both a long-term "Permissible Exposure Limit" (PEL) and a "Short-Term Exposure Limit" (STEL).[63] In its required review under Executive Order No. 12,291, the OMB objected to the STEL regulation on grounds of cost-effectiveness. To satisfy both the OMB and to stay within its judicially imposed timetable, OSHA simply scratched out STEL from its final rule by hand.[64] The Public Citizen Health Research Group again sued OSHA, claiming, among other things, that there was no basis in the rulemaking record to exclude STEL. Again, the court agreed, but because the court decided the issue on statutory and evidentiary grounds, it failed to reach the constitutional issue of the OMB's very substantive role in this process.[65] Citing *Thomas*, however, the court nevertheless noted *in dicta* that "OMB's participation in the ETO rulemaking presents difficult constitutional questions concerning the executive's proper rule [*sic*] in administrative proceedings and the appropriate scope of delegated power from Congress to certain executive agencies. Courts do not reach out to decide such questions."[66] In 1987, the same court ruled that any delay of the issuance of OSHA's final rule on STEL for ETO beyond the extended deadline of March 1988 could expose OSHA to liability for contempt of court.[67]

The reluctance on the part of the courts to reach these constitutional issues is understandable. The executive branch is expected to play an important interpretive role when it comes to supervising agency policymaking. But reinterpretation of statutes to make them conform to the executive branch's notion of efficiency and, in effect, what the new global era of competition requires can easily go beyond constitutional authorization. The courts, Congress, and the executive all need to take part in the interpretation of the regulatory matrix. To leave this task largely to only one branch at a significant transition point in our regulatory history before Congress itself has attempted to define legislatively the contours of this new age invites serious constitutional risks. It is with this perspective that we now turn to the use of constitutional formalism and the doctrine of presidential deference in the global era.

CONSTITUTIONAL FORMALISM AND EXECUTIVE POWER

If the New Deal–APA era was marked by judicial deference to congressional judgments and the environmental era was marked by a more vigorous form of judicial activism, the deregulatory era seems increasingly to be marked by judicial deference to the executive.[68] This deference is reflected most clearly in the Supreme Court's approach to judicial review of administrative decision making in Chevron v. NRDC. As will be argued below, deference to the executive in a deregulatory context such as this can be excessive, depriving both the courts and Congress of important decision-making roles. But the growth of presidential control is not confined to doctrines of administrative law dealing with agency discretion. The role that the executive can or cannot play in controlling or influencing various bureaucratic decisions was a very important constitutional concern in the 1980s.

The rise of the administrative presidency coincides with the re-emergence of constitutional issues that have been largely moribund since the early days of the New Deal.[69] Once again, the constitutionality of independent agencies have been in contention,[70] the nondelegation doctrine has shown some signs of life, and even the ghost of Crowell v. Benson[71] has appeared. As doctrines of administrative and constitutional law have evolved in the transition from a regulatory era dominated by a national perspective to a deregulatory era typified by a more global point of view, the kind of fundamental changes in regulatory perspectives that triggered agency deregulation put constitutional issues in a new light. Judicial attempts to resolve separation-of-powers issues have generally favored expanded executive power and discretion, and, on occasion, been quite formalistic in their overall constitutional approach and tone.

This formalistic discourse is a constitutional analogue of the hard-look doctrine. It invariably makes the court the ultimate arbiter of the extent to which executive, legislative, and judicial power can be combined in new ways. But formalism is not the only doctrinal choice available for resolving separation-of-powers issues. Just as a reviewing court may invoke either the deference of Chevron v. NRDC or the hard-look approach of State Farm Mutual Auto. Ins. Co. v. DOT[72] in certain kinds of cases, the Supreme Court has also used a more pragmatic functional approach to separation-of-powers questions, as in Morrison v. Olson[73] and Mistretta v. U.S.[74] Our primary purpose in the following section will be to examine the bases of the more formalistic constitutional approaches to separation-of-powers questions and their relationship to two important doctrines of administrative law: nondelegation and presidential deference. In so doing, we shall also highlight the significance of the very different constitutional approach taken by the Court in *Morrison* and *Mistretta*.

A Hard-Look Approach to the Doctrine of Separation of Powers

Inherent in the New Deal approach courts ultimately took to the Constitution was great tolerance for the substantive results reached by legislative processes. Congress was permitted to delegate legislative responsibilities relatively freely to administrative agencies. It also treated the regulatory tasks of a modern, activist government pragmatically and, thus, as essentially overlapping in nature. The lines between legislative and executive and legislative and judicial functions were not distinct. The Court's practical approach to such questions[75] was less concerned with possible contamination of legislative with executive powers, or vice versa, than with the overall effect that certain legislation was likely to have on the balance of powers between and among the three branches of government.[76] Inherent in a pragmatic approach is a concept of "checks and balances": though the balance may, at times, require separation, a combination of the different perspectives and different voices represented by the various branches of government best achieves the overall balance of powers established in the Constitution.[77]

This relatively deferential judicial approach to the structure and location of agencies within our constitutional system contributed to the growth of the administrative state.[78] The national government's extensive new role that began during the New Deal differed significantly from the relatively minimalist role the national government played at the beginning of our history.[79] To the extent that separation-of-powers principles are viewed procedurally, rather than substantively, they are consistent with a more flexible, legislatively defined concept of individual liberty. They are not themselves a source of substantive constitutional protection. As Philip Kurland has noted "the doctrine of separation of powers was not a rule of decision."[80] Protection of individual liberty ultimately had to be found in other, more specific provisions of the Constitution, particularly in the Bill of Rights.[81] So far as the economic legislation of the New Deal was concerned, these protections were largely procedural, not substantive. The legislative process was allowed to work its will.

The Court's more tolerant approach to separation-of-powers issues, however, did no more than make legislation possible. Congress itself had to implement its vision of progress. Once this was done, the New Deal interpretations of the Constitution offered relatively little resistance to such legislative efforts. This approach constitutionalized broad congressional discretion to act, but in so doing, it also underscored the theoretical ability for legislative and political change to occur and reoccur continually. The New Deal's emphasis on the relative autonomy of the legislature and ultimately, its agents as well, enabled the New Deal vision of progress to be statutorily institutionalized, but, since Congress and not the Court was the agent of change, not necessarily constitutionalized. Congress had wide powers to pass and, at least theoretically, to amend or repeal its own laws.[82]

A formalistic conception of the Constitution, at its most extreme, emphasizes a categorical approach to separation-of-powers issues. Is a specific governmental action legislative, executive, or judicial? Is it being performed by someone in the appropriate branch of government and, therefore, in accord with the Constitution? Separation-of-powers concepts certainly point to fundamental differences in governmental functions, but attempts to capture these complexities under the terms "legislative," "executive," or "judicial" are inevitably arbitrary. Since it is virtually impossible to describe fully and accurately the complex functions of modern government functions with these three labels, most exercises of governmental power lend themselves to descriptions that include some combination of these functions.[83] As a consequence, when a formalistic approach is rigorously applied, regulatory legislation becomes constitutionally vulnerable to a new judicial activism. In this sense, formalism is a kind of constitutional hard-look doctrine. Moreover, it resonates with the relatively minimalist role played by the federal government from the early days of the Republic to World War I and with the emerging viewpoint of these deregulatory, cost-conscious times in which it has reemerged as a significant approach to governmental issues.

As applied in some Supreme Court cases decided during the 1980s, formalism and its rhetoric indirectly support a strong antiregulatory bias that can have deregulatory side effects. Just as there is a substantive side to the administrative law hard-look doctrine, so too is there a substantive side to this constitutional hard-look approach. The more formalistic the Court, the more substantive separation-of-powers principles become. Carried to their logical extreme, they can easily serve as an independent constitutional basis for protecting individual rights, including the individual economic rights generally disregarded by New Deal statutes. A vigorous application of formalism would, for example, render regulatory statutes such as the Federal Trade Commission Act constitutionally suspect.[84] By making it more difficult constitutionally for the federal government to pass regulatory legislation creating agencies that combined executive, legislative, and judicial functions, such an approach could also, albeit indirectly, revive the concept of federalism.

The framers, however, intended the separation of powers to help preserve liberty, but not necessarily to constitutionalize a specific, negative concept of individual liberty, one in which freedom is defined primarily as an absence of federal governmental action.[85] Freedom could, instead, be defined positively as the passage of federal legislation furthering the freedom of a majority of citizens.

Formalistic approaches to separation-of-powers issues, however, establish, or reestablish, a set of constitutional limitations on the exercise of federal power, particularly of federal legislative power, that resemble those exercised prior to the regulatory eras we have been examining. These formalistic limitations on how power can be shared among the branches of government are somewhat akin, at least in the results they are likely to produce, to the constraints that predated the Seventeenth Amendment when federalism was a much more important structural, constitutional limitation on the power of the central government.[86] They also are of a piece with the Supreme Court's narrow interpretation of the commerce clause prior to 1937. Both the election of senators by state legislatures prior to the Seventeenth Amendment and a narrow reading of the commerce clause greatly enhanced the power of state governments and limited that of the federal. A strict separation-of-powers approach can have a similar effect by making federal regulatory legislation that in any way shares or mixes legislative, executive, and judicial functions more difficult to uphold in the courts. A functional checks-and-balances approach to separation-of-powers issues, however, would place federalist concerns in the hands of federal legislators and the protection of individual rights solely in the Bill of Rights and other specific constitutional clauses. It would also underscore the existence of a freely functioning federal legislature, constrained only by political forces and ultimately, the Bill of Rights. The federal legislature could thus act in a timely way on the basis of new or varying conceptions of liberty, as it saw fit.[87]

Quite apart from the federal, deregulatory side effects that may result from the rigorous application of a formalistic approach to regulatory statutes, the use of this approach, coupled with an expansive view of executive power, can have significant structural effects. Formalism, as it has been invoked by the Court, has tended to expand the executive's role in the supervision and control of the administrative process.

Formalism and Executive Control over Administrative Discretion

INS v. Chadha[88] and Bowsher v. Synar[89] exemplify the formalistic constitutional approach applied to issues arising from the administrative process. The decisions in both these cases protect, if not expand, the executive's role in controlling the administrative process; however, they do so with a rhetoric that, if carried to its logical extreme, places the constitutional status of administrative agencies in jeopardy. A true formalistic approach can just as easily assume a narrow executive role when applied to the exercise of executive power over the administrative process. Executive orders that have broad legislative effects could thus also be considered constitutionally suspect.[90] Whatever the substantive result, however, of a constitutional attack based on formalistic assumptions and its ultimate impact on the legislative or executive power in question, a formalistic constitutional approach clearly increases the power of the court. It makes governmental action, both executive and legislative, constitutionally vulnerable and subject to close judicial review.

INS v. Chadha sets forth an approach to constitutional issues and uses a rhetoric that encourages such attacks. In that case, the Supreme Court struck down a unicameral legislative veto provision as unconstitutional and in violation of fundamental separation-of-powers principles.[91] The statute in question was the Immigration and Nationality Act. It authorized one house of Congress, by resolution, to invalidate the decision of an immigration judge to allow Chadha, a deportable alien, to remain in the United States. The Court's sweeping opinion made very clear that the Court was not at all interested in reviewing the various forms of legislative vetoes already in place.[92] This is consistent with the all-or-nothing rhetoric that typifies the formalistic approach. The rhetoric itself does not easily countenance ambiguity or gradations in the legislative, judicial, or executive effects of governmental action.[93] Thus, despite the Court's recognition that governmental functions are not hermetically sealed,[94] the Court's analysis treated all legislative vetoes as legislative in nature and, by implication, strongly suggested that meaningful lines existed between various governmental functions. Writing for the majority, Chief Justice Warren Burger thus assumed that all legislative vetoes, in effect, constituted amendments to the enabling statutes involved and were essentially new pieces of legislation.[95] As such, they could not short-circuit the full legislative process. For these vetoes to have legal effect, they not only had to pass both houses of Congress, but they had to be presented to the president for his approval or veto. Failure to provide for presentment would require even bicameral vetoes to be struck down as unconstitutional.[96]

The formalistic rhetoric the Court used in reaching this result conflicts with the New Deal's overall tolerance for what Landis called "intelligent realism."[97] The Court in *Chadha* focused not on the democratic nature of the overall structure of government, but on the application of a rather crude litmus test to the complicated and delicate power relationships Congress sought to balance.[98] By choosing such a test, the Court substituted a hard-look approach for a more pragmatic deferential approach. The New Deal's James Landis had looked to industry for his model of government, but Chief Justice Burger looked to the Founding Fathers: "In purely practical terms, it is obviously easier for action to be taken by one House without submission to the President; but it is crystal clear from the records of the Convention, contemporaneous writings and debates, that the Framers ranked other values higher than efficiency."[99]

In Bowsher v. Synar, the Court took a similarly formalistic approach to the Balanced Budget and Emergency Deficit Control Act of 1985.[100] In the process, the Court also attempted to ensure an appropriate role for the executive in the supervision of the budgetary process. Enabling the executive branch to infuse current political sentiments into regulatory processes may be an important goal, but doing so in a way that risks constitutionalizing a substantive, deregulatory approach to the legislative issues dealt with by Congress is quite another matter. The logic of formalism and the radical separation-of-powers model implicit in it leans very far in this direction. Whether the Court sees the separation of powers as substantive rules for decisions in individual cases or as a procedural guide to the manner in which power should be allocated among the branches will greatly influence the extent to which the logic of this doctrine is applied. The more the Court chooses to use the doctrine of the separation of powers as a means of protecting individual rights in individual cases, the more it risks judicial activism bordering on a kind of substantive due process.[101] Given the complexity of modern government, formalistic analyses that ignore the wider perspective of the overall power relationships among the branches of government inevitably render much regulatory legislation constitutionally suspect. But short of this possible substantive result, the formalistic perspective implies a very different conception of the administrative process. This conception appears particularly clearly in the lower court's opinion in *Bowsher*.

The purpose of the Gramm-Rudman-Hollings Act[102] was to eliminate the federal budget deficit by requiring, under certain circumstances, "automatic" across-the-board cuts in federal spending. Each year, the directors of the Office of Management and Budget (OMB) and the Congressional Budget Office (CBO) were to estimate the federal budget deficit for the coming year independently of one another. If the estimates exceeded the maximum targeted deficit amount for that fiscal year by a particular amount, the OMB and CBO directors were to calculate, independently, on a program-by-program basis, the budget reductions necessary to meet the maximum deficit amount. They were then to report jointly their deficit and budget-calculation estimates to the comptroller general. The comptroller general was to review these reports, which theoretically might differ both in their approaches to the calculations made and in the actual numbers produced. The comptroller general, presumably, was to resolve these conflicts and report his conclusions to the president.[103] The president would then issue a sequestration order mandating the spending reductions specified by the comptroller general.[104] Congress then had an opportunity to act and obviate the need for this order. If Congress failed to act, the sequestration order would become effective.

This statute was challenged before a three-judge district court almost immediately after passage. In striking down the act in a *per curiam* opinion widely reported to have been authored by then Judge Scalia, the lower court focused on Humphrey's Executor v. United States,[105] taking aim at what it called "the political science preconceptions characteristic of its era and not of the present day.[106] The court noted:

> It is not as obvious today as it seemed in the 1930s that there can be such things as genuinely "independent" regulatory agencies, bodies of impartial experts whose independence from the President does not entail correspondingly greater dependence upon the committees of Congress to which they are then immediately accountable; or, indeed, that the decisions of such agencies so clearly involve scientific judgment rather than political choice that it is even theoretically desirable to insulate them from the democratic process.[107]

Along with its substantial doubts about the policy justifications for independent agencies, the district court also expressed serious concern about the overall constitutionality of the so-called headless fourth branch: "It has . . . always been difficult to reconcile *Humphrey's Executor's* 'headless fourth branch' with a constitutional text and tradition establishing three branches of government."[108] The lower court emphasized that changes had occurred since *Humphrey's Executor* had been decided. Specifically, the court focused on INS v. Chadha, and noted that, at a minimum, "some of the language of the majority in

Chadha does not lie comfortably beside the central revelation of *Humphrey's Executor* that an officer such as a Federal Trade Commissioner occupies no place in the executive department and that an agency which exercises only 'quasi-legislative or quasi-judicial powers' is 'an agency of the legislative or judicial departments of the government.'"[109]

The district court, however, ultimately chose a narrower ground for its decision, noting that "[t]he Supreme Court's signals are not sufficiently clear . . . to justify our disregarding the rationale of *Humphrey's Executor*."[110] Relying on *Humphrey's Executor*, rather than overruling it, the court found the Balanced Budget Act unconstitutional. According to the court, the Comptroller General was neither a "purely executive officer" nor an officer like the one involved in *Humphrey's Executor*. Though he or she exercised some powers that were unquestionably legislative, the official's powers under the automatic deficit-reduction provisions of the act were neither exclusively legislative nor exclusively judicial.[111] The lower court thus found the comptroller general to be "in the no-man's land described by *Humphrey's Executor*."[112]

The lower court also suggested that this case could be decided on broader grounds:

> We think it at least questionable whether the power would be approved even with respect to officers of the United States who exercise only "quasi-legislative" powers in the *Humphrey's Executor* sense—since it would dramatically reduce the value of the right to appoint such officers which the Constitution has assured to the Executive or to the Courts of Law, a right that the Supreme Court has regarded as an important element of the balance of powers, prompted by the founders' often expressed fear "that the Legislative Branch of the National Government will aggrandize itself at the expense of the other two branches."[113]

The Supreme Court majority did not take this bait, and affirmed on narrower grounds.[114] Writing for the majority once again, Chief Justice Burger had little trouble reaching the merits of the case.[115] The majority used this case as an opportunity to reiterate the separation-of-powers rhetoric of INS v. Chadha.[116] Quoting from Buckley v. Valeo[117] and *Chadha*, the Court set forth its major premise:

> The dangers of congressional usurpation of Executive Branch functions have long been recognized. "The debates of the Constitutional Convention, and the Federalist Papers are replete with expressions of fear that the Legislative Branch of the National Government will aggrandize itself

at the expense of the other two branches" (Buckley v. Valeo). . . . Indeed, we also have observed only recently that "[t]he hydraulic pressure inherent within each of the separate Branches to exceed the outer limits of its power, even to accomplish desirable objectives, must be resisted.[118]

In light of these pressures, the Court reasoned that if the comptroller general exercised executive powers and only Congress could remove him, it would be tantamount to a congressional veto and thus in violation of the principles set forth in *Chadha*. Equating congressional removal with a legislative veto, the Court reasoned further that "Congress could simply remove, or threaten to remove, an officer for executing the laws in any fashion found to be unsatisfactory to Congress."[119] This, the Court said, was precisely what *Chadha* disallowed.[120] In so holding, the Court took a formalistic separation-of-powers approach.[121] It examined the activities of the comptroller general, determined whether they could be labeled executive, legislative, or judicial, and then examined the place of the comptroller general in the administrative structure to determine whether that official was under the control of the appropriate branch of government. The majority found the act to be unconstitutional on those grounds, but sidestepped the more fundamental issue raised by then Judge Scalia: the constitutionality of the "headless fourth branch."[122]

The Return of Pragmatism

With Judge Scalia now sitting as a justice of the Supreme Court, this issue was very much alive once again in Morrison v. Olson. Yet in that case the Court not only resisted the opportunity to declare a degree of independence from the executive unconstitutional, it also rejected the formalistic rhetoric used by the Burger Court. The Rehnquist Court, at least in this case, opted for the pragmatic rhetoric of functional balancing and chose to defer to the bargains struck by Congress and the executive. In so doing, the Court refused to constitutionalize its conception of the administrative process, but its overall approach was not necessarily inconsistent with the more political conception typified by Chevron v. NRDC and some of the underlying assumptions of constitutional formalism.

The Ethics in Government Act of 1978[123] created the office of "independent counsel," whom Congress sought to make as independent from executive control as possible, since his or her primary function was to investigate and possibly prosecute high-ranking executive officials suspected of criminal conduct. Congress assumed that a conflict of interest would be built into any such investigation if it were carried out by Department of Justice prosecutors in the usual manner. To assure a high degree of independence, Congress required the attorney general to request the appointment of an independent counsel, to be named by a "Special Court."[124] The attorney general could demand removal of this person only for cause.[125] Both the appointment and removal clauses of the act were attacked on constitutional grounds. The question regarding the ability of Congress to restrict the president's discretion to remove the independent counsel to a "for cause" standard raised the issue of how much Congress could interfere with a core executive function. The primary argument of the petitioners was that prosecutorial power of this sort was completely executive in nature and could not, constitutionally, be shared. As Justice Scalia argued in dissent, Article II vests *all* executive power in the president.[126]

The majority in *Morrison* rejected this argument and upheld the act. It distinguished this case from Bowsher v. Synar by noting that in *Bowsher*, the comptroller general performed executive functions and his removal could be initiated *only* by Congress. In this case, however, Congress exercised no such monopoly. The executive clearly had a role to play; it could, if it wished, initiate removal proceedings. The Court implied, however, that Congress's role in passing the statute with a "good cause" removal provision did not really affect its analysis: "Unlike both *Bowsher* and *Myers*, this case does not involve an attempt by Congress itself to gain a role in the removal of executive officials other than its established powers of impeachment and conviction."[127] Presumably this was one reason why the constitutional hard-look approach of *Bowsher* was not employed. Indeed, the Court further reasoned that the "[a]ct instead puts the removal power squarely in the hands of the Executive Branch; an independent counsel may be removed from office, only by the personal action of the Attorney General, and 'only for a good cause.'"[128] While emphasizing the executive's role in initiating removal of an independent counsel, the Court seemed to ignore the fact that Congress was nevertheless involved when it conditioned that removal on "good cause." As Justice Scalia argued in his fiery dissent, "limiting removal power to 'good cause' is an impediment to, not an effective grant of, presidential control."[129] This, of course, was precisely the issue that Scalia had felt too constrained to reach as a lower court judge in *Bowsher*. It was one of the key issues he was now eager to reach, with, he hoped, a majority of his colleagues.

As in *Bowsher*, the majority reaffirmed the vitality of *Humphrey's*

Executor as a precedent, but, in so doing, it applied a different approach to the resolution of separation-of-powers issues: "[T]he real question is whether the removal restrictions are of such a nature that they impede the President's ability to perform his constitutional duty, and the functions of the officials in question must be analyzed in that light."[130] This approach triggers a separation-of-powers analysis that the dissent disparagingly characterized as a "balancing approach."[131] The majority was, at best, very vague on what factors should or should not go into future judicial balancing.[132] Moreover, since the majority concluded that "this case does not involve an attempt by Congress to increase its own powers at the expense of the Executive Branch,"[133] the fact that purely executive power may have been involved was not decisive. The Court rejected the all-or-nothing discourse of formalism and the microanalysis of governmental functions that it encouraged. In its place the Court substituted a more functional constitutional discourse and a macro perspective of the overall balance of power between the governmental branches that the Supreme Court majority thought this act *actually* mandated.[134]

Taking into account the approach to separation-of-powers issues the Court took in *Chadha* and *Bowsher*, it is, perhaps, difficult to explain how seven justices now supported not only the result in this case, but also the pragmatic approach by which it was achieved.[135] One could, somewhat cynically, contend that the new Rehnquist Court was unwilling to go down in history in so politically charged a case as this as a predictable supporter of executive power in general, and executive power wielded by the Reagan administration in particular.[136] One could also contend that this was a rather special kind of conflict-of-interest legislation. By upholding it, the Court, in fact, protected and enhanced the overall integrity of the executive branch. One could also argue, however, that, on a doctrinal level, the facts of this case simply did not trigger the hard-look rhetoric of constitutional formalism. *Morrison* did not as easily lend itself to the all-or-nothing constitutional discourse that typified *Chadha* and *Bowsher*. In *Chadha*, the executive was completely by-passed by vetoes the Court viewed as legislative in nature. In *Bowsher* the power to remove an official exercising important executive functions was initially monopolized by Congress.[137] In both cases the executive was essentially cut out of an important executive decision.

Morrison also involved an important exercise of executive power, but in Morrison the executive was not completely excluded from either the appointment or the removal of the independent counsel. For appointment purposes, the executive initiated the proceedings, which culminated in the naming of an inferior officer. Since the Court saw the independent counsel as "inferior," the appointment role played by the special court set up by the Ethics Act fit easily within the textual authority of the Constitution.[138] More importantly, the executive had a distinct and, in the Court's view, dominant role in the removal of independent counsel. The attorney general had removal power over this official, albeit only "for good cause."[139] Congress would not be involved in the actual application of these provisions. Congress would not make the decision that a particular independent counsel should be removed from office. Congress's only involvement was abstract and legislative: specifying the criteria of "good cause." The executive branch was not excluded from a decision-making process that might ultimately result in removal; indeed, when it came to the removal of a particular individual, the executive branch was largely on its own.[140] The issue in this case was thus whether this minimal sharing of power between the executive and legislative branches so undercut the executive prosecutorial role that it presented a violation of constitutional dimensions. The fact that Congress was not directly involved with the removal of a particular individual arguably triggered the majority's functional-balancing approach to separation-of-powers questions.

As the dissent forcefully argued, however, this case could have been conceptualized in all-or-nothing terms if one began with the premise that *all* executive power—or at least every core executive function—was vested exclusively in the executive branch. Any intrusion by Congress into an area controlled solely by the executive branch would necessarily trigger the hard-look approach of constitutional formalism.[141] The majority of the Court was unwilling to see this case in such all-or-nothing terms because Congress was not to be involved at all in the removal of particular individuals. The Court's approach, however, suggests yet another way of understanding *Morrison* and, more important for our purposes, of fitting this case into the emerging administrative-constitutional framework of the global era.

In end effect, the majority in *Morrison*, like Justice Scalia, also believed that this case was about power,[142] but it focused on the power of the political process to pass legislation and resolve political problems. The majority thus took a procedural approach to the question of the proper allocation of power in order to ensure the overall functioning of the political process, not necessarily the vindication of individual

rights in individual cases. Implicitly, at least, individual-rights questions were matters best left to the interpretation and application of
more specific constitutional provisions. For the majority, only a dramatic shift in power among the branches of government would trigger
the judicial activism typified by the hard-look approach of formalism.
Anything short of such a dramatic shift would involve the Court in
political value choices for which there were no judicially principled
bases for decision.

The *Morrison* balancing approach is, thus, consistent with the judiciary's increasingly political view of the administrative process and with
the overall trend toward greater executive influence over the administrative process. As noted above, the flexibility of functionalism can
favor executive as well as legislative power, while the logic of formalism
is potentially very restrictive of both. In a practical sense, *Morrison*
may, in the long run, provide for even greater executive flexibility in
supervising administrative discretion because it will presumably be
very tolerant of the executive use of legislative power. It also seems to
put to rest some persistent attempts to repeal parts of the New Deal
through the courts rather than through Congress. The majority at least
implied that if certain administrative agencies had outlived their usefulness, Congress, not the courts, would have to act. The courts could
not make such decisions because they were not judicial or constitutional decisions.

The Supreme Court's decision in Mistretta v. United States supports
the approach taken in *Morrison*. *Mistretta* involved a constitutional
attack of the Sentencing Reform Act of 1984 premised on separation-of-
powers principles. John M. Mistretta, who plead guilty to the charge of
conspiracy to distribute cocaine, attacked his eighteen-month prison
sentence issued pursuant to guidelines established by the United
States Sentencing Commission. Specifically, he took issue with the
placement in the judicial branch of the seven-person independent
sentencing commission created by the act. In addition, he challenged
the constitutionality of requiring that three of the seven commissioners
be federal judges appointed and subject to removal by the president.
The thrust of his argument was that the various mixtures of judicial,
legislative, and executive power that resulted undermined the integrity of the judicial branch.

Though the majority of the Court found Congress's requirement of
judicial service on the part of three judges "troublesome," it had little
difficulty rejecting such separation-of-powers concerns. The Court

cited Madison in support of its view that some combinations of functions, as long as they are limited, present no danger. Indeed, they may even be desirable: "We have recognized Madison's teaching that the greatest security against . . . the accumulation of excessive authority in a single branch lies not in a hermetic division between the Branches, but in a carefully crafted system of checked and balanced power within each Branch."[143]

Though the rhetoric of checks and balances does not necessarily resonate with the deregulatory or antiregulatory substance of certain agency actions, it does underscore two other important points: the political nature of the decisions made by Congress and, by implication, administrative agencies, and the very limited role of the judiciary in reviewing fundamentally political decisions. The judicial deference in *Morrison* and *Mistretta* is deference to the political bargains struck by Congress and the executive. It provides a very supportive constitutional framework for both the skepticism on value questions and the increasing willingness of the judiciary to rely on political rationality that underlie the doctrine of presidential deference.

We shall now pursue these constitutional themes in a more explicit administrative-law context by examining, first, the nondelegation doctrine opinions of Justice Rehnquist and, second, the doctrine of presidential deference as conceived and applied in Chevron v. NRDC. Although there is much to be said for active executive supervision of administrative agencies,[144] judicial deference to agency change in the face of congressional inaction and aggressive executive decontrol, particularly in global deregulatory contexts, raises serious institutional issues. The implications of the checks-and-balances analysis in cases like *Morrison* is that all branches should have a role to play in such decision-making contexts. *Chevron*, however, and the nondelegation rhetoric of Chief Justice Rehnquist are more consistent with a formalistic interpretive approach.

The Rise of Political Rationality

The Supreme Court has not struck down an act of Congress on the grounds that it was in violation of the nondelegation doctrine since A.L.A. Schechter Poultry Corp. v. United States.[145] Yet Chief Justice Rehnquist's special concurrence in Industrial Union Department, AFL-CIO v. American Petroleum Institute[146] and his dissent in American Textile Manufacturers' Institute v. Donovan,[147] represent serious

attempts to resurrect this doctrine. Though his arguments are intellec-
tually plausible and appropriately encourage Congress to play a more
responsible role in law making, they do not differ significantly from
those made in the past. Nor are they any more practical or likely to
achieve the results they advocate.[148] Yet, what made their reiteration
so compelling in these cases was the global context in which they now
appeared and the value-laden social regulation to which they were
applied.

The Chief Justice Rehnquist's application of the nondelegation doctrine
to the Occupational Safety and Health Act[149] under review in *American Petroleum* and *Donovan* focused principally on the value choices
Congress was asking the secretary of labor to make. How much safety
had Congress mandated? Should the working environment be essentially risk free? Underlying these questions was an even more fundamental issue: What is the value of a human life?[150] Chief Justice
Rehnquist found no legislative answer to that question in the text or
history of the act. He concluded that this failure of legislative will was
fatal to the overall legitimacy of Congress's attempt to delegate rulemaking authority to the secretary.[151]

The Chief Justice's emphasis on the fundamentally political nature of
value choices relied on the Lockean notion that these kinds of choices
can be made only with the consent of the governed—and thus are
properly decided by legislatures, not courts. Consistent with this approach was a skepticism that assumes that value choices are fundamentally political because they are incapable of any truly principled resolution. The nondelegation doctrine invoked by Chief Justice Rehnquist
thus required clear textual and historical guidance before a court could
engage in a legitimate interpretive role.[152] If the legislature did not
decide the fundamental political issues, a court had no basis upon
which to construct a principled opinion. Thus, Chief Justice Rehnquist
looked first to the Founding Fathers for his basic premises, then to the
legislative fathers of the Occupational Safety and Health Act.[153] Finding no legislative basis for any of the possible judicial interpretations of
this statute,[154] he concluded that the legislature had not done its job. It
was not just silent on an unforeseeable issue. Rather, the legislature
was silent on the very issue upon which this statute should have been
based. These were legislative issues precisely because they involved
fundamental political value choices.

The nature of the health and safety regulation involved in these cases
underscored the political nature of these value choices and gave Justice

Rehnquist's arguments a flavor and relevance that is not found in the regulatory contexts of the New Deal. Application of the nondelegation doctrine in this context differed from invocations of the doctrine in the context of statutes raising conflicts of economic interest.[155] The fundamental conflicts of value involved in these cases did not translate into purely economic discourse. They invoked at least two world views that were not easily, if at all, reconcilable. One world view, economic in nature, would require an agency to consider explicitly the economic consequences of its regulatory actions and weigh these costs against the potential benefits of its actions. The other, absolutist in nature, emphasized the supreme value of life and the need to preserve it, whatever the cost. The nature of the issues involved made Justice Rehnquist's institutional preference for legislative resolution of these conflicting world views more compelling. Indeed, his basic argument was that the choice of the appropriate perceptual glasses for dealing with such issues was not the province of bureaucrats or judges. Such issues were fundamentally political and, thus, clearly legislative.

The application of the nondelegation doctrine in these cases also resonates with a minimalist conception of the role of the federal government. Like the application of formalism in the separation-of-powers cases discussed above, a vigorous application of the nondelegation doctrine would have a strong deregulatory or antiregulatory bias. It would be very difficult to reenact health and safety statutes that have been declared unconstitutional for failing to resolve more definitively the conflicts of value involved. Such life-and-death questions call out for "right" answers, but the variety of answers suggested by the different world views these questions invoke engenders a conflict that is not easily susceptible to the give-and-take of the legislative process. This is undoubtedly one reason why such statutes usually reflect political compromises in a procedural, rather than substantive, manner. Thus, they often reject the Administrative Procedure Act's informal rulemaking and incorporate a statutory hybrid rulemaking that is more procedurally complex.[156] The nondelegation doctrine, by invalidating procedural substitutes for substantive legislative bargaining clearly expressed in terms of definitive legislative choices, would make it much more difficult to propose and pass new statutes that contain fundamental conflicts of value.[157]

These possible deregulatory results are, of course, neither a sufficient nor a necessary condition to the rigorous application of the nondelegation doctrine. Nor do these by-products necessarily confirm the political and constitutional foundations of the doctrine. Nevertheless, the nondelegation doctrine gains a new freshness and force precisely because of the overall context in which the doctrine now applies. In these global deregulatory times it no longer seems quaint. Chief Justice Rehnquist's nondelegation opinions are even more forceful because their formalistic aspects represent more than the voice of a single justice. They also resonate with the implications of the formalistic approach taken in Bowsher v. Synar and INS v. Chadha. The deregulatory overtones of the nondelegation doctrine highlight the fact that the doctrine is consistent with the negative concept of liberty—freedom is best preserved when the federal government acts infrequently or not at all, and if the federal government must act, then only with the explicit consent of the governed. As former Chief Justice Burger noted in INS v Chadha: "With all the obvious flaws of delay, untidiness, and potential for abuse, we have not yet found a better way to preserve freedom than by making the exercise of power subject to the carefully crafted restraints spelled out in the Constitution."[158]

Finally, Chief Justice Rehnquist's attempt to resurrect the nondelegation doctrine and its resonance with the cost-conscious, global regulatory age comports with the view of the administrative process expressed in his dissent in Motor Vehicle Manufacturers Association v. State Farm Mutual Automobile Insurance Co.,[159] which was, to a large extent, reflected in the majority opinion in Chevron v. NRDC. The nondelegation doctrine's emphasis on the political nature of the value choices involved, some of which must be made by Congress and most of which usually are made by agencies, challenges the idea that agency legitimacy flows from agency expertise. For example, agencies may be experts at analyzing the possible health and safety effects of certain toxic substances, but they are not qualified to choose among the alternative remedial approaches, for that question is political, not technical, in nature. The emphasis on the political nature of these decisions encourages a more uniformly political perspective on the administrative process. There is seldom a clear line between expert analysis and political choice. A perception of agencies that emphasizes politics tends to resolve all doubts in favor of politics, rather than expertise. Judicial deference to political rationality and executive control may thus make it easier for agency decisions to withstand substantive judicial scrutiny.[160]

Political questions involve values, yet there are no real experts on values. The value skepticism implicit in Chief Justice Rehnquist's opinions thus reinforces his argument that a legislature must make such fundamental political choices and emphasizes the political nature of the administrative process. Assuming Congress has properly delegated its powers, agencies engaged in policymaking are also making value choices that are statutorily constrained. These choices are political and are best supervised, not by judicial reasoning with its incrementalism and judicial rationality, but by political control and accountability. With that control in place, political rationality can legitimately replace judicial rationality because principled decisions in the realm of values and political choice are not, in any event, really possible.[161]

Political rationality is more likely to be steeped in some new vision of the future than in the precedents inherited from the past. By allowing breaks with the past, the use of political rationality to uphold agency decisions tends to maximize agency flexibility. Such an approach can more easily disregard judicially reasoned, incremental change constrained by precedent and leaves open the possibility of more dramatic changes in agency policy.

Fundamentally, political rationality is premised on power, not reason. Political value choices need not be principled, but simply authorized by the legislature. Thus, the administrative process is a means for implementing political value choices. The primary role of the courts is to ensure agency value choices are statutorily authorized. But agency discretion in making these choices is best controlled by the political branches of the government, particularly by the president. It is, therefore, no surprise that along with the more political view of agency decisions comes a greater executive role, one which a formalistic approach is able to constitutionalize in the ways described above.[162]

An examination of presidential deference in the context of deregulation, however, will show why political rationality alone is generally not enough to justify agency deregulatory actions, particularly when we are entering a new age, an age that should, and ultimately must, be defined by both the president *and* the Congress.

DEFERRING TO EXECUTIVE DEREGULATION

The administrative law doctrine of presidential deference very much complements the constitutional trends discussed above, including the formalistic separation-of-powers approach, which generally favors the executive, the value skepticism inherent in the pragmatism of Morrison v. Olson, and the nondelegation doctrine opinions of Chief Justice Rehnquist. As we shall see in detail, Justice John Paul Stevens in Chevron v. NRDC applies a kind of originalist interpretive approach to statutes.

Chevron—An Overview

Chevron v. NRDC began as a challenge to the EPA's repeal of rules promulgated during the Carter administration pursuant to the mandates of the 1970 Clean Air Act,[163] as amended in 1977.[164] These statutes directed the EPA to establish primary and secondary national standards of ambient air quality for various pollutants. Each state was to devise an implementation plan for each pollutant, setting forth its program for achieving the required air quality standards by a certain date.

In 1977, Congress amended the act to impose even more stringent requirements on states that had not yet reduced pollution to levels below the ambient standards in what were called nonattainment areas.[165] These provisions required permits "for the construction and operation of new or modified stationary sources" of air pollution.[166] A state could issue a permit for the construction of a new or modified major source in a nonattainment area only if the proposed source met these stringent requirements.[167] The primary goal of these amendments was to reduce pollution in nonattainment areas. The legislative history suggests that cost was to be a factor in attempts to achieve this goal, but arguably not to the extent argued by the government in Chevron.[168]

Consistent with the apparent stringency of the 1977 amendments, the Carter EPA viewed all individual pieces of plant equipment as "stationary sources" of pollution within the meaning of the act. The relevant statutory provisions required all new sources of pollution, or modifications to major stationary sources that increased the amount of pollution by more than one hundred tons per year to comply with the "lowest achievable emission rate."[169] The Carter EPA applied this stringent standard to each piece of equipment in the plant that might potentially be replaced. In this way, the Carter EPA hoped that pollution in nonattainment areas would, in fact, begin to improve.

In response to President Reagan's directive that agencies conduct a "[g]overnment-wide reexamination of regulatory burdens and complexities,"[170] the Reagan EPA conducted an informal rulemaking proceeding, which resulted in the repeal of the Carter EPA rules and the implementation of a so-called bubble concept.[171] Under the "bubble" approach, the EPA defined a major stationary source as the entire plant, rather than the individual facilities within the plant.[172] It was thus possible to replace individual pieces of equipment within a plant without any pollution controls whatsoever, if the owner could show that the net increase in *total* pollution would not exceed one hundred tons per year. The entire plant was, in effect, encased in an imaginary bubble for purposes of determining whether the requirements of the 1977 Act should apply.

The net effect of the bubble concept was to lessen considerably the stringency of the Carter rules. It allowed for the possibility that plants in nonattainment areas could essentially maintain the status quo when they replaced individual pieces of equipment rather than actually lower their overall level of pollution. The bubble concept thus helped replace the less cost-conscious regulatory approach to pollution control espoused by the Carter EPA and affirmed by the courts with a new regulatory approach designed to mitigate the costs borne by those creating the pollution. In so doing, it allowed the essentially consumer-oriented Clean Air Act to take on a distinct producer orientation.[173]

Achieving statutory goals in a more cost-efficient manner is always a valid goal, but the bubble approach arguably did more than lower the costs of achieving the act's regulatory goals. The bubble approach was also likely to have a substantial impact on the curtailment of pollution in nonattainment areas. It enabled polluters to upgrade their equipment without necessarily lowering their total pollution rate. It was at least questionable whether Congress had authorized a regulatory approach that emphasized the costs of regulation while possibly maintaining the status quo in nonattainment areas.[174] This was, however, the way the government argued the case in court.

In its brief to the Supreme Court, the EPA "spoke" economics. It asked the Court to "[s]uppose that it is economically desirable to modernize and expand the capacity of machine A, leading to an increase in its emissions to 700 units, and that at the same time emissions from machine B could be correspondingly reduced from 500 to 300 units."[175] The EPA went on to argue that, under these circumstances, review prior to the granting of a construction permit would be useless because the project would not adversely affect air quality. Though this argument disregarded completely the distinct possibility that Congress might not have wanted to maintain the status quo in nonattainment areas, the EPA continued its cost-based argument by assuming that the cost of the two-hundred-unit reduction from machine *B* was $1 million. If machine *A* had to have the "lowest achievable emission rate," the unit would emit six hundred units, but this would cost $2 million. To effect a one-hundred-unit increase in emissions from machine *A*, machine *B* would have to be cut back by one hundred and this would cost $0.5 million. The EPA argued that, without the bubble, the total cost would be $2.5 million, but with it, the cost would only be $1 million and the effect on air pollution would be the same. Thus, the EPA concluded:

> [The bubble approach] ensures that emissions from new or modified sources *do not prejudice attainment*; it requires review of those projects that could interfere with achievement of national air quality standards. It also facilitates the statutory policies of industrial growth and modernization by eliminating the costs necessary to comply with new source review for projects that do not adversely affect air quality. And it gives a plant owner the flexibility to control emissions in the most efficient manner.[176]

This is, essentially, an argument for accepting the environmental status quo at the least possible regulatory cost, but one that gives little weight to the fact that the 1977 act, as applied to nonattainment areas, was intended to achieve more than the status quo. The EPA's approach is seemingly at odds with the overall structure of the Clean Air Act, its legislative history, and at least one previous judicial interpretation of the act by the United States Court of Appeals for the District of Columbia Circuit.[177]

More important, using a market-oriented approach as the primary means of assuring environmental quality arguably changed significantly the very ends of the program mandated by Congress. This regulation did not easily lend itself to the use of the market as a means for achieving the *same* regulatory ends. The use of the market transformed the statute from a consumer-oriented statute to one with a distinct producer bias.[178]

The Clean Air Act Amendments of 1977 were premised on a common-pool conception of market failure. They anticipated a technology-based standard designed to reduce pollution in nonattainment areas. As one commentator noted, "the 1970 Amendments imposed Draconian mandates for the abatement of pollution, regardless of cost."[179] The 1977 amendments built on that approach. The act and its amendments highlighted a set of value judgments that emphasized environmental goals not easily reducible to mere dollars-and-cents discourse.[180] EPA's approach was not necessarily unwise, but in the context of the Clean Air Act and its 1977 amendments, it should have at least raised some serious judicial questions. In short, the nature of the issues at stake, the nature of the statute, the market failure involved, and the change in policy direction represented by the bubble concept all pointed to closer judicial scrutiny. On its face, this case would appear to have had much more in common with Motor Vehicles Manufacturers Association v. State Farm Mutual Automobile Insurance Co. than with FCC v. WNCN Listeners' Guild.[181]

The Court in Chevron v. NRDC[182] nevertheless took an approach to the appropriateness of the EPA's new definition of stationary sources that not only maximized agency discretion, but also avoided any real examination of the agency's dramatic change in philosophic perspective. The Court's approach is particularly disturbing because the EPA's policy shift changed not only the regulatory means by which Congress could achieve its ends but, arguably, the regulatory ends as well. Even if one resolves the complicated questions of legislative history and intent to support the bubble approach, the Court's approach in *Chevron* is still problematic.

The *Chevron* Court was unwilling to take a hard look at the questions of law in this case, much less the questions of policy. It advocated, instead, a two-step approach to judicial review:

> When a court reviews an agency's construction of the statute which it administers, it is confronted with two questions. First, always, is the question whether Congress has directly spoken to the precise question at issue. If the intent of Congress is clear, that is the end of the matter; for the court, as well as the agency, must give effect to the unambiguously expressed intent of Congress. If, however, the court determines Congress has not directly addressed the precise question at issue, the court does not simply impose its own construction on the statute, as would be necessary in the absence of an administrative interpretation. Rather, if the statute is silent or ambiguous with respect to the specific issue, the question for the court is whether the agency's answer is based on a permissible construction of the statute.[183]

To be acceptable the agency's construction need not be "the only one it permissibly could have adopted to uphold the construction, or even the reading the court would have reached if the question had arisen in a judicial proceeding."[184] The *Chevron* approach thus maximizes agency discretion by defining narrowly the legal category in which courts are usually expected to intervene to "the precise issue in question," thereby enlarging considerably the residual discretionary functions of the application of law and the determination of policy, in which agencies are generally expected to excel. Underlying this deferential approach, however, was not necessarily a faith in agency expertise, but rather, a view of politics that placed great weight on the fact that agencies were controlled by the president and thus, their discretionary judgments were the responsibility of the executive branch, which is accountable to the electorate. If Congress had not decided the precise issue in question, neither would a court, even though that issue had important legal and policy implications. Not unlike Justice Rehnquist's dissent in *State Farm Mutual*,[185] Justice Stevens thus spoke in terms of presidential deference:

> Judges are not experts in the field, and are not part of either political branch of the Government. Courts must, in some cases, reconcile competing political interests, but not on the basis of the judges' personal policy preferences. In contrast, an agency to which Congress has delegated policymaking responsibilities may, within the limits of that delegation, properly rely upon the incumbent administration's views of wise policy to inform its judgments. While agencies are not directly accountable to the people, the Chief Executive is, and it is entirely appropriate for this political branch of the Government to make such policy choices resolving the competing interests which Congress itself either inadvertently did not resolve, or intentionally left to be resolved by the agency charged with the administration of the statute in light of everyday realities.[186]

Chevron—An Analysis

The *Chevron* Court's two-step approach to reviewing relevant questions of law is akin to the Court's formalistic constitutional approaches described above in the following ways. The Court defines the issue as an agency value choice. Its implicit assumption that such value choices are fundamentally political in nature places the issue outside the bounds of principled judicial resolution. If Congress did not address "the precise question at issue,"[187] it is thus inappropriate for the Court to second-guess a reasonable agency interpretation.

The Court reaches this result by opting for an all-or-nothing discourse, similar to the discourse of constitutional formalism. Along with Justice Rehnquist's recent attempt to revive the nondelegation doctrine, *Chevron's* textualist statutory approach is reminiscent of the delegation-doctrine debate between Justice Benjamin Cardozo and Justice Charles Hughes in the early delegation cases. In Panama Refining Co. v. Ryan,[188] for example, Justice Hughes focused on specific statutory language and sought a "precise" indication that the power to be exercised by the president over the transport of "hot oil" was, in fact, specifically delegated by Congress. Finding no such decision in the delegation clause of the statute, he voted to strike it down. Justice Cardozo, on the other hand, was willing to examine the overall purpose of the statute, its preamble, its legislative history, and to infer Congress's basic intent and the apparent limits of an agency's power.[189]

Like Justice Hughes's approach in *Panama Refining*, the majority's approach in *Chevron* provides a very narrow, formalistic reading of statutory language and congressional intent. Only questions involving *ultra vires* matters are considered fair game by the *Chevron* Court, but to be *ultra vires* the actions must be violations of *precise* statutory terms. The Court is not about to examine the overall substance of the subject involved, nor the nature of the regulation and the value conflicts that underlie it; rather the Court formalistically construes statutes in a manner that defers to the agency in the name of presidential deference whenever Congress has failed to resolve the *precise* issue. The policymaking area left to the president and his agents is thus significantly expanded.

The bright line that *Chevron* draws between questions of law and questions of agency discretion is also similar in approach to the bright lines that the formalists draw among legislative, executive, and judicial functions in INS v. Chadha and Bowsher v. Synar. But just as it is impossible to capture the complexity of governmental actions by applying the labels of legislative, executive, and judicial in a constitutional context, clear distinctions between legal and discretionary issues at the agency level seldom exist. To create them, however, the *Chevron* court takes a textualist rather than a contextualist approach to statutory interpretation, that is, an approach that is most reluctant to use a statute's legislative history to determine the legal meaning of an ambiguous term. The reasons for this approach have been more fully expressed in various cases following *Chevron*, in which the Court has increasingly and openly engaged in a spirited methodological debate.[190]

In Blanchard v. Bergeron,[191] for example, the Court dealt with a judicial rather than an agency interpretation of a statute. Justice Scalia, however, forcefully articulated why he, at least, does not rely on legislative history in any context. In rejecting the Court's use of a Senate report that cited three district court cases favoring a particular statutory interpretation of an attorney's fee provision, he stated:

> Congress is elected to enact statutes rather than point to cases, and its members have better uses for their time than poring over District Court opinions. That the court should refer to the citation of three District Court cases in a document issued by a single committee of a single house as the action of Congress displays the level of unreality that our unrestrained use of legislative history has attained. I am confident that only a small proportion of the Members of Congress read either one of the Committee Reports in question, even if (as is not always the case) the Reports happened to have been published before the vote. . . . As anyone familiar with modern-day drafting of congressional committee reports is well aware, the references to the cases were inserted, at best by a committee staff member on his or her own initiative, and at worst by a committee staff member at the suggestion of a lawyer-lobbyist; and the purpose of those references was not primarily to inform the Members of Congress what the bill meant, . . . but rather to influence judicial construction.[192]

This view of legislative history refuses to interpret the statutory *products* of the democratic process in light of the democratic *processes* that produced them. Given the diverse, self-interested, and often manipulative role played by interest groups, as well as the fact that the *whole* Congress is unlikely to be aware of such interpretive subtleties,[193] any judicial quest for "genuine" legislative intent is doomed to failure.[194] This is true when a regulatory statute initially interpreted by an administrative agency is involved. An examination of congressional intent would only engage the Court in a review of the unprincipled give and take of the political process. If Congress was not precise in its intentions, the Court should defer to the agency, rather than enter the intensely political thicket of interpretation. Such a judicial approach to statutory interpretation may even encourage Congress to be more specific in its future legislation, knowing that failure to do so will give the final word to an agency, not a court. It will in any event, represent another bright line between the agencies and the courts, making the legislative process less of a sporting event.[195]

These are powerful arguments and they gain strength from their real-world understanding of the legislative process. But being realistic about the legislative process does not require an all-or-nothing judicial approach to legislative history. A sophisticated judicial analysis of a statute's history need not result in interest-group manipulation of a court, nor would it unduly expand the judicial role. Courts have the institutional competence to engage in such interpretation and, more important, they have the obligation to ensure that an administrative agency does not exercise any more power than Congress originally gave to it. Closing judicial eyes to the help that an examination of a statute's legislative history may provide only makes the fulfillment of that judicial role more difficult. Quite apart from attempts by interest groups to manipulate future statutory interpretations, an examination of a statute's legislative history can be very helpful. It can deepen considerably the court's understanding of the kind of regulation Congress may have intended, the type of market failure it sought to correct, and the regulatory values Congress sought to further with the statutory framework it created. It is particularly these value questions that often are not at all reflected on the face of the statute. This is not to say that recourse to legislative history will, in all cases, be illuminating, but it will often either reinforce a court's view of the statutory language in contention or raise serious questions when a purely textual interpretation of a statute is juxtaposed with its legislative history. As Judge Wald has argued:

> As a general matter, interpreting statutes is more difficult than one might think from reading judicial opinions. Once a decision is reached, we often mask much of the angst that is involved in getting there. Although judges' opinions often refer to "plain statutory" language, the truth is that statutes are increasingly complex and technical, and a judge may not always be certain as to the meaning of the small print. As we conscientiously embark on our duty to ascertain what the words mean in the context of the statute's aims and purposes, we are almost inevitably drawn to the historical record of what the men and women who proposed and sponsored the legislation intended to enact. We feel better when their words confirm our reading of the text; we worry more when it contradicts the text. This does not mean, as the textualist Justices accuse, that we "transform" every "snippet of analysis" in congressional reports into "the law of the land" or "elevate to the level of statutory text a phrase taken from the legislative history. . . . " It does mean, however, that we think again when we face a contradiction between text and history, and we should. [196]

The judicial willingness to "think again" in the face of contradictions between text and history should extend to judicial review of agency interpretations of law as well. Being willing to resort to legislative history when reviewing the legality of agency action presumably authorized by an ambiguous statutory term represents a mode of judicial interpretation that is more in accord with the underlying assumptions of a checks-and-balances approach. A contextualist approach that includes an examination of legislative history assumes that there is and should be overlap between the oversight responsibilities of the courts and the executive branch because there may be some contexts, however rare, in which exclusive executive oversight might result in too much power being exercised by that branch of government. The executive has the duty to take care that the laws are faithfully executed, and it plays an important supervisory role when it comes to the federal bureaucracy. The courts, however, must make sure that the actions agencies take pursuant to executive directives fall within the powers that Congress gave to them. Such a judicial role is particularly necessary in deregulatory contexts. The evolutionary approach to change that accompanied the expansion of the New Deal is not the same as the process of change typified by the deregulatory context involved in *Chevron*.

Most *ultra vires* questions involve affirmative regulatory actions that arguably exceed the authority of the agency that undertakes them. The primary question is one of power: did the agency have the power to take this step? In the New Deal context, these cases usually raised purely jurisdictional questions and came about due to agency attempts to extend their regulatory reach. In resolving these kinds of questions, courts, sometimes explicitly, but often implicitly, examined the relevant congressional history and statutory language and resolved all doubts in favor of agency power. Similarly, courts deferred to policy decisions, which were fully within agency discretion, but the context was always that of affirmative regulatory action. In a deregulatory context, *ultra vires* questions of this sort do not usually arise as such. If an agency has had the power to take certain affirmative actions, it may be assumed that it has the legal authority to pull back. The only real questions are *why* an agency would choose to exercise its power in this way. This requires an examination of what, in fact, the agency offers to put in place of the rules it seeks to withdraw.

As the *Chevron* case shows, some statutes require affirmative regulatory action to ensure that legislative goals will be attained. This is particularly the case when it comes to lowering pollution levels in nonattainment areas.[197] Deregulation or the substitution of a market-based regulatory approach, however, may very well undercut the substantive goals of the statute involved. Using market means to achieve regulatory ends can transform those ends into something quite at odds with what Congress intended. It can, for example, result in a cost-conscious regulatory regime that encourages the maintenance of the environmental status quo, rather than its improvement. These are issues about which reasonable people may differ, and they are, by no means, easy issues to decide. A court should not, of course, automatically veto such agency change. But such change does raise *ultra-vires* concerns, even in the context of a contraction, rather than an extension of regulatory power. It may seem that the legal power to do less at a lower cost would automatically be within the power of an agency that had previously tried to accomplish more at a higher cost, but the substitution of market means can result in a significant shift of statutory goals. Such questions of policy, law, or a mixture of the two require close judicial scrutiny because the very values Congress sought to promote may be at stake.

This is particularly true in light of another important contextual factor—in this case—the kind of market failure involved. *Chevron* dealt with a form of market failure that should not immediately lend itself to an economic discourse without careful consideration of the differing philosophic perspectives that underlie the common-pool and natural-monopoly conceptions of market failure. This is not to argue that it is impossible to approach common-pool failures with an economics mind-set as the EPA did in 1981. Rather, it is to argue that the EPA's approach should have raised additional judicial concerns since it may amount to the adoption of new regulatory ends. When this occurs, something more than a rational-basis approach and a cursory discussion of the legislation and its history are required. Such a case should turn on substance, not on the invocation of a seemingly neutral deference doctrine that bows to the electoral accountability and legitimacy of the executive. Presidential deference is substantively tied to market values that are much more questionable in the deregulatory environmental context of this case than the Court's analysis implies.

Even if we were to conclude that issues such as whether or not to resort to a bubble policy in pursuing the goals of the 1977 Clean Air Act were well within the EPA's powers, the deregulatory context in which they arise requires that a court reach that result after engaging in the same judicial soul searching applicable in most *ultra vires* cases. The agency is, in effect, reinterpreting its legal mandate. In a deregulatory context, this usually means that it intends to further market values that may or may not be part of the agency's enabling act or, more broadly, its regulatory constitution. The focus in such cases cannot simply be on the fact that policy issues are involved as if all policy issues were the same. The relationship of policy to statute differs, particularly in deregulatory contexts. Characterizing deregulatory decisions simply as an exercise of policy discretion blurs the usual pro-regulatory policy approaches of agencies with deregulatory and, quite possibly, anti-regulatory policy goals. Decisions such as these should be based on the substantive legislative bargains that are exemplified by the statute, its history, and the regulatory regime it creates. In such contexts, courts have an important oversight role to play.

Chevron Revisionism

There is increasing evidence to suggest that the apparently clear two-step approach in *Chevron* is not nearly as clear when it is applied. Courts often disagree over what is and what is not an ambiguous statutory term. As one judge has remarked, "Some will find ambiguity even in a No smoking sign."[198] More important, in applying *Chevron*, courts are not at all in agreement on when and to what extent they should use legislative history to discern the meaning of an ambiguous statutory term. *Chevron* itself resorted to legislative history to assess the reasonableness of the agency's interpretation. Some courts, however, and some justices on the Supreme Court are willing to resort to a detailed examination of a statute's legislative history to determine whether a statutory term is, in fact, ambiguous or clear in the first instance. In INS v. Cardozo-Fonseca,[199] for example, the Supreme Court majority examined the legislative history of an immigration act to determine whether Congress's intent on a particular issue was clear. If it was not, then the Court would defer, but only after an intensive search of the legislative history to determine what certain conflicting statutory terms apparently meant. Justice Scalia, the most ardent defender of *Chevron* on the Court, argued that the majority's approach to interpretation and a determination of statutory ambiguity could render "deference a doctrine of desperation." It authorizes "courts to defer only if they would otherwise be unable to construe the enactment at issue."[200] Such disagreements over when and to what extent a legislative history should be examined and what legislative histories actually mean continue to arise in the application of *Chevron*. These disagreements go to the heart of the textual/contextual debate discussed above.[201] The outcome in the courts remains to be seen. At stake, is the role that courts will ultimately play in assuring that the executive branch does not go too far in its attempt to adapt old statutes to a new era without congressional involvement. In *Chevron*, itself, however, there were other, broad contextual factors involved that may also narrow the applicability of that case as precedent, factors that went well beyond the four corners of the statute involved and its legislative history.

The Court was undoubtedly aware of the impact of the EPA's policies, particularly on the economically hard-hit northeast. The case involved important and enormous political trade-offs: jobs in the northeast rust belt, where old smoke-stack industries were dying a slow death, versus acid rain in New York, dead lakes in the Adirondacks, and similar negative effects on our neighbors in Canada. These trade-offs involve questions that do not necessarily yield to agency or judicial expertise. So perceived, they are political; and if, as in this case, Congress's intent concerning the statutory term "source" was opaque, so be it. The Court was not about to make the value choices Congress either could not or would not make. Such issues are indeed best left to the "other political branch." But this conclusion could also have resulted in a delegation decision, one that remanded the statute to Congress for further consideration. The Court, however, too easily assumed away any delegation concerns,[202] choosing, instead, to treat the Clean Air Act as if it were a much more discretionary public-interest statute.

Congress's silence and the opaqueness of the statutory term "stationary source" enabled the Court to act as if this act were a typical New Deal public-interest statute. Since Congress was not "precise" in what it authorized the agency to do, the Court read the agency's powers broadly. It assumed that power was delegated to the agency to act in the public interest, leaving to the agency discretion how best to exercise that power.

But not just any exercise of power could qualify for the hands-off treatment in *Chevron*. The case does have some definable limits.[203] Though the statutory term was ambiguous and the Court was predisposed to defer to the agency, it was necessary for the agency to show that it was reasonable to assume that the statute allowed it to "speak economics." Though one could argue, as we have, that the Court was not sufficiently rigorous in its analysis of this claim because it treated it as a question of discretion rather than law, the agency did, at least, address these points, and it used legislative history to bolster its conclusion that its policy was reasonable.[204] Concerning the regulatory ends of the program, the Court focused on the House Committee Report accompanying the 1977 amendments.[205] Specifically, it noted that "Section 117 of the bill . . . had two main purposes: (1) to allow reasonable economic growth to continue in an area while making reasonable further progress to assure attainment of the standards by a fixed date; and (2) to allow States greater flexibility for the former purpose than EPA's present interpretative regulations afford."[206] Having rather easily satisfied itself that economics could, in fact, be utilized, the Court then focused on the market oriented means the agency proposed to use. As in the New Deal cases, the EPA proposed its market approaches in public-interest terms. As the Court noted:

> [The EPA] pointed out that the dual definition "can act as a disincentive to new investment and modernization by discouraging modifications to existing facilities," and "can actually retard progress in air pollution control by discouraging replacement of older, dirtier processes or pieces of equipment with new, cleaner ones." Moreover, the new definition "would simplify EPA's rules by using the same definition of 'source' for PSD, nonattainment, new source review, and the construction moratorium. This reduces confusion and inconsistency." Finally, the agency explained that additional requirements that remained in place would accomplish the fundamental purposes of achieving attainment with NAAQS's [National Ambient Air Quality Standards] as expeditiously as possible.[207]

Thus, unlike the Court in Motor Vehicles Manufacturers Association v. State Farm Mutual Automobile Insurance Co., the *Chevron* Court could point to some legislative history that authorized these economic ends. In addition, the Court could now entertain and address what sounded like public-interest reasons for pursuing more market-oriented means to these ends. The *Chevron* Court, like the Court in FCC v. WNCN Listeners Guild, was then able to conclude: "[T]he plant-wide definition is fully consistent with one of those concerns— the allowance of reasonable economic growth—and, whether or not we believe it most effectively implements the other, we must recognize that the EPA has advanced a reasonable explanation for its conclusion that the regulations serve the environmental objectives as well."[208] The Court emphasized the need for agency flexibility in this area. That the EPA's interpretation represented a major change in policy was not a "danger signal." Indeed, quite the contrary. "The fact that the agency has from time to time changed its interpretation of the term 'source' does not . . . lead us to conclude that no deference should be accorded to the agency's interpretation of the statute. An initial agency interpretation is not instantly carved in stone."[209]

This approach obviously allows agencies much more flexibility to change with the times and circumstances. Yet the Court's willingness to embrace the economic ends of the regulation in this case does so at the expense of the more serious value conflicts raised by the incorporation of market approaches into this kind of regulatory regime. The Court's formalistic approach to the statute and its legislative history converted a case involving potentially serious conflicts of value into one involving an economic discourse more appropriate for the economic regulatory concerns of the New Deal.

Just as judicial deference during the New Deal was not neutral in terms of the vision of progress that motivated and legitimized the various legal and policy approaches employed, deference in a deregulatory context also has very definite substantive results: It helps advance the goals of efficiency. Before those goals become the norm, however, a court should determine whether Congress ever intended an efficiency discourse to apply to the statute in the first place. Article II requires that the executive take care that the laws are "faithfully," not necessarily "efficiently," executed. There can be a difference between these two standards. The overall trends of the new global era, however, threaten to blur that distinction by too easily deferring to executive power. For this reason, the Court should have played a more active role in *Chevron*. Its failure to do so emphasizes new power relationships among courts, agencies, Congress, and the executive that may represent not only a change in substantive regulatory policy, but also a change in the very processes of change itself.

The Rise of the Administrative Presidency

Perhaps the most significant trend in administrative law, particularly since the beginnings of the environmental era, is the steady increase in presidential power over the administrative process. Gone are the days when an effective president merely managed legislative policymaking and carried out traditional executive functions—such as foreign affairs.[210] As the bureaucracy has grown, particularly with the addition of the legislative programs and new bureaucracies established in the 1970s, it has become unwieldy and has produced a great quantity of new law.[211] As we have seen, effective executive coordination of these various law-making centers, many of which are executive in character,[212] requires greater executive influence over policy initiation and implementation as well as greater executive control over the legal output of the bureaucracy.[213] This is particularly true for strong presidents who seek to effect sweeping policy changes through comprehensive administrative reforms. Too much executive influence, however, can transform the administrative presidency into a modified form of parliamentary government. The executive does not control the legislative process, but it does control the administrative process. To the extent Congress fails to constrain the executive or participate more directly in the creation of a regulatory framework for a new era, the executive's increasing domination of the law-making power of the administrative process begins to suggest the control of a prime minister rather than the supervisory role of a president.

The significant increase in the scope of executive management of the law-making processes of agencies, both executive and independent,[214] coincides with the increasing failure of Congress to act authoritatively or consistently regarding comprehensive regulatory reforms, particularly when those reforms have global consequences. By nature, Congress's outlook is more domestic and regional, if not parochial, than that of the president.[215] From an institutional point of view, the president is the official one can expect to have not only a national, but also an international, perspective. His responsibility for foreign affairs and for our nation's role in the interdependent global economy, at least hypothetically, obliges him to take a more global outlook. It is more difficult to capture a decision maker with such a broad and varied constituency. To the extent comprehensive regulatory reforms that recognize global realities are possible, they are more likely to be generated more consistently at the presidential level.[216] Nevertheless, Congress is theoretically the body that can create new regulatory histories and new beginnings by passing new laws or repealing old ones. It can, if it chooses, wipe clean the statutory slate, leaving only the market in its place.[217] The fact that Congress rarely takes such radical action is due, in part, to what political scientists have described as the "science of muddling through."[218] Congress often acts as if it collectively has a predominantly common-law cast of mind and usually effects change incremen- tally. Moreover, an institution created to represent local and regional interests may have a particularly difficult time coping with issues that have a significant global component. Indeed, some of the institutional changes in Congress arguably have exacerbated these gradualist ten- dencies, transforming Congress's penchant for moderation into inac- tion, making Congress too easily manipulated by groups whose main goal is to maintain the status quo.

The increased emphasis on reelection in Congress, and the excessive careerism and parochialism that this preoccupation can spawn, coupled with the breakdown of party hierarchy and discipline, make decisive, innovative congressional action increasingly rare.[219] Institutional changes in Congress's own in-house structure and procedures can also mitigate against decisive change. As one commentator has noted, "the organization of Congress meets remarkably well the needs of its mem- bers."[220] Interest-group politics accord a disproportionate amount of power to those seeking to preserve the status quo and enable elected officials to pursue an increasingly narrow conception of their job.[221]

Perhaps even more important, the rise of political action committees (PACs) and the role that money plays on Capitol Hill make Congress too responsive to short-term political demands. This does not neces- sarily result in rapid or radical change. Rather, it increases the ability of one interest group to stymie the goals of another, particularly when comprehensive change is demanded. Change that requires some clear commitment to an overriding vision is likely to provoke a variety of powerful, wealthy groups, both for and against the change.[222]

The global era will accelerate these forces of fragmentation in Con- gress by raising a series of new issues and concerns that ultimately will require major, comprehensive legislative change, the kind of change most difficult for Congress to accomplish. More fundamentally, how- ever, the global era highlights the institutional limits of Congress. Congress is an institution created to focus largely on local and regional concerns. As an institution, Congress often has conceptualized global regulatory concerns in protectionist terms. Thus, the ability of Con- gress as an institution to take a truly global perspective on future issues is and will likely remain a major institutional and political challenge.

Along with the application of market approaches to regulation in this global era is an increase in the use of market approaches to explain congressional behavior.[223] Public choice theories tend to see individual congressmen as subject to various political vectors capable of moving them in directions directly proportional to the strength of the political force represented. These theories almost always assume passive venality on the part of legislators.[224] Whatever their empirical merits, these theories illustrate quite clearly a perspective on legislative politics as removed from, if not antithetical to, principled deliberation in the public interest.[225] Congress is increasingly a collection of local enterprises in which legislators act as independent contractors, rather than as representatives of an organic body with a definitive national purpose.[226] In the absence of an almost overwhelmingly strong political force for change, Congress seems increasingly content to live with a stalemate rather than risk comprehensive change, especially before the politics of new situations are fully sorted out.[227] Unfortunately, stasis can often be worse than inappropriate reforms.

Increased executive control over agency policymaking in the 1970s and 1980s has occurred largely at the expense of congressional control. To some extent, however, Congress has apparently approved of this shift, both affirmatively and passively. Congress has affirmatively created many agencies that are more executive in nature than the independent agencies of the New Deal. One would expect the president to exercise control over these entities. But the executive control that has resulted is not limited to increased coordination and clarity of purpose. The executive has introduced substantive changes as well, particularly in the context of deregulation. Many of the substantive, deregulatory policies of the executive have been implemented by agencies, and Congress has neither affirmed these new directions nor disapproved of them.[228] The New Deal and environmental eras we have examined have been marked by the passage of specific congressional programs, inspired or at least backed by the president. Congress passed the laws that courts ultimately interpreted and extended in the New Deal era and in the environmental era that followed. While agency deregulation under these acts can be interpreted as similar to the regulatory extensions that agencies adopted in previous eras, it is important to emphasize that the most distinctive feature of the politics of efficiency is that no specific legislative program marks this new era. With the exception of congressional deregulation of the Civil Aeronautics Board and a few other deregulatory statutes, deregulation is essentially a program carried out by the executive branch through executive orders,[229] appointments of efficiency-minded individuals, vigorous executive control over decisions not to enforce certain existing rules and regulations,[230] and agency attempts to rescind some rules and replace them with more cost-effective or market-oriented approaches.[231]

With few exceptions, Congress has neither repealed nor amended the statutes now used to effect these changes. Its primary contribution to deregulation has been indirect, in the form of budgetary legislation[232] and tax reductions.[233] These statutes have pressured agencies to scale down their programs, goals, and statutory mandates. But such statutes differ markedly from those of the New Deal and environmental eras. Their impact on substantive law is indirect. They do not provide the legal guidance to courts that statutory interpretation usually requires. They are more like presidential speeches, hortatory rather than prescriptive. They are all part of the atmosphere or mood of the times—a mood that agencies have tried to read, and, occasionally force, into their own statutory mandates.[234]

The rise of the administrative presidency is, in short, spurred by the management needs of an unwieldy bureaucracy and the new substantive demands of a global era. But management evolves into legislation when the market becomes an end in and of itself. If the same processes of change used in the environmental and New Deal eras are to be used to define the contours of the global era, Congress must play a more direct and substantive role. There are constitutional and statutory limits to the extent of change possible if only an administrative strategy is employed. Congress *and* the president must define the global scope of our regulatory structure. Both branches must help to shape the contours of a new globally relevant body of law.

ADMINISTRATIVE LAW AT THE START OF A GLOBAL ERA

A number of basic trends in the doctrines of constitutional and administrative law have emerged: the adoption of a global regulatory perspective that encourages deregulation and fuels a politics of efficiency; the rise of the administrative presidency; the further decline of Congress in the wake of increasing presidential control over the administrative process; the declining role of agency expertise as the fundamental source of agency legitimacy; and the gradual erosion of a legal discourse focusing primarily on the relationship of agency rationality to judicially determined congressional goals by a more political discourse that is epitomized by deference to executive interpretations of the laws involved, which has resulted in a tendency toward agency actions justified in terms of presidential power and electoral accountability. These trends provide a perspective on larger patterns of change that form the context of doctrines of constitutional and administrative law such as formalism and presidential deference. These trends also indicate a distinct break with the formal and procedural assumptions of the regulatory eras that preceded the global era. The following table sets forth a brief summary of the critical parameters of this evolution.

The larger patterns of change that now dominate administrative law have been increasingly global in character. The new era of global competition among corporate entities and nation states has manifested itself in the form of a rather crude, *realpolitik*. In the words of the musical, *Chess*, "Nobody's on nobody's side. Everybody's playing the game, but nobody's rules are the same."[235] Much of our domestic regulation seems to have exacerbated our inability to compete internationally. The deregulatory tendency currently dominating administrative activity is an attempt to redress that problem in a rather narrow and extreme manner, offering only microeconomic solutions to problems of global interdependence and interconnectedness. Our system of public law has begun to transform itself, and it can be argued that in so doing, nothing very fundamental has changed. Thus, in place of the myth of agency expertise, we have substituted another, the myth of executive accountability. Agencies have continued to further their (and presumably Congress's) visions of progress, and the courts, by deferring, made these visions possible.

Some hold that the flexibility of our system of public law has allowed the stiff wind of global economic reality to blow through our institutions. Agencies, once again, have become the primary agents of change, and some important modifications to our doctrines of administrative and constitutional law have begun to take shape. Expertise, independence, and other myths designed to insulate New Deal agencies from day-to-day control by the political branches have given way to a greater emphasis on the political nature of agency tasks. Agencies make and implement value choices that are political and, as such, are arbitrary, for no one is an expert when it comes to making difficult value choices. Value skepticism goes hand in hand with global market realities. Perhaps it is appropriate for Congress to leave the supervision of regulatory, political decision making to the president. Article II, after all, gives the executive the duty to take care that the laws are faithfully executed, and the increase in presidential supervisory power need not necessarily undermine agency expertise or congressional authority. Moreover, because agencies have proliferated and because their mandates have crossed over industry lines, there is an enormous need to

Table 1. The processes, justifications, and sources of legal change in three eras

Regulatory era	Locus of expertise	Regulatory problems	Social goals	Sources of change	Modes of change
New Deal–APA	Independent regulatory commissioners as agents of Congress	Chaotic markets	Economic recovery and stability	Congress and the president	New statutes and agencies—incremental change through adjudication
Environmental	Executive agencies as agents of the president	Pollution, disease, and injury	Environmental recovery and preservation	Congress and the president	New statutes and agencies—increased use of rulemaking powers
Global	Personal values and market responses	Regulatory costs and regulated markets	Recovery of efficiency and economic growth	The president	Agency statutory interpretations, OMB reviews, rule rescissions, agency inaction, budget cuts

coordinate and control their vast policymaking powers. Agencies can still set forth the appropriate range of alternatives from which administrators must choose, and courts can continue to be sure that agencies choose only those alternatives within their statutory powers, but policy preferences are best controlled by an elected branch of government—the president.

A stronger case, however, can be made for the proposition that something fundamental is indeed transpiring. This is particularly clear when one begins with the proposition that the processes of change themselves are as significant as the substantive results that they achieve. In the deregulatory era a number of factors suggest that the processes of change are themselves changing in fundamental and constitutionally dangerous ways that warrant careful monitoring. The executive has used the "take care" clause to transform enabling statutes into efficiency-minded pieces of executive legislation. This change is not simply a process of exploring and implementing the implications of congressional statutes. Discontinuity with the past is typical of the processes of change in the global era. Moreover, the executive frequently replaces Congress's goals with its own. These economic policies and approaches to regulatory issues may or may not be wise, but Congress has been remarkably silent and passive regarding their development, their implementation, and their origin. Making the executive the ultimate interpreter of the regulatory matrix in a deregulatory context has created a new source of law and policy, one that creates the possibility for rapid and often dramatic change. There are, or should be, institutional limits to this kind of change. Accordingly, without more active congressional involvement, greater judicial supervision, not less, is demanded.

A line distinguishing expertise and politics makes sense in a regulatory setting, but in a deregulatory setting it is not that easy to separate law from policy and politics from technical alternatives, particularly when these alternatives consist of market solutions applied in regulatory contexts. The perceptions and the politics of an era, not to mention the economic stakes involved, can blur these distinctions. More significantly, emphasizing political rationality rather than judicial analysis of regulatory reasoning can also mask Congress's relatively nonexistent role in defining the modern era, thus underemphasizing the need for true political involvement and fundamental reform at the legislative level.

An emphasis on political rationality has another effect on change. It encourages the blurring of categories such as law and policy by too easily resolving all doubts in favor of power, rather than power constrained or expressed in reasoned analysis. When power is not firmly anchored in a statutory regime passed by Congress, political rationality not only provides flexibility, but perhaps too great an opportunity for executive officials to respond to the moment, to the relatively new and fickle demands of the media, and to the increasingly short-term political view of what is needed. The rationality and change explored in earlier regulatory eras emphasized gradualism, precedent, history, and a link with the past. Political rationality lends itself to more abrupt change and to greater flexibility. Yet, what legitimates such change is a sense of democracy that, ironically, may be undercut by the structure of administrative and constitutional law now taking shape. Deferring to the president when he implements a Global Regulatory Reform Act passed by Congress is one scenario. But deferring to change that our interest-group-bound political system is not really able to accomplish on its own is quite another. Change that occurs in this manner does not further democratic principles, though it may further some new economic reforms.

Indeed, the theory of democracy that underlies the current executive-oriented administrative state does not differ substantially from the "thin democracy" of the New Deal. Rather than independent, expert agencies connected to Congress, we have more politically oriented agencies directly connected to the executive. Today, policy and power do not come from the people; we do not have a "strong" form of democracy.[236] Power and policy continue to come from technocratic decision makers who gain legitimacy because, theoretically, they are controlled directly by an official that is subject to all of our votes. This, of course, is a myth. Executive accountability has its own limitations. More important, it is constitutionally limited when it becomes a source of legislative change. Without a more active Congress, placing more and more supervisory control in the executive's hands risks moving the processes of change in very undemocratic directions. "Thin democracy" can only become threadbare in such contexts.

The change in the deregulatory context reviewed thus far places a great deal of legislative power in the executive. Congressional programs defined the New Deal and environmental eras. The president and Congress worked together. Much of the deregulatory reform that has occurred in recent years, however, has taken place through the executive's aggressive reading of the "take care" clause. Thus, an intense contradiction exists between the democratic tone of the constitutional and administrative rhetoric of the deregulatory era and the lack of congressional participation in the change that has occurred. The global era, however, continues to evolve. The economic discourse of global competition and world trade is now being tempered by global environmental and developmental perspectives. The environmental perspective, in particular, helps place such regulatory concerns as ozone and greenhouse gases not only on the international agenda, but domestic regulatory agendas as well. Domestic problems must be seen in a new light and in relationship to global forces and actors over which local legislators and regulators have little direct control. Global agreements such as the Montreal Protocol and its amendments represent a form of global legislation. This legislation sets forth a broad regulatory framework and defines a new sense of regulatory progress. It also offers a global regulatory model for change—change based on gradual yet frequent and responsive amendment of its basic legislative goals in light of additional scientific information. It represents the creation of a new global regulatory framework, one that may help set forth the broad parameters of new international and domestic regulatory goals. Courts ultimately may have something specific to defer to, and Congress may find itself "reenergized" by an important legislative agenda.

To better understand these possibilities, it is necessary to examine more fully the Montreal Protocol and the new global discourse it generates. While the forces of global competition and the economic perspective and discourse they encourage dominated the beginnings of the global era, the issues now developing are much more complex. They involve not only economics and global trade, but the concerns raised by the poverty of the third world and the ability of science to identify problems of global dimension the solutions to which will require collective international action. This new discourse places new issues on the international regulatory and domestic regulatory agendas and resurrects older domestic issues as well. Moreover, it is changing the way we think of all of these issues, both old and new. On an institutional level, the new discourse is likely to accelerate some of the trends identified here, especially the flow of power to the president and the continuing institutional and political challenges faced by domestic legislatures with regulatory agendas that are increasingly global in their significance.

4

Global Regulation

Global competition and the technology necessary to create and take advantage of global markets are helping to shape a new context for U.S. domestic regulatory and deregulatory discourses. Global trade puts a premium on efficiency in both the private and public sectors. It also favors a political attitude that, at times, can encourage reform well beyond the demands of efficiency per se. This politics of antiregulation derives in part from the application of microeconomic principles to government, and in part out of a general sense that regulation has failed. This sense of frustration is exacerbated by the perception that other countries play by more permissive rules or no rules at all and by a general nostalgia for that period of U.S. economic dominance, when there was little, if any, significant foreign competition.

This latter-day, worldwide "rise of the trading state"[1] and the intensification of global competition that goes with it is but one facet of a global perspective, albeit a very important one. Markets have become more global, but the law has also become global in important ways. For example, global regulation is now developing around certain environmental issues. Its language is complex and rich, for it speaks to two other crucial worldwide issues, the environment and the disparities in wealth that exist between developed and less developed nations. These three global issues—competition, the environment, and development—are directly linked to an important domestic concern of global significance: national security.

The complex global regulatory discourse generated by these factors is now shaping a new body of international law that will inevitably temper antiregulatory and deregulatory domestic initiatives. World-wide agreements that seek to regulate or ban certain environmentally harmful substances usually put these issues on domestic regulatory agendas. Moreover, the effort to create global regulation helps shape national institutions. By blurring the lines between domestic and international issues, global regulatory processes might contribute significantly to increases in executive power, for the more international an issue becomes, the more likely it is that it will be seen as a presidential responsibility.

At the same time, the elimination of bright-line distinctions between the domestic and the foreign could also, at least theoretically, encourage the revival of a Congress strong enough to treat as domestic what the executive branch will argue are international policy concerns. One can imagine growing conflict between the branches over differing congressional and executive approaches to global problems. But to the extent that congressional approaches to such issues are regional or arguably protectionist in nature, power will most likely continue to flow to the executive branch. Global problems require global solutions, and the executive branch is more likely than the Congress to have the necessary global perspective. The use of executive orders, particularly in conjunction with the executive's use of its constitutional treaty-making powers could become an increasingly important source of both international and domestic law. Whether Congress can play a responsible and effective role in the resolution of interrelated domestic and international issues will, therefore, most likely depend on its ability to incorporate a truly global perspective into its thinking. Congress will have to redefine individual and collective interests in global terms in order to respond appropriately at the domestic level.

To act in this manner, Congress will have to take a much longer view of what constitutes the self and collective interests of its constituents. Given the nature of a legislative body and its more local and regional focus, it is difficult to predict whether and how the wisdom to discern this longer view will be created. In previous regulatory eras, however, it seems that the ability to take a longer view coincided with the creation of a broad cultural and legal framework that helped define a new sense of progress and the steps necessary to achieve it. The global regulatory discourse now taking shape on certain environmental issues may be the beginnings of such a framework.

In this chapter I chart at least the outlines of this new framework and the new sense of progress that drives it. I begin by examining the nature of the global-environmental issues involved and then analyze the Montreal Protocol on Substances That Deplete the Ozone Layer, a major piece of global legislation that successfully accommodates three very different perspectives on the ozone problem—science, trade, and development—without necessarily resolving fully the conflicts among them.

THE NATURE OF INTERNATIONAL ENVIRONMENTAL ISSUES

Global-environmental problems are very much a part of the world's legal agenda for the 1990s and, most likely, well beyond.[2] The increasing ability of science to take the globe's environmental pulse by measuring the impact of various forms of industrialization has helped to place important global-commons issues on the world's political agenda *before* any discernible environmental catastrophes occur. Global warming and the threat posed to the earth's ozone layer by certain pollutants have generated an international scientific discourse that has raised the world's environmental consciousness and awareness of the long-range consequences of current patterns of modernization and industrialization. In addition, the external costs imposed by modern technology in an interconnected world make the boundaries between nations relatively meaningless when it comes to the damage caused by acid rain, oil spills in international bodies of water, or nuclear accidents. This situation is made clear when the various international environmental issues are placed on a continuum with transboundary environmental issues at one end and global-commons issues at the other.

Transboundary Environmental Issues

Transboundary legal questions vary in complexity in terms of the facts and issues involved, but also in terms of the number of countries necessary to resolve the dispute. At one end of the regulatory spectrum, international law attempts to deal with environmental harm within one nation caused by actions taken by individuals, entities, or governments in another, usually adjacent, country. An oil spill in a river that crosses only one national boundary involves only two different legal jurisdictions. The relevant period is the recent past. The damages are accidental. Questions of liability predominate. Though such legal issues can be complex,[3] such a dispute involves only two jurisdictions and can be resolved with the application of traditional common-law remedies.

The explosion of the Soviet nuclear power plant at Chernobyl is a more complicated situation. The cause of the harm is clear. Whatever liability flows from such an accident is very much a retroactive determination traceable to a single, catastrophic event. But the victims of this harm and the extent of their damage may not be known for some time. Moreover, several jurisdictions are involved.[4]

Acid rain is an even more complex problem. It involves multiple, ongoing, economically productive causes of harm that is not at all accidental. Several countries are likely to be both the victims of this harm and have within them various perpetrators of it as well. Canadian enterprises, for example, produce acid rain that adversely affects their own environment and that of the United States; U.S. concerns do the same here and to Canada. Solutions to such chronic pollution problems usually involve both regulation of the manufacturing processes within the countries involved and international determination of the relative contribution each country makes to the harm inflicted on other countries. Domestic regulatory reforms without international cooperation cannot cure this problem. The international component of a solution to acid rain thus often comes in the form of bilateral or multilateral treaties.[5] Such treaties are possible only when each of the countries involved determines that the international solution is worth the economic and, perhaps, political costs necessary to deal with the issue domestically. The inability to solve the acid rain problem or even to ignore it effectively without engaging in international negotiation makes the entanglement of domestic policy and domestic politics with international policy and politics inevitable. Nevertheless, in terms of the political and legal questions they raise, the blurring of the distinction between international and domestic, and the scientific challenges involved, global-commons issues are even more complicated than transboundary issues in both scope and content.

Environmental Issues and the Global Commons

Problems such as the depletion of the ozone layer or the buildup of greenhouse gases in the atmosphere are global-commons issues in several respects. First, they deal with potential environmental damage to a resource that no one owns. From an economic point of view, it is precisely because no one can own the atmosphere that there is no system in place to protect it. Second, the harm involved is common to all. Third, virtually all countries contribute to the problem. It is in this sense that such global-commons issues suggest our viewing, in this case, the earth's atmosphere as a "common heritage of mankind."[6]

Questions of responsibility for damage to the ozone layer differ at least in degree from those of a nuclear accident or an oil spill. Decision makers must look both to the past and to the future. Many developed countries are responsible for past contributions to environmental damage, but virtually all countries, including the less developed, are likely to contribute to future environmental degradation. Given the damage to the atmosphere that has already occurred, additional pollution, from whatever source, could have profound ecological consequences. Rather than liability in a common-law sense of fixing responsibility for damage to a particular individual or entity for a one-time, accidental occurrence, fixing responsibility in such global contexts is a much more complicated matter. Regulation must attempt to deal with future environmental problems that have not yet fully manifested themselves and also take into account the effects of past actions.

Among the complications of defining the problem is the fact that, as with acid rain, potential damage may be a result of ongoing processes that are economically beneficial for many of the countries involved. Accordingly, determining the degree of potential responsibility for environmental harm usually involves complex developmental issues and the concerns over the equitable, distribution of wealth inherent to them. Global-environmental problems such as ozone depletion and the greenhouse effect are largely the results of certain forms of modernization such as industrialization and the use of the automobile and other consumer goods. Wealthy countries have long had the luxury of affluence by engaging in activities that now appear to be the main causes of environmental damage. They were able to achieve relatively high standards of living without having to internalize the costs of environmental harm in any way. Today's poorer countries bent on moving into the mainstream of the global economy can often ill afford the costs that regulation would add to their attempts to industrialize.

A global-environmental perspective thus highlights the need for collective regulatory action on the part of virtually all countries, but not in a way that ignores the wealth-creating potential of global competition. Poorer countries may not be able to absorb the regulatory costs of global-environmental concerns and remain competitive in world markets. The interrelationship between environmental issues and economic growth, particularly the growth of less developed countries, thus makes both the overall cost of global regulation and the ability of certain economies to cope with it an important international concern. In addition, the likelihood that both environmental protection and traditional forms of economic growth can coexist indefinitely, of course, raises even more fundamental questions, quite apart from the equitable demands of countries with developing economies. At this stage in the emerging process of global ordering, regulatory effort must minimize future environmental damage and permit traditional forms of economic growth for reasons of both economic policy and equity for developing nations. The domestic political support necessary for industrialized countries to participate effectively in such global agreements also requires sensitivity to the impact of international regulation on economic growth.

These three aspects of globalism—trade, development, and the environment—define the broad outlines of the debates that preceded the Montreal Protocol on Substances That Deplete the Ozone Layer and continue in its aftermath. They suggest three very different starting points and perspectives, all of which are reflected in the body of the protocol and its amendments. This agreement has been effective even without the prior resolution of these debates over approach. It has provided a new and important regulatory framework that encourages progress on the ozone problem and serves as a possible model for other international regulatory efforts. To explain more fully the nature of the global regulatory discourse it encourages as well as the kinds of viewpoints and interests that had to be accommodated for an agreement of this kind to attract enough support to be effective, I shall examine these three lines of debate as they emerged in the context of the Montreal Protocol.

THE MONTREAL PROTOCOL

The Montreal Protocol on Substances That Deplete the Ozone Layer was agreed to by twenty-four countries on September 16, 1987.[7] This agreement was a protocol to the Vienna Convention for the Protection of the Ozone Layer, opened for signature on March 22, 1985.[8] The signatories to that convention agreed to "take appropriate measures . . .

to protect human health and the environment against adverse effects resulting or likely to result from human activities which modify or are likely to modify the ozone layer."[9] The Montreal Protocol was based on the general framework set forth in this convention. It calls for scheduled reductions in the consumption and production of several chlorofluorocarbon (CFC) compounds. As an interim measure, it required a freeze at 1986 levels on annual consumption of CFCs and certain bromine (halon) compounds as well.[10] Following that, the protocol required scheduled, long-term reductions in annual consumption—29 percent by 1994 and 50 percent by 1999.[11] These regulatory goals have since been amended to require a total phaseout of certain CFCs by the year 2000.[12]

Scientists now generally agree that CFCs can and have had a devastating effect on the earth's ozone layer.[13] These compounds do not break down quickly.[14] The impact of their release into the atmosphere is cumulative. The chlorine gas they emit triggers a chemical reaction that depletes the stratosphere of ozone, thereby making radiation damage from the sun a serious long-term health concern. The reduction in ozone levels they cause does not necessarily affect all countries equally, though virtually all countries contribute to this kind of damage.[15] Along with the buildup of carbon dioxide in the earth's atmosphere, CFCs also contribute to global warming.

The Montreal Protocol's initial substantive response to the problems created by CFCs and related compounds was less significant than the global regulatory process it established and the international precedent it set. Though discovery of an actual hole in the ozone layer caused worldwide concern that facilitated later negotiations and the 1990 amendments, the 1987 protocol itself "represents the first time that the world community committed itself to imposing controls on an important industrial sector *before* actual damages to human health and ecology were registered."[16] The initial agreement was frequently criticized as being too little too late,[17] but the important aspect of the agreement is the gradual regulatory approach to the phasing out of certain substances coupled with frequent reassessment of its substantive goals in light of new scientific evidence that it initiated. The protocol was thus written not as an end in itself but as the beginning of a cooperative effort that would continue to extend its regulatory prohibitions as scientific discoveries and circumstances warranted.[18] The 1990 amendments to it, which both clarify and considerably extend the obligations of the original protocol, bear this out.[19]

To examine both the nature of this agreement and the global regulatory process it has engendered, we shall consider the Montreal Protocol from the point of view of the implicit and explicit interrelation-
ships of the three components discussed thus far: environment, trade,
and development. This more complex discourse reinforces some aspects of domestic regulatory discourses and tempers others. The new
global discourse involves the economic, competitive concerns identified and discussed in Chapter 3. At the same time, it recognizes the
needs of less developed countries in a manner that recalls both the
concerns for financial equity and the market skepticism of the New
Deal. Its emphasis on science and the ability of science to identify and
suggest solutions for major environmental problems recalls too the
public-interest, regulatory perspectives of the environmental era.

The Montreal Protocol and Science

Science proved to be an effective discourse for moving debate on the
Montreal Protocol from particular national and regional interests to
larger environmental issues on which general agreement was more
likely. The primary motivating factor for the Montreal Protocol and its
amendments was thus the environmental problem it defines and seeks
to correct. Even so, the mere pointing to future environmental disas-
ters possible from the depletion of the ozone layer could not have
overcome national and regional calculations of short-term economic
self-interest. In effect, the agreement asked potential signatories to
redefine their national interests. Science and the credibility of scientific discourse provided the central terms of that project. Science
offered the possibility of an analysis of environmental problems that
could be shared by all countries. It facilitated a conception of the
problem, a solution to it, and a language for discussing it that transcended a solely (and overtly) political view of the issues involved.
Unlike the language of law, the language of science is not tied to any
one state; the credibility of scientific claims of objectivity and univer-
sality created important substantive and symbolic aspects of the agreement. Even if one does not accept the universal truth claims of science,
it remains true that in the case of the Montreal Protocol and especially
its amendments, the scientific discourse served best as the one that
could fairly and comprehensively translate individual positions and
preferences into a collective vision that seeks action in the interest of
the global body politic.

How a country responds to scientific findings and risk assessments and how a country chooses the options it will pursue are political questions. The scientific perspective, however, can and did provide a concrete basis for action capable of attracting general agreement on at least a definition of the problem and its urgency.

Ozone is a pollutant at ground level, but in the upper stratosphere it plays an extremely helpful role. By absorbing ultraviolet rays from the sun, it protects life on earth from the harmful effects of overexposure to this radiation.[20] There is substantial evidence that an increase in ultraviolet radiation induces certain kinds of skin cancer, suppresses the human immune system, causes cataracts, and adversely affects plant and aquatic life.[21]

In the early 1970s, the research of two independent teams of scientists suggested that the release of chlorine into the atmosphere could devastate the ozone layer. In 1973, Richard Stolarski and Ralph Cicerone, scientists at the University of Michigan, researched the effects of the chemical emissions of rocket fuel. They hypothesized that the chlorine gas emitted by these rockets would act as a catalyst in such a way as to allow a single chlorine atom to destroy tens of thousands of ozone molecules.[22] Given the small number of rockets involved and the minor amount of chlorine they emitted, their findings were not immediately alarming, from an environmental point of view. The amount of chlorine gas ultimately released into the stratosphere by the growing use of CFCs, however, was enormous. This finding shaped the context in which the 1974 research of Mario Molina and Sherwood Rowland was appreciated as being environmentally significant.[23]

Molina and Rowland's research analyzed the chemical properties of chlorofluorocarbons.[24] These compounds had a number of important economic uses. They were used extensively as propellants in aerosol sprays, as coolants in refrigerators and air conditioners, as blowing agents for insulation and foam, as solvents for cleaning computers, and in a variety of other consumer goods. They were not dangerous or harmful to human beings when used in these ways, and they were inexpensive to produce. More important, CFCs and halons are very stable compounds. This property makes them useful for many practical applications, but it also causes a problem. As they escape from refrigerators, air conditioners, and the like, they rise to the stratosphere where they can remain intact for several decades or longer. As they are slowly broken down by solar radiation, they then release significant amounts of chlorine that react with ozone in an extremely destructive manner over a long period of time.

The fact that CFCs are very useful and apparently safe and economic meant that they were being produced and used at an increasing rate. Their chemical longevity meant that their impact on the stratosphere was cumulative and long lasting. If Molina and Rowland's hypothesis regarding the interaction of chlorine atoms with ozone molecules was correct, the gradual buildup of CFCs in the stratosphere was, therefore, likely to have a long term, devastating effect on the earth's ozone layer. These research findings and their implications had potentially significant bearing on the efforts of others concerned to protect the environment.

Initially, however, the reaction of the scientific community to this hypothesis and its implications was mixed. As Richard Benedick points out in his book *Ozone Diplomacy*:

> The research complexities involved were enormous. Ozone amounts to considerably less than one part per million of the total atmosphere, with 90% of it concentrated above 6 miles in altitude. The intrinsically unstable ozone molecules are constantly being created and destroyed by complex natural forces involving solar radiation and interactions with even more minute quantities of other gases. Ozone concentrations fluctuate widely as a result of natural causes on a daily, seasonal and solar cyclical basis. . . . Further, there are great geographical variations in ozone abundance over different latitudes as well as at different altitudes in the atmosphere. Amid all these large-scale fluxes, scientists thus faced an enormous challenge in attempting to detect a minuscule "signal" of the beginnings of the postulated long-term downward trend in stratospheric ozone concentrations.[25]

These "signals" were eventually to come as scientists detected not only a hole in the ozone layer above the Antarctic in 1985, but also an even larger depletion of the ozone layer than had been predicted initially. Prior to these "signals," however, scientific debate, and the dissemination of information within the scientific community as well as among the public at large led to a growing awareness among policymakers in various nations of the need to act collectively despite scientists' uncertainty. The Vienna Convention and the Montreal Protocol were well along before these signals became as clear as they now appear to be.

Indeed, Molina and Rowland's findings quickly led to widespread discussion and debate among scientists and the lay public. The scientific community in the United States almost immediately involved the National Academy of Sciences in a major research campaign focusing on the earth's ozone layer. Congress also became interested in the science involved and held hearings dealing with possible adverse effects on the ozone layer in 1974 and 1975. At the international level, the United Nations' Environmental Program (UNEP), based in Nairobi and headed by Dr. Mostafa Tolba, called for international meetings to discuss the implications of the chlorine hypothesis for the global environment. This international effort ultimately led to UNEP's call for a "World Plan of Action on the Ozone Layer" and the establishment in 1977 of a "Coordinating Committee on the Ozone Layer." That U.N. committee produced annual reviews of the evidence dealing with ozone depletion. Ultimately, these international scientific efforts culminated in an international report involving over 150 scientists from various nations, published by UNEP and the U.N.'s World Meteorological Organization (WMO) in 1986.[26] It was "the most comprehensive study of the stratosphere ever undertaken: three volumes containing nearly 1,100 pages of text plus 86 reference pages listing hundreds of articles."[27] Among other things, that report fully supported the chlorine theory of ozone depletion and, significantly, noted that the accumulations of certain CFCs had nearly doubled from 1975 to 1985. It predicted that this rate of increase would have a devastating effect on the ozone layer over the last half of the twenty-first century and result in extremely harmful effects on the Northern hemisphere. In addition, the report identified a number of new CFCs and bromine compounds that threatened the ozone layer. It was crucial background for the negotiations that preceded and ultimately led to the Montreal Protocol in 1987.

Dissemination, debate, and a recitation of the risks eventually had significant political effects, both domestically and internationally. The willingness to consider seriously the report's predictions was enhanced by the fact that in the 1970s, particularly in the United States, the domestic political climate was most receptive to analyses that suggested environmental reforms. Molina and Rowland's 1974 findings and their implications for the environment coincided with the peak of the environmental era of regulation in the United States, discussed in Chapter 1. The United States was one of the first countries to ban the use of CFCs in aerosol spray cans.[28] In retrospect, it now appears that perhaps the most significant factor leading to the United States's willingness to undertake a leadership role in negotiating the Montreal Protocol in 1987 was passage of the Clean Air Act in 1977, specifically section 7457(b). That provision set forth a proactive form of regulation vis-à-vis potential ozone-destroying agents. It was not necessary that it be proven that substances like CFCs, in fact, injured the ozone layer. Rather, section 7457(b) of the Act authorized the administrator of the Environmental Protection Agency to regulate "any substance . . . which in his judgment may reasonably be anticipated to affect the stratosphere, especially the ozone layer in the stratosphere, if such effect may reasonably be anticipated to endanger public health or welfare."[29] This kind of proactive domestic regulation when analyzed from the point of view of global trade and competition, creates an important incentive for encouraging a nation to participate in an international regulatory approach to a global problem.

The Montreal Protocol and Trade

The Montreal Protocol is a response not only to scientific debate and the global-commons problem posed by atmospheric pollution but also to the conflicting, self-interested economic goals of its actual and potential signatories and adherents. From a trade perspective, the existing incentives for not joining in such an agreement are enormous. They are not unlike those that made the abolition of child labor difficult, if not impossible, to achieve on a state-by-state basis in late nineteenth- and early twentieth-century United States. Few states at that time were willing to impose additional costs on their own industries because local manufacturers could easily avoid them by shifting their operations across state lines. International regulation of various industrial processes that does not bind all or at least most nations is similarly unlikely to succeed, particularly if it provides a significant competitive advantage to countries that choose not to comply. Piecemeal regulation is likely to impose costs on domestic manufacturers competing with entities in countries that make no such regulatory demands. These costs create an incentive for industry to move to or expand production in those countries that do not impose them.[30] Partial regulation can even stiffen the resolve of some nations to resist the imposition of new global regulatory costs, for such resistance not only gives present domestic manufacturers a competitive advantage but also helps to attract new business. For these reasons, many countries are likely to be extremely reluctant, to impose global-commons regulatory costs on themselves unless there is a reasonably level regulatory playing field that includes their competitors. In the case of the Montreal Protocol, the nature of the potential environmental harm involved overcame this cost-conscious reluctance to engage in unilateral regulatory restrictions. Clearly defined environmental dangers, albeit in a somewhat hypothetical future, can provide the domestic and international political motivation "to do something." Substantial risk helps redefine nations' sense of their own interests in relation to interests of the global commons. At the same time, when the economic costs of change are high, there are also compelling incentives for nations to emphasize the uncertainty that inevitably accompanies scientific analyses of such complex global problems. This resistance, however, did not materialize to obstruct the formulation of the Montreal Protocol.

One important reason for the lack of opposition was the existence of substitutes for CFCs.[31] The allure of a technological fix is that it allows for change with a minimum of lifestyle disruption for consumers and economic disruption for producers. Though U.S. producers such as DuPont initially resisted any restrictions on CFCs, they were, in fact, able to develop substitute propellants spray cans even before the federal government introduced its aerosol ban in 1978.[32] Other alternatives to CFCs were also considered at least possible, making the gradual phaseout approach adopted by the Montreal Protocol seem economically realistic.

Closely related to the creation of substitutes is the development of markets for those products. Regulation that either bans outright or establishes a reliable timetable for the gradual elimination of certain kinds of pollutants helps ensure a market for their substitutes, particularly if those substitutes can be created, produced, and sold at a reasonable price. Substitutes that are significantly more expensive may encourage a market for lower-priced goods produced with banned pollutants, creating an incentive for production of such goods in states not subject to the regulation involved. A reasonably priced substitute or comprehensive regulation, or both, creates a strong economic incentive to innovate and adopt new products. Indeed, the producers of these new products have an opportunity to participate in the creation and, perhaps, domination of new worldwide markets.

When U.S. producers such as DuPont, Allied, and Pennwalt appeared willing to accept strict international CFC regulation, some European producers suggested that these U.S. companies had developed a "secret substitute" and planned to enter the profitable European markets with a substantial competitive advantage over their European counterparts. As Richard Benedick has noted, however, "this suspicion was unfounded. To the dismay of environmentalists, DuPont admitted in 1986 that it had ceased research into alternatives for non-aerosol CFC uses five years earlier."[33] This lack of existing substitutes was treated far differently by European producers. As Benedick also notes, "for their part, the primary objectives of European companies, exemplified by France's Atochem, Britain's Imperial Chemical Industries, Italy's Montefluos, and West Germany's Hoecht, were to preserve market dominance to avoid for as long as possible the costs of switching to alternative products."[34]

The willingness of U.S. industry at least to entertain the possibility of strict international CFC regulation was, perhaps, not as surprising as the U.S. government's ultimate decision to play a major leadership role in securing such an agreement. The United States was not initially an enthusiastic supporter of a global ozone treaty.[35] The deregulatory philosophy that dominated the domestic legal agenda of the Reagan administration determined to a great extent its overall approach to international law and international legal solutions. For example, during the 1980s, the United States chose not to sign the Law of the Sea Treaty, objecting, in large part, to some of the treaty's more bureaucratic aspects.[36] It opted out of the Paramilitary Activities case, brought in the International Court of Justice by Nicaragua against the United States, when that court determined it had jurisdiction to hear the case;[37] and it unilaterally engaged in the armed invasion of Grenada without the authorization of either the Security Council of the United Nations or the U.S. Congress for reasons arguably controversial in terms of international law.[38] With the assistance of Congress, which enacted the Kassebaum amendment, the United States also withheld the full share of dues it was assessed by the U.N. during the 1980s, which drove the U.N. and some of its agencies nearly to bankruptcy.[39] Given such developments, it would have been inconsistent for the United States to participate, much less play a leadership role, in the creation of the Montreal Protocol.

But an individual country's domestic politics and laws can also provide an important incentive to pursue an international agreement that seeks to impose regulations on other countries that are at least as stringent as its own. Indeed, the desire to attain a level regulatory playing field encouraged, and may have even determined the U.S. decision not only to join in the Montreal Protocol, but actively to advocate and work for its adoption by other countries as well. The U.S. domestic position was made quite clear by a lawsuit filed in federal court by the National Resources Defense Council (NRDC), a public interest, environmentally activist organization. The NRDC alleged that the proactive regulatory authority granted to the EPA in the 1977 Clean Air Act amendments in fact required the United States to take unilateral regulatory action designed to limit substantially its own production and use of CFCs. The litigation they initiated against EPA resulted in a consent order,[40] which triggered EPA regulations and a series of domestic and international workshops that substantially affected both the perception of the ozone problem within the Reagan administration as well as that administration's assessment of its own domestic and international legal obligations.[41] This changed consciousness helped put global treaty negotiations in a new light. If the United States had to adhere to regulatory restrictions concerning CFCs, it was best, particularly from a competitive trade point of view, if the producers and consumers of CFCs in other nations did the same. The domestic regulation of the 1970s thus played a crucial role in determining the U.S. role in the international negotiations leading to the 1987 protocol.

The Montreal Protocol and Development

The developmental perspective is closely related to the competitive on the issue of global regulation. It differs from the kind of cost-benefit calculation just described in that it explicitly includes concerns of equity or fairness. These concerns are manifested in at least two ways. First, when less developed countries weigh their costs and benefits of entering into a worldwide regulatory agreement, they (by definition) do so against a backdrop of poverty and a level of material and economic well-being substantially below that of the developed world. This self-interested pressure for economic growth is not unlike that of the more developed world, but the relative impact of even small increases in growth on the day-to-day lives of people in many less developed countries is likely to be far greater than similar growth increments in more affluent nations. Put negatively, the impact of regulation on the standards of living in the developed world is likely to be negligible when compared with the third world's confrontation with the choice between mere subsistence and economic health.

Second, when wealthier nations weigh *their* costs and benefits of entering into a worldwide regulatory agreement, they may be more willing than developing countries to do so. They can absorb new regulatory costs more easily than less developed countries because the wealthier nations can incorporate new regulatory requirements more efficiently and make use of available and perhaps more costly substitutes more easily than competitors that utilize less sophisticated manufacturing approaches. Indeed, these more developed countries may actually secure an actual competitive advantage by imposing regulation on themselves and others. Further, wealthier nations (to the extent that they have adopted the developmental perspective) should have a sense of culpability. Global-commons issues such as ozone depletion or the buildup of greenhouse gases are very much the product and problems of industrialized societies. Developed countries achieved their economic affluence after many years of polluting, which exacted a significant toll on the environment. Though all such future pollution—whatever the source—is just as damaging to environment, in all fairness developed countries should scale back their harmful pollutants at a greater rate than developing countries. So long as industrialization is the means by which developing countries enter the economic mainstream, some damage to the environment is inevitable. From this point of view, developed nations should bear a disproportionate burden of the regulatory costs, as a way of compensating poorer countries for the environmental damage inflicted by the developed world in the past.

The Montreal Protocol was sensitive to these perspectives and their underlying rationales. It permits those developing countries with low levels of CFC use per capita to delay their compliance with the protocol for up to ten years.[42] It also helps give a developing country's easier access to alternative substances and technologies.[43] As we shall see, these provisions have facilitated discussion and resulted in amendments to the protocol that substantially strengthen it from a developmental point of view.[44]

Accommodating the Scientific, Competitive, and Developmental Perspectives

Science. The Montreal Protocol creates an ongoing regulatory process driven by growing scientific understanding of the effects of CFCs and other related chemical compounds on the earth's ozone layer. A process for reassessing the protocol's substantive regulatory provisions as new scientific evidence comes to light is built into the body of the agreement. This is a crucial feature of the protocol that helps renew the links between the participation by the signatories and the scientific discourse that first made agreement possible. Article 6, for example, guarantees that at least every four years "the Parties shall assess the control measures provided for in Article 2 on the basis of available scientific, environmental, technical, and economic information."[45] In fact, the process of reassessment began only five months after the protocol had entered into force. At a meeting in Helsinki on May 2, 1989, the parties to the protocol considered new evidence of even greater ozone depletion than had been anticipated. This meeting resulted in a nonbinding document called the Helsinki Declaration on the Protection of the Ozone Layer, which called for a total phaseout of CFCs by the year 2000. In addition, the reassessment that occurred at this meeting put other damaging CFCs and halons, not originally controlled in the Montreal Protocol, on the agenda for future control.[46]

This meeting served as an important background reason for another meeting of the parties, which took place in London in June 1990, for the purpose of amending the protocol. The London amendments to Article 2 of the protocol dealt with both the timing and the nature of the products to be controlled or phased out. They required, among other things, that the original CFCs controlled by the Montreal Protocol be phased out at a much faster rate and within ten to fifteen years; ten new CFCs and halons were added to the phase-out list as well as two other chemicals that adversely affect the ozone layer, carbon tetrachloride and methyl chloroform.[47] Various other "transitional substances" were also noted as possibly harmful for the ozone layer and marked as subjects for further scrutiny and control.[48]

The ongoing process of reassessment and regulatory change triggered by the protocol is facilitated by its distinction between an adjustment and an amendment. An adjustment is a change in the stringency and timing of CFCs already controlled by the Montreal Protocol and is binding on all parties, even those who did not vote for the change adopted by the majority. Controls on new chemicals, however, constitute amendments, and enter into force only after two-thirds of the parties ratify them. Such changes are not binding on those who do not.[49]

In addition to building in processes for reassessment and change in light of new scientific evidence, the protocol also encourages not only the creation of new scientific understandings of the problems involved, but the widespread dissemination of that information. Article 9, for example, requires that the parties shall cooperate "in promoting, directly or through competent international bodies, research, development, and exchange of information on" the "best technologies for improving the containment, recovery, recycling, or destruction of controlled substances or otherwise reducing their emissions." They are to seek "possible alternatives" to the controlled substances as well as exchange information on the cost and benefits of "relevant control strategies." This information is to be public. Indeed, the parties must cooperate "in promoting public awareness of the environmental effects of the emissions of controlled substances that deplete the ozone layer." Moreover, they must submit reports every two years listing the activities undertaken pursuant to Article 9.[50]

Such an approach to information gathering and dissemination helps create and maintain the regulatory environment required for progress. It encourages necessary research. More important, it helps create new ways of talking about global issues informed by research and the latest findings that science has to offer.

The gradualism reflected in the phase-out approach to CFCs initially adopted by the Montreal Protocol has thus been tempered significantly by a regulatory process that encourages the creation and dissemination of information aimed at providing the scientific basis for reassessing and changing the substantive goals of the protocol. Article 9 also calls for a cost-benefit analysis of "relevant control strategies." Providing new scientific information on just what those costs and benefits might be is an extremely important part of the political process. Indeed, such an approach allows global environmental regulation to move beyond a basic-rights discourse to a language that addresses the economic and practical problems that must be solved before real change is possible. This kind of scientific and cost-benefit discourse can thus speak more directly to the self-interested concerns of all of the parties involved.

The question of how to deal with those countries that choose not to participate as well as with participants that violate the agreement is closely related to the basic issue of how best to encourage participation in global regulation. Are there substantive incentives to encourage nonparties to join the agreement and signatories to adhere to its terms?

Article 4 of the Montreal Protocol uses trade as a sanction against those who do not choose to participate in the protocol's regulatory obligations. In fact, Article 4 is, in effect, the only compliance provision in the treaty. It bans imports of bulk CFC and halon chemicals by parties from nonparties.[51] It also effectively bans the export of CFCs to nonparties by stating that such exports could not be subtracted from a party's own consumption level. Any exports that did occur would result in cuts in the exporting country's domestic sales. Within three years of the Montreal Protocol's entry into force, the parties were to determine whether it was feasible to control the trade of products containing CFCs or any other controlled substances from any nonparty.[52] This provision addresses the very significant, potential problem of off-shore production. A signatory to the protocol could, in effect, arrange to shift production of products with CFCs offshore and then import the end products that use CFCs. The protocol begins to try to close this potential loophole by "determining the feasibility of banning or restricting from States, not a party to the Protocol, the import of imported products produced with but not containing" CFCs.[53] In addition, parties are to "discourage" the export to nonparties of technologies for producing and utilizing CFC substances. The protocol also restricts parties from providing new subsidies, aid, credits, guarantees, or insurance programs for the export to nonparties of products, equipment, plants, or technologies that might facilitate the production of CFCs.[54]

The nature of the regulatory problem with which the Montreal Protocol deals easily lends itself to using trade as a sanction. CFCs are identifiable chemical compounds associated with specific manufacturing processes and well-known consumer uses. The specificity of the harm and the ability to trace it back to specific sources, products, and the technologies that produce them makes it relatively easy to ban the trade of such goods and thereby discourage their continued production and use.

Prohibiting technology transfer for the production and use of CFCs rather than simply "discouraging" it would have significantly improved this article. Nevertheless, trade sanctions provide a significant incentive to participate in the protocol. At worst, they restrict CFC production and use to nonparties. This restriction can be particularly effective from both an economic and a regulatory point of view *if* the primary producers of and markets for CFCs are found in the countries that are signatories to the protocol. Economically speaking, nonparty producers would be denied access to major markets; nonparty consumers could also be deprived of major sources of CFCs, which would require them to deal with fewer suppliers at higher prices. Of course, some less developed countries such as China are so large that were they to develop their own internal, domestic markets for CFCs, they would have a considerable demand for these products within their own borders. In this event, the amounts of CFCs produced and used could be extraordinarily harmful to the global environment. Thus, the development and use of economically feasible and environmentally compatible substitutes is necessary to ensure that the market for CFCs is destroyed in all countries. The protocol attempts to encourage this development as well.

The gradual regulatory approach to phasing out certain CFCs adopted by the protocol can be viewed as technology-forcing regulation. A more positive, economic description of the approach, however, is that it is regulation designed to create new markets for substitute products. The gradual phase-out of CFCs required by Article 2 of the protocol and its amendments does two things. First, it gives major producing and consuming states the time to adjust to the new approaches and new products necessary to avoid major economic disruption. Second, the use of firm deadlines for the phase-out of certain CFCs provides incentives for the creation of substitute products.[55] Assuming that substitutes could be developed within the transition period provided, those countries and manufacturers capable of inventing these new products have the prospect of creating and perhaps dominating new and substantial global markets.

In short, the protocol accommodates the trade perspective both by using trade as a sanction and by taking a gradual approach to regulatory stringency, creating realistic incentives to produce environmentally sound substitute products. The 1990 amendments used this approach and extended it even further. They provided that the same trade restrictions apply for all newly controlled CFCs and halons; the ban on exports of controlled CFCs and halons that originally applied only to nonparties was now extended to all parties; and any existing party that did not accept the London amendments would be considered a nonparty with respect to those substances and subject to the same trade restrictions.[56]

The initial protocol also addressed issues associated with the trade perspective in other, less direct ways. For example, the Vienna Convention established the basic governing principle of one nation, one vote. This principle, carried to its logical conclusion, would give countries with little or no economic interest in CFCs the opportunity to impose heavy regulatory costs on those with much to lose. Article 16 of the protocol thus adopted a two-step voting process that recognized every country's equal right to vote for or against certain regulatory provisions, but stipulated that before the protocol could enter into force at least eleven parties representing two-thirds of global consumption would have to sign it. This, in effect, meant that it was necessary to draft an agreement capable of attracting the signature of a "critical mass" of the major producing and consuming countries if the protocol were to succeed. Failure to do so would result in little or no effective reform.

A protocol that reflected only the trade perspective, or only the scientific perspective, or even both of them could not necessarily attract the broad participation among the nations of the world requisite for such global legislation to work. The perspective of the less developed world was also reflected in the protocol and especially its amendments.

Development.   The Montreal Protocol attempted to deal with questions of equity inherent in a regulatory scheme designed to apply to rich and poor nations alike. Less developed countries were allowed initially to continue their use of CFCs for ten years without compliance with the protocol if their present use of CFCs was less than 0.3 kilograms per capita. Moreover, the parties were to assist less developed countries in acquiring environmentally safe alternative technologies with subsidies, aid, credits, guarantees, and the like. To accommodate the needs of less developed countries for CFCs, the protocol permitted producers in industrial countries to increase production 10 percent above baseline levels as long as the excess is for export to less developed, signatory countries.[57] This provision was designed to discourage developing countries from constructing new CFC production facilities while providing them with their "basic domestic needs" until substitutes were available. Presumably, this kind of offer would also encourage participation in the agreement on the part of less developed countries wanting to use CFCs, but not necessarily able to manufacture or interested in manufacturing their own.

These provisions in the Montreal Protocol were important symbolically. They made development issues a part of the ongoing negotiation process. They were not, however, effective. Under the Montreal Protocol as first adopted, developed countries were only to "facilitate" access to technology and subsidies.[58] The initial offer to be a facilitator must be seen in light of the substantive requirements that the agreement imposed at the beginning: within ten years, developing countries were not to exceed an emission level of 0.3 kilograms per capita. This figure was extremely low—well below the unspecified 1986 baseline average for developed countries. Thus, less developed countries were being asked to bind themselves permanently to a level of CFC consumption well below that of the developed world in exchange for the mere hope of access to new technologies and financial aid. Large developing countries such as India and China found the promises of technological help in the future too vague to provide any real assurances. Nor was there any direct financial aid forthcoming in the protocol as first drafted.

The 1990 London amendments go considerably beyond these basic provisions in at least two fundamental ways. First, Article 10 is designed to assist less developed countries financially as they try to adopt to new technologies and more environmentally sound products and manufacturing processes. Specifically, a mechanism is proposed to establish a multilateral fund to "meet . . . according to criteria to be decided upon by the Parties, the agreed incremental costs" of shifting to new technologies.[59] Second, Article 10A makes more explicit the goal of technology transfer than the provisions of the initial protocol. "Each Party shall take every practicable step . . . to ensure (a) That the best available, environmentally safe substitutes and related technologies are expeditiously transferred to" less developed countries.[60] These two amendments, in effect, impose substantial responsibility on the developed world for the ability of less developed countries to live up to the accelerated control provisions of the amended protocol.[61]

There are, to be sure, a number of problems yet to be solved. The "incremental costs" that result as various less developed countries adapt to new technologies and approaches are not easy to determine. More important, the willingness of participating nations to agree to a transfer of technology may not be enough, since the patents involved are not owned by states but by private companies eager for new markets, or by profitable joint ventures that the legal structures of some less developed countries may not be able to accommodate. Nevertheless, what is significant at this stage is the fact that the approaches set forth in the Montreal Protocol established a regulatory process that ultimately did lead to further discussions and more generous proposals vis-à-vis the developing world.

In short, substantive equitable requirements are ultimately required to ensure the participation of developing countries such as India and China, both of whom chose not to join the Montreal Protocol but whose representatives now recommend adoption of the agreement as amended. It may, however, be necessary to go further to ensure the participation of the less developed world as well as to ensure the effectiveness and perceived objectivity of the science that underlies this agreement. The protocol as amended assumes that each nation will be developing its own information or that various groups or nongovernmental organizations will be doing so. It is crucial that this information be depoliticized and result from independent analysis. An international science commission devoted to the collection, analysis, and open dissemination of data not contaminated by political bias could help further the creation of a regulatory discourse for dealing with the common problems of humankind.

Closely related to the development of such a commission is the research and development for new technologies. Individual countries, even developed countries, may not have the resources or political will to focus on the long-term benefits of basic scientific research. Indeed, the market does not always provide the incentives necessary for the long-term research that can lead to the kinds of technologies that could, for example, lower the world's consumption of fossil fuels. Developing practical solar energy, or fusion-power sources or evaluating the medicinal potential of insects and plant life found in rain forests require basic research for which there is no immediate payoff.

Such substantive proposals assume the importance of the creation of an objective, independent discourse that can command the respect of the world community, even when some of its findings point in the direction of added economic costs for some nations. They also assume the necessity of international funds to accomplish these ends. These monies may have to come from international taxes or at least in part from voluntary or mandatory contributions by participating parties, as the 1990 amendments now require. Other sources could be fees for the use of common spaces such as oceans, outer space or carbon taxes on gasoline, a small portion of which could be dedicated to such an international fund.

In the final analysis, a public-interest discourse that transcends the short-run, economic self-interest of individual nations is now being created at the international level. This discourse will encourage more sophisticated cost-benefit calculations by all governments involved—cost-benefit calculations that begin to reflect the true costs of certain manufacturing processes and lifestyles by taking into account the damage to the global environment that they cause.

This international discourse is closely related to domestic regulatory and deregulatory discourses. Indeed, had the Congress not passed the 1977 Clean Air Act, particularly section 7457(b) dealing with ozone depletion, it is not nearly so likely that the United States would have played the aggressive leadership role in negotiating the Montreal Protocol that it ultimately did. Thus, even at the international level, the importance of the legislative and the executive branches of government working together cannot be underestimated. There also are other key factors that can facilitate acceptance of such agreements. The science involved must be sufficiently developed to be persuasive regarding the likelihood of future environmental damage, even when the exact nature and extent of that damage remains uncertain. The technology involved must have produced substitutes for commodities that can damage the environment or at least be reasonably capable of developing such substitutes at a reasonable cost. This is critical, for the higher the cost of these substitutes, the greater the likelihood that scientific uncertainties will be accentuated at the expense of potential environmental harm. Finally, as the Montreal process makes clear, the developed world must remain committed to the continued economic growth of less affluent nations.

Domestic Implications and the Future

The implications of the emerging global regulatory discourse for future change and the creation of new international and domestic regulatory matrices are significant. The true value of the Montreal Protocol and its amendments lies not in the substantive provisions of these agreements, but in their development of a *process* that can continually adjust to and renew itself in light of future scientific developments. Such a process creates a language, new forums, and new partnerships across national boundaries for dealing with problems common to us all. It is but the first stage of a multistage endeavor that will include not only further international action but domestic as well.

The global discourse is complex. It addresses both competitive concerns and issues of environmental integrity and economic equity. By deepening the regulation-deregulation debates of the 1980s, this complexity helps place new regulatory issues on the U.S. domestic political agenda. In the 1980 elections, all three presidential candidates—Ronald Reagan, Jimmy Carter, and John Anderson—advocated some form of deregulation. In the 1988 election, both George Bush and Michael Dukakis sought to be "the environmental president." The antiregulatory aspects of a global competition perspective have been and will continue to be tempered. The fact that the global discourse combines important aspects of the domestic regulatory discourses from each of the earlier regulatory eras identified and examined in this book is likely to have an integrative effect on domestic regulatory discourses. Not only might environmental problems appear on the political agenda once again. Issues involving poverty and the crippling effects of great disparities in wealth on individuals and society are also highlighted by the new global discourse.

For a variety of reasons, the executive branch of government is most likely to play a leadership role in resolving global issues. That such formerly domestic issues as the environment are now also international will enable power to continue to flow to the president. Executive initiative in this area will seem necessary because the international quality of these problems more easily justifies the global perspectives the executive branch can take and the global solutions it can propose. The relatively open-textured nature of international law and policy and the dominant role that states as opposed to individuals and nongovernmental entities within those states play when formulating this law and policy ensure that the executive branch will have wide discretion in deciding which global solutions it should propose or adopt. Without domestic legislation such as section 7457(b) of the 1977 Clean Air Act, that discretion is likely to remain relatively unstructured, as will the role of individuals and nongovernmental entities in the policymaking process.

The cost of regulation and its relation to economic growth will continue to be key issues in the years ahead. Economic sensitivity to regulation should receive encouragement from the success of the regulatory approach taken in the Montreal Protocol and the attention that agreement gives to economic growth in both the developed and the developing world. But looming large on the political horizon are new economic issues that will have direct relevance to the day-to-day concerns of the developed world in particular. Foremost among these is the issue of economic growth: how much more growth that relies heavily on fossil fuels will be possible before the conflict with environmental survival is so severe that it becomes a critical political issue? This question will be asked and answered in relation to developing countries and their ability to alleviate poverty: to what extent is economic growth accomplishing that goal for the majority of these countries' populations, and at what cost to the environment? At the very least, new conceptions of economic growth and new means of achieving it will have to be developed. Moreover, population growth, especially in the developing world, is another issue with major international and domestic implications for the future.

As such issues, particularly those directly affecting lifestyle, are delineated, a larger question will have to be addressed. How long can the logic of economic growth as we have known it continue to dominate domestic and international regulatory and (more generally) political discourses? Perhaps we are at the threshold of an environmentally sensitive global era based on growth-oriented regulation which will survive indefinitely. It is more probable, however, that a fourth era will evolve—one dominated by the needs of the environment and the ecological limits of resource-intensive economic growth and the political limits of environmental management. In the ecological era yet to come, regulatory approaches that emphasize nature rather than economic growth may require new modes of discourse introduced by new types of change. Whatever regulatory issues the future may bring, it is likely that the new discourse will be grounded in consideration of science, economics, and equity. These components will have been imported from the global era now emerging. Market forces and market discourses will remain relevant, but primarily as regulatory tools. The New Deal and environmental-era discourses examined in this book will continue to play important conceptual roles in the processes of global ordering now under way.

More significantly, the nature and democratic quality of U.S. responses to international problems will continue to be shaped by the ability of the legislative and executive branches of government to work together. If the Congress is to play a significant and positive role in an increasingly internationalized United States, where the boundary between the domestic and the global is already rapidly disappearing, then it must participate in charting a course for these new developments. The globalization of markets, politics, and law proceeds apace. Though it may seem paradoxical, the global era is emerging as one in which domestic law and politics have a scope and importance far greater than in earlier times when the world began only beyond a nation's borders.

Notes

PREFACE

1. See Louisville Joint Stock Land Bank v. Radford, 295 U.S. 555 (1935) (Frazier-Lemke Act); A.L.A. Schechter Poultry Corp. v. United States, 295 U.S. 495 (1935) (section 3 of National Industrial Recovery Act); Railroad Retirement Bd. v. Alton R.R., 295 U.S. 330 (1935) (Railroad Retirement Act); Panama Ref. Co. v. Ryan, 293 U.S. 388 (1935) (section 9 of National Industrial Recovery Act). But see the following, which all sustained the validity of Joint Resolution of June 5, 1933, which declared gold payment contracts illegal: Perry v. United States, 294 U.S. 330 (1935) Nortz v. United States, 294 U.S. 317 (1935); Norman v. Baltimore & Ohio R.R., 294 U.S. 240 (1935).

2. R. H. Jackson, *The Struggle for Judicial Supremacy* (New York, 1949), p. 106.

3. In declaring the Frazier-Lemke Act unconstitutional, a unanimous Court held that "the Fifth Amendment commands that, however great the Nation's need, private property shall not be thus taken even for a wholly public use without just compensation" (295 U.S. at 602).

4. Pub. L. No. 73–67, 48 Stat. 195 (1933).

5. 295 U.S. at 528.

6. Id.

7. 295 U.S. 602 (1935).

8. 272 U.S. 52 (1926).

9. See Agins v. City of Tiburon, 447 U.S. 255 (1980) (land use regulations upheld as reasonable); Goldblatt v. Town of Hempstead, 369 U.S. 590 (1962) (restrictions on landowner's ability to excavate upheld). But see Richard Epstein, *Takings: Private Property and the Power of Eminent Domain* (Cambridge, Mass., 1985).

10. See Arizona v. California, 373 U.S. 546, 626 (1963) (Harlan, J., dissenting in part).

11. See United States v. Causby, 328 U.S. 256 (1946) (U.S. warplanes, in following a flight path approved by the Civil Aeronautics Authority, flew only eighty-three feet above Causby's farm, which constituted taking, congressional determination that navigable airspace is in public domain notwithstanding).

12. See Bowsher v. Synar, 106 S. Ct. 3181 (1986); Northern Pipeline Construction Co. v. Marathon Pipe Line Co., 458 U.S. 50 (1982).

13. See Industrial Union Department, AFL-CIO v. American Petroleum Institute, 448 U.S. 607, 671–88 (1980) (Rehnquist, J., concurring).

14. Address by Attorney General Edwin Meese III to the Federal Bar Association, September 13, 1985, pp. 2–3 (on file at the *Cornell Law Review*).

15. Ibid., p. 3. He elaborates his position: "In other words, federal agencies performing executive functions are themselves properly agents of the executive. They are not 'quasi' this, or 'independent' that. In the tripartite scheme of government a body with enforcement powers is part of the executive branch of government. Power granted by Congress should be properly understood as power granted *to the Executive.*"

INTRODUCTION

1. See Executive Order No. 12,287, 3 C.F.R. 124 (1981), reprinted in 15 U.S.C. sec. 757 (1982).

2. 15 U.S.C. sec. 751–56 (1976).

3. See 15 U.S.C. sec. 753(a) (1976). President Carter had already used this authority to begin deregulating the price of oil. President Reagan accelerated the process. See Alfred Aman, "Institutionalizing the Energy Crisis: Some Structural and Procedural Lessons," *Cornell L. Rev.* 65 (1980): 491.

4. For a procedural and substantive case study of this regulatory program, see Aman, "Institutionalizing the Energy Crisis."

5. Deregulatory proposals were made during Ford's administration, and deregulation was also vigorously pursued during the Carter administration. For a history and analysis of the deregulation that occurred in the trucking, airline, and communications industries, see Martin Derthick and Paul Quirk, *The Politics of Deregulation* (Washington, D.C., 1985).

6. See Stephen Wermiel, "Washington Lawyers Seeing Signs That the Boom Times Have Passed," *Wall Street Journal*, March 18, 1982, p. 29.

7. See R. D. Hershey, Jr., "Need for Lawyers in Capital Cut," *New York Times*, June 1, 1981, p. D1.

8. See "Program for Economic Recovery—Address before Joint Session of Congress," *Weekly Compilation of Presidential Documents* 17 (February 18, 1981): 136; "Program for Economic Recovery—White House Report," *Weekly Compilation of Presidential Documents* 17 (February 18, 1981): 138.

9. See "Deregulation Carried Out with Zeal," *New York Times Magazine*, January 10, 1982, p. 32. See also, Lief Carter, "Judicial Review of the Reagan Revolution," *Judicature* 65 (1982): 458.

10. See "Workers Wait Numbly for Probable Oblivion," *New York Times*, November 26, 1981, p. B1. The head of the Department of Energy noted that he wished to "work [him]self out of a job."

11. See Aman, "Institutionalizing the Energy Crisis," p. 491.

12. I shall refer to these three regulatory eras throughout this book. The "New Deal era" covers roughly the years from the Great Depression through the end of World War II. The "APA Era," covers the post-war years from the mid to late 1940s to the 1960s. (The Administrative Procedure Act, 5 U.S.C. sec. 551–59, 701–06, 1304, 3105, 3344, 5372, 7521 [1982], was passed in 1946.) I collapse these two into a "New Deal–APA era." The "environmental era" begins in the late 1960s and reaches its peak during the 1970s. The Administrative Procedure Act was significantly glossed by much of the legislation passed during this period. The environmental era lasts until 1981 when what I call the "global deregulatory era" begins. For an excellent history of the substance of the federal regulation during these times as well as a different breakdown of the historic eras involved, see Robert Rabin, "Federal Regulation In Historical Perspective," *Stan. L. Rev.* 38 (1986): 1189.

13. This is not to say, however, that Congress did not initially jump on the deregulatory bandwagon when it appeared that a general consensus was emerging regarding the deregulation of the airline, communication, and transportation industries. See Merrick Garland, "Deregulation and Judicial Review," *Harv. L. Rev.* 98 (1985): 505, 507–8, and note 4, for a

citation of pertinent statutes. Most of these statutes, however, effected only partial decontrol. Only the Airline Deregulation Act of 1978, Pub. L. No. 95–504, 92 Stat. 1705 (codified in 49 U.S.C. sec. 1301 et seq.), led to the complete deregulation of one phase of the airline industry and the elimination of a federal agency, the Civil Aeronautics Board.

Some of Congress's deregulatory actions arguably had a re-regulatory effect. See Motor Carrier Act of 1980, Pub. L. No. 96–296, 94 Stat. 793 (1980) (current version at 49 U.S.C. sec. 10927 (Supp. 1982)). Working within the framework of existing legislation, the Interstate Commerce Commission sought to increase competition in the trucking industry by deregulating various aspects of the industry. See P. S. Dempsey, "Congressional Intent and Agency Discretion—Never the Twain Shall Meet: The Motor Carrier Act of 1980," *Chi. Kent L. Rev.* 58 (1981): 1, 14–21; J. F. Hayden, "Teamsters, Truckers, and the ICC: A Political and Economic Analysis of Motor Carrier Deregulation," *Harv. J. Legis.* 17 (1980): 123, 145–47. Congress responded to the commission's deregulatory attempts by passing the Motor Carrier Act of 1980. The act included an amendment that set forth increased competition and efficiency as goals. (94 Stat. 794 sec. 4[3]), however, also maintained significant regulatory control. Congress promised vigorous oversight review of the ICC to ensure that it remained within its statutory authority. In addition, although Congress lessened the burden of proof on new applicants to obtain new trucking routes, it did not eliminate it entirely (94 Stat. 794 sec. 5). Applicants would continue to have to produce evidence that showed that the transportation service they sought to provide served a useful public purpose and was response to a public need. Courts, however, subsequently interpreted such provisions liberally to justify further deregulatory action, arguably beyond that which Congress intended. See Dempsey, "Congressional Intent," pp. 31–53.

14. See M. P. Fiorina, *Congress: Keystone of the Washington Establishment* (New Haven, Conn., 1977), pp. 5–14.;D. R. Mayhew, *Congress: The Electoral Connection* (New Haven, Conn., 1974), pp. 25–45.

15. See Charles Lindbloom, "The Science of Muddling Through," *Pub. Admin. Rev.* 19 (1959):79.

16. For an analysis of how market values, approaches, and norms often become a part of an overall regulatory scheme, see Alfred Aman, "Administrative Equity: An Analysis of Exceptions to Administrative Rules," *Duke L. J.* 1982, no. 3: 277.

17. Some commentators have suggested that the New Deal programs are best understood as examples of presidential power, with Congress doing the bidding of a very strong president. See Theodore Lowi, *The Personal President* (Ithaca, N.Y., 1985) pp. 44–66; see also, Martin Shapiro, "APA: Past, Present, Future," *Va. L. Rev.* 72 (1986): 447, 447–52. Though this may be true to a large extent, it is important for our discussion to recognize a very fundamental point: Congress at least passed the legislation generally authorizing the regulatory activities of federal agencies. Some of this legislation may have been unacceptably vague, but contrast this level of congressional involvement with the comparative roles of Congress and the president set forth in Chapter 3 where deregulation often occurs without any major deregulatory legislation, but rather through agency and executive power as well as through budgetary constraints on agency action.

18. 467 U.S. 837 (1984).

CHAPTER 1 AGENCY REGULATION AND JUDICIAL REVIEW

1. See Lon Fuller, *The Morality of Law* (New Haven, Conn., 1964), pp. 79–81, who lists constancy in the law as one of eight desiderates of an effective system of rules. See also, H.L.A. Hart, *The Concept of Law* (New York, 1961); and R. M. Unger, *Knowledge and Politics* (New York, 1975), pp. 89–90.

2. This is one reason why it is important to place reasonably clear statutory limits on an agency's duties and powers. See Theodore Lowi, *The End of Liberalism: The Second Republic of the United States*, 2d ed. (New York, 1979), pp. 92–126.

3. An example of this is discussed in Chapter 2. For a critique of the broad delegation of power to agencies that allowed changes in agency law and policy to occur in an arguably

unconstitutional manner, see Lowi, *The End of Liberalism*, pp. 130–31. See also P. H. Aranson, Ernst Gellhorn, G. O. Robinson, "A Theory of Legislative Delegation," *Cornell L. Rev.* 68 (1982) 1; James Freedman, "Review: Delegation of Power and Institutional Competence," *U. Chi. L. Rev.* 43 (1975): 307; Theodore Lowi, "Two Roads to Serfdom: Liberalism, Conservatism and Administrative Power," *Am. U. L. Rev.* 36 (1987): 295. But see K. C. Davis, *Administrative Law Treatise*, 2d ed. (San Diego, Calif., 1978), pp. 207–8; Louis Jaffee, "An Essay on Delegation of Legislative Power: II," *Colum. L. Rev.* 47 (1947): 561; Jerry Mashaw, "Pro-Delegation: Why Administrators Should Make Political Decisions," *J. Law, Econ. & Org.* 1 (1985): 81; Richard Pierce, "Political Accountability and Delegated Power: A Response to Professor Lowi," *Am. U. L. Rev.* 36 (1987): 391; Richard Stewart, "Beyond Delegation Doctrine," *Am. U. L. Rev.* 36 (1987): 323, and "The Reformation of American Administrative Law," *Harv. L. Rev.* 88 (1975): 1667, 1700–01.

4. See Aranson, Gellhorn, and Robinson, "A Theory of Legislative Delegation," pp. 17–21.

5. Ibid.

6. L. L. Jaffe, *Judicial Control of Administrative Action* (Boston, 1965), p. 575.

7. Ch. 324, 60 Stat. 237 (1946) (current version codified in 5 U.S.C. sec. 551–59, 701–6, 1305, 3105, 3344, 5372, 7521 [1982]).

8. See Packard Motor Car Co. v. NLRB, 330 U.S. 485 (1947); NLRB v. Hearst Publications, Inc., 322 U.S. 111 (1944); Gray v. Powell, 314 U.S. 407 (1941). But see the judicial-review provisions of the Administrative Procedure Act, ch. 324, 60 Stat. 237, 243 (1946) (current version codified in 5 U.S.C. sec. 702–6 [1982]).

9. This is not to argue, however, that the APA itself did not represent a significant change in the overall supervisory power of courts over administrative agencies. Most agency decisions, including policy decisions, were made in an adjudicatory context (pursuant to sections 554, 556, and 557). Moreover, the Administrative Procedure Act's substantial-evidence standard concerning questions of fact, though applied in a relatively deferential manner, nevertheless represented a toughening of earlier standards, particularly for those courts which believed substantial evidence need not be found in the record *as a whole* (see Universal Camera Corp. v. NLRB, 340 U.S. 474, 489 [1951]). Concerning questions of policy, however, the act seemed to codify the rational-basis approach taken by courts prior to its passage. The "arbitrary, capricious, and an abuse of discretion" standard was applied much like the reasonableness standard for legislation in the post-*Lochner* era, which appears to be what the drafters of the act intended. See Pacific States Box & Basket Co. v. White, 296 U.S. 176, 185 (1935); H.R. Rep. No. 1980, 79th Cong., 2d sess., 1946, reprinted in *Administrative Procedure Act: Legislative History* (Washington, D.C., 1946), p. 233. But when it came to policymaking, even policymaking in an adjudicatory context, the Court was willing, after the passage of the APA, to demand that a federal agency rather than a court provide the reasons that justify a particular policy. (see SEC v. Chenery, 332 U.S. 194 [1947]). Moreover, section 706 of the act, which applied to questions of law, did not state what level of deference an agency's interpretation of the law should receive from reviewing courts. Nevertheless, the courts developed elaborate deference doctrines. See NLRB v. Hearst Publications, Inc. See James DeLong, "New Wine for a New Bottle: Judicial Review in the Regulatory State," *Va. L. Rev.* 72 (1986): 72.

10. For a discussion of these economic issues, see Martin Shapiro, *Who Guards the Guardians?: Judicial Control of Administration* (Athens, Ga., 1988), pp. 39–41.

11. 98 U.S. 45 (1905).

12. Id.

13. Felix Frankfurter, "Social Issues before the Supreme Court," *Yale Rev.* 22 (1933): 476.

14. Oliver Wendell Holmes, cited in Frankfurter, "Social Issues," p. 478.

15. Ibid., p. 480.

16. Ibid., p. 486.

17. Ibid.

18. Ibid.

19. United States v. Carolene Products Co., 304 U.S. 144, 152 n. 4 (1938).

20. Id. at 152.

21. Id.
22. Id. at 152 n. 4.
23. Id.
24. F. D. Roosevelt, "The Second Inaugural Address" (January 20, 1937), reprinted in *The Public Papers and Addresses of Franklin D. Roosevelt*, ed. Samuel Rosenman (New York, 1941), p. 5.
25. 239 U.S. 441 (1915).
26. Id. at 445.
27. F. D. Roosevelt, "The Second Inaugural Address," p. 123.
28. 295 U.S. 495 (1935).
29. There were, of course, exceptions. Even judges sympathetic to the New Deal recognized, at least initially, that other legitimate constitutional limitations on legislative primacy existed. They felt it was their duty to impose these limitations, no matter how serious the conditions of the times. Writing for the majority in Louisville Joint Stock Land Bank v. Radford, 295 U.S. 555 (1935), Justice Brandeis declared the Frazier-Lemke Act an unconstitutional taking of private property. In so doing, he emphasized that "the Fifth Amendment commands that, however great the Nation's need, private property shall not be thus taken even for a wholly public use without just compensation" (Id. at 602). Similarly, the Court in Schechter Poultry Corp. v. United States, struck down important New Deal legislation on delegation grounds. Although that decision was viewed at the time as a serious setback to the administration, the basis of the decision was sound. By demanding that Congress be more precise in delegating power to agencies and, perhaps even more important, by demanding that this power not be given to private industrial groups, the Court staked out a legitimate constitutional position. Nevertheless, though theoretically there may be a constitution for all seasons, the overwhelming political spirit of the age can ultimately shape constitutional perceptions of problems as well as constitutional interpretation. Indeed, both the delegation and the takings doctrines largely fell into disuse in the post–New Deal era. They were never repudiated in quite so definitive a way as the application of the substantive-due-process clause to economic legislation, yet they were never serious obstacles to the rise and expansion of the administrative state.
30. See U.S. v. Darby, 312 U.S. 100 (1941). The use of the Tenth Amendment as a check on federal power was revived in National League of Cities v. Usery, 426 U.S. 833 (1976). This revival was short-lived. In Garcia v. San Antonio Metro. Transit Auth., 469 U.S. 528 (1985), the Court apparently put this doctrine to rest once again. But Justice Rehnquist dissented, noting that he was "confident" that the National League of Cities approach would "in time again command the support of a majority of the Court" (id. at 580).
31. Contracts-clause doctrine went the way of substantive due process. See Home Building & Loan Ass'n v. Blaisdell, 290 U.S. 398 (1934). See also Gerald Gunther, *Constitutional Law*, 11th ed. (Mineola, N.Y., 1985), p. 487; R. L. Hale, "The Supreme Court and the Contracts Clause: III," *Harv. L. Rev.* 57 (1949): 852, 890. For some recent examples of an apparent revival of the contracts clause, see Allied Structural Steel Co. v. Spaunous, 438 U.S. 234 (1978); United States Trust Co. v. New Jersey, 431 U.S. 1 (1977).
32. See M. M. Shapiro, "The Constitution and Economic Rights," in *Essays on the Constitution of the United States*, ed. M. J. Harmon, pp. 74–98 (Port Washington, N.Y., 1978); Bruce Ackerman, "The Storrs Lectures: Discovering the Constitution," *Yale L. J.* 93 (1984): 1013, 1056–57, 1064–65.
33. This is not to imply, however, that the New Deal consisted only of economic regulation. A major portion of New Deal legislation dealt with social issues such as unemployment compensation and social security. See A. M. Schlesinger, *The Coming of the New Deal* (Boston, 1988), pp. 263–82, 297–315. See also Social Security Act, ch. 531, 49 Stat. 620 (1935) (codified at 42 U.S.C. sec. 301–1399 [1982]).
34. Air Carrier Economic Regulation Act, ch. 601, tit. IV, sec. 401–16, 52 Stat. 987 (1938), repealed by Federal Aviation Act of 1958, Pub. L. No. 85–726, 72 Stat. 731 (current version at 49 U.S.C. sec. 481–96 [1982]). Federal Communications Act of 1934, ch. 652, 48 Stat. 1164 (codified in various sections of 47 U.S.C.). Natural Gas Act, ch. 556, 52 Stat. 821 (1938) (codified at 15 U.S.C. sec. 717–717w [1982]). Securities Act of 1933, ch. 38, tit. I, 48 Stat. 74

(codified at 15 U.S.C. sec. 77a–77aa [1982]). National Labor Relations Act, ch. 372, 49 Stat. 448 (1935) (codified at 29 U.S.C. sec. 151–66 [1982]).

35. See E. W. Hawley, *The New Deal and the Problem of Monopoly* (Princeton, N.J., 1966), pp. 472–94. See also B. D. Karl, *The Uneasy State* (Chicago, 1983), pp. 153–54; Norman Thomas, "Socialism, Not Roosevelt's Pale Pink Pills," in *New Deal Thought*, ed. Howard Zinn (Indianapolis, 1966), p. 398.

36. See Schechter Poultry Corp. v. United States, which strikes down the NRA because the act improperly delegated legislative power to private groups. See Hawley, *The New Deal*, p. 398.

37. See Robert Rabin, "Federal Regulation in Historical Perspective," *Stan. L. Rev.* 38 (1986): 1248.

38. See the Social Security Board, which received its statutory authority from the Social Security Act, ch. 531, tit. VII, 49 Stat. 620, 635 (1935).

39. Independent commissions usually required that the commissioners be appointed for a specific term of years. They could not be removed during that term except for cause. See Federal Communications Act of 1934, at 1102; Securities Act of 1933; National Labor Relations Act. See also M. H. Bernstein, *Regulating Business by Independent Commission* (Princeton, N.J., 1955), p. 53.

It is interesting to note that New Deal commentators criticized independent commissions because they combined executive, prosecutorial, and judicial functions. See President's Commission on Administrative Management, *Report of the Committee with Studies of Administrative Management in the Federal Government* (Washington, D.C., 1937), pp. 36–38. See also R. E. Cushman, *The Independent Regulatory Commissions* (New York, 1944), p. 701.

40. James Landis, *The Administrative Process* (New Haven, Conn., 1938), pp. 10–12.

41. Ibid., pp. 11–12.

42. 295 U.S. 602 (1935).

43. Id. at 631–32.

44. Id. at 628.

45. Id. This case and its reasoning are now once again very much under attack. See D. P. Currie, "The Distribution of Powers after Bowsher," *Sup. Ct. Rev.* 1986:19, 34–36; G. P. Miller, "Independent Agencies," *Sup. Ct. Rev.* 1986:41, 44 n. 17, 45–50. But see Morrison v. Olson, 108 S. Ct. 2597 (1988).

46. 272 U.S. 52 (1926).

47. R. H. Jackson, *The Struggle for Judicial Supremacy* (New York, 1949), p. 106.

48. Landis, *The Administrative Process*, pp. 10–12.

49. See B. P. Ackerman and W. T. Hassler, "Beyond the New Deal: Coal and the Clean Air Act," *Yale L. J.* (1980): 89. For a view that disagrees somewhat with this conception of New Deal regulatory activity, see Rabin, "Federal Regulation in Historical Perspective," p. 1263 n. 236.

50. As one commentator has noted: "In the science of politics expounded by Hamilton and Madison it was precisely this 'scheme of representation' that 'promised the cure. . . . ' [T]he founders expected elected representatives to be wiser and more virtuous than the average voter. In addition, the powerful offices created by the Constitution, with their fixed and fairly lengthy terms, would appeal to able men, those who 'possess most wisdom to discern, and most virtue to pursue the common good of the society.'" (S. E. Rhoads, citing *Federalist Papers*, nos. 9, 10, 57, in *The Economist's View of the World* (New York, 1985), p. 203. See also J. G. Pocock, *The Macchiavellian Moment* (Princeton, N.J., 1975), pp. 506–52. See C. R. Sunstein "Interest Groups in American Public Law," *Stan. L. Rev.* 38 (1985): 29, 47.

51. See B. R. Barber, *Strong Democracy* (Berkeley and Los Angeles, Calif., 1984), pp. 3–25.

52. Ibid., p. 4.

53. Independence and expertise were two by-products of setting up administrative agencies as independent commissions. They were not ends in and of themselves, but rather the result of a much broader goal—the accomplishment of the substantive tasks set by Congress. In this sense, the concept of representation subsumes expertise and independence in the

same sense a speaker's inherent right to speak is the actual basis of theories of speech that present themselves as based on the value of the speech that results.

54. See D. W. Brogan, *American Character* (New York, 1956).

55. See Hawley, *The New Deal*.

56. See H.R. Rep. No. 1980, 79th Cong., 2d sess., 1946, pp. 7–16, reprinted in *Administrative Procedure Act: Legislative History*, pp. 241–50; S. Doc. No. 248, 79th Cong., 2d sess., 1946, pp. 241–50. See generally Walter Gellhorn, "The Administrative Procedure Act: The Beginning," *Va. L. Rev.* 72 (1986): 219, 226–33. See also *The Final Report of the Attorney General's Commission on Administrative Procedure, Administrative Procedure in Government Agencies*, S. Doc. No. 8, 77th Cong., 1st sess., 1941 (hereafter *Attorney General's Comm. Report*). This report led to the introduction of the legislation that became the Administrative Procedure Act.

57. Wang Yang Sung v. McGrath, 339 U.S. 33, 40 (1950).

58. See B. B. Boyer, "Alternatives to Administrative Trial-Type Hearings for Resolving Complex Scientific Economic and Social Issues," *Mich. L. Rev.* 71 (1972): 111; M. G. Dakin, "Ratemaking—The New Approach at the FPC: Ad Hoc Rulemaking in the Ratemaking Process," *Duke L. J.* 1973, no 1: 41.

59. As Louis Jaffe noted in *Judicial Control of Administrative Action*, p. 575 "In the 1940s the Supreme Court, particularly in Gray v. Powell and NLRB v. Hearst Publications, Inc., recognized perhaps more openly than had been customary in the recent past the law- or policy-making functions of the agencies. It was a time when the agencies were fast growing in power and were being viewed by the courts—particularly the Supreme Court—with exceptional tolerance." For more recent analysis and theory concerning the various contexts in which courts will or will not defer to questions of law, see R. W. Levin, "Identifying Questions of Law in Administrative Law," *Geo. L. J.* 74 (1985): 1.

60. See Packard Motor Car Co. v. NLRB (Court does not defer to agency legal interpretations but upholds the Board's decision and thus its extension of jurisdiction). For a reconciliation of this case with *Hearst* and *Powell*, see Levin, "Identifying Questions of Law," pp. 23–27.

61. See NLRB v. Hearst Publications, Inc. (Court defers to agency extension of the National Labor Relations Act to "newsboys"). After the Court essentially foreclosed most constitutional attacks on regulatory statutes, statutory challenges to the jurisdictional basis of agency regulation were often the only realistic substantive legal arguments available. The broad delegation clauses upheld by the courts gave the agency and ultimately the reviewing court broad discretion in determining how an agency could or should extend its reach to new situations not explicitly covered by their enabling acts. In most New Deal and post–New Deal cases, the courts almost invariably upheld the agency's power to regulate. See Federal Power Commission v. Louisiana Power and Light Co., 406 U.S. 621 (1972) (Court extended power to control price to the power to control curtailments and allocation of scarce natural gas supplies); Red Lion Broadcasting Co. v. Federal Communications Commission, 395 U.S. 367 (1969) (Court rejected attempts to narrow the scope of the FCC's regulatory powers by equating a First Amendment right to broadcast with an individual's First Amendment right to speak, write, or publish); Phillips Petroleum Co. v. Wisconsin, 347 U.S. 672 (1954) (Court applied the price controls of the Natural Gas Act to natural gas produced and sold at the well head); National Broadcasting Co. v. United States, 319 U.S. 190 (1943) (Court upheld the FCC's power to issue regulations that extended its jurisdiction from the regulation of technical and engineering matters to more direct control of licensee behavior).

62. This was often true even if the agency resisted an extension of its own jurisdiction. See, for example, *Phillips Petroleum Co.*, 347 U.S. at 676. It is interesting to note that this extension of jurisdiction to cover natural gas purchases was not necessarily what Congress had in mind. Congress, however, was never politically able to master the votes to roll back these controls. See S. G. Breyer and W. P. Macavoy, *Energy Regulation by the Federal Power Commission*, (Washington, D.C., 1974), pp. 56–58. Similarly, it is interesting to note that the Court's extension of jurisdiction under the National Labor Relations Act to cover foremen as supervisory employees in *Packard Motor Co.*, 330 U.S. at 491, was corrected by Congress the next year. Congress amended the Taft Hartley Act to specifically exclude foremen as "super-

visory employees." For a discussion of this amendment, see NLRB v. Bell Aerospace Co., 416 U.S. 267, 279–80 (1974).

63. For an example and discussion of common law rhetoric, see E. H. Levi, *An Introduction to Legal Reasoning* (Chicago, 1958), pp. 1–6.

64. See Communications Act of 1934, ch. 652, sec. 309(a), 48 Stat. 1085 (codified in various sections of 47 U.S.C.) (FCC can grant licenses if they serve the "public interest, convenience, and necessity").

65. See *Phillips Petroleum Co.*, 347 U.S. 672, 682–83 (1952). See also Chevron v. NRDC, 467 U.S. 837, 851 (1984). Of course, even when the legislative history seems clear, it may speak very differently to those with different theories of the case. See P. M. Wald, "Some Observations on the Use of Legislative History in the 1981 Supreme Court Term," *Iowa L. Rev.* 68 (1983): 195, 214: "It sometimes seems that citing legislative history is still, as my late colleague Harold Leventhal once observed, akin to 'looking over a crowd and picking out your friends.'"

66. See United States v. Midwest Video Corp., 406 U.S. 649 (1972) (FCC); United States v. Southwestern Cable Co., 392 U.S. 157 (1968) (FCC); United States v. Drum, 368 U.S. 370 (1962) (ICC); Phillips Petroleum Co. v. Wisconsin (FPC); NLRB v. Highland Park Mfg. Co., 341 U.S. 322 (1951) (NLRB); Rochester Tel. Corp. v. United States, 307 U.S. 125 (1939) (FCC); Public Serv. Comm'n v. Havemeyer, 296 U.S. 506 (1936).

More recently, however, courts have shown a tendency to resolve close jurisdictional cases against any extension of agency power. See FCC v. Midwest Video Corp., 440 U.S. 689 (1979) (Midwest II) (holding that certain access rules violated a provision of the Communications Act of 1934). The First Amendment has also been playing a more significant role, at least when FCC regulation is involved. See Century Communications Corp. v. FCC, 835 F.2d 292 (D.C. Cir. 1987) (the First Amendment and the FCC's must-carry rules); 1985 Fairness Report, Inquiry into Section 73. 1910 of the Commission's Rules and Regulations concerning the General Fairness Doctrine Obligations of Broadcast Licenses, 58 Rad. & Reg. (P&F) 137 (1985) (elimination of doctrine based, in part, on First Amendment concerns). See Bowen v. American Hosp. Ass'n, 476 U.S. 610 (1986); Capital Cities Cable, Inc. v. Crisp, 467 U.S. 691 (1984).

67. See J. L. Mashaw and D. L. Harfst, "Regulation and Legal Culture: The Case of Motor Vehicle Safety," *Yale J. on Reg.* 4 (1987): 257, 267–79.

68. Northrop Frye, *The Modern Century* (Toronto, 1967), p. 31.

69. See Schaffer Transp. v. United States, 355 U.S. 83, 94–95 (1957).

70. 15 U.S.C. sec. 717a(6) (1982).

71. 15 U.S.C. sec. 717c(a) (1982).

72. 205 F.2d 706 (D.C. Cir. 1953).

73. 347 U.S. at 685.

74. Natural Gas Act, ch. 556, sec. 1(b), 52 Stat. 821 (1938) (current version codified at 15 U.S.C. sec. 717[b]).

75. Id. at sec. 2(b) (current version at 15 U.S.C. sec. 717a[b] [1982]).

76. For a discussion of the history of the Natural Gas Act, see M. E. Sanders, *The Regulation of Natural Gas* (Philadelphia, 1981), pp. 35–42.

77. 347 U.S. at 682 and n. 10.

78. Id. at 678, 682. An example of the extreme to which the Court went to grant the Commission jurisdiction is the Court's dismissal of the solicitor's testimony as irrelevant. The Court argued that the testimony concerned a version of the act far different from the one finally passed. In so doing, the Court ignored a second version, which was nearly identical to the final bill, and the hearings connected with it. The Court also apparently forgot that seven years earlier it had used the very testimony it now discounted, to construe the meaning of "production and gathering."

Justices William O. Douglas, id. at 687, and Tom C. Clark, id. at 690, dissented. Justice Douglas questioned the value of the legislative history because it contained no discussion of independent producers (id. at 688). He also noted that the Commission's construction of the Act was consistent with the Court's past decisions (id. at 689–90). More important, he argued that the Court was imposing upon the Commission power that Congress had refused to grant (id. at 690). Justice Clark added that the Court was tampering with the balance of power between the federal government and the states by giving the federal government absolute control where previously it could exercise control only if the states failed to do so (id. at 691).

79. Id. at 685.

80. Id.

81. Id.

82. Report of the Federal Trade Commission, S. Doc. No. 92, 70th Cong., 1st sess., 1936, pp. 589, 591, 593, 600–601.

83. 331 U.S. 682 (1947).

84. 347 U.S. at 689–90.

85. Id. at 682.

86. See Natural Gas Policy Act of 1978, 92 Stat. 3350 (current version at 15 U.S.C. sec. 3301–3432, 42 U.S.C. sec. 7255 [1982]). See Alfred Aman, *Energy and Natural Resources Law: The Regulatory Dialogue* (New York, 1983), chap. 4.

87. Of course, as mentioned at note 36 above, the New Deal also dealt extensively with more direct forms of redistribution such as social security and unemployment compensation. But an important and relatively long-lasting contribution of the New Deal was the establishment of five of the "big seven" independent agencies: The Civil Aeronautics Board (1938); the Federal Communications Commission (1934); the Federal Power Commission (1930); the National Labor Relations Board (1935); and the Securities and Exchange Commission (1934). Along with the Interstate Commerce Commission and the Federal Trade Commission, these agencies directly affected "the national economy and the quality, service, and prices paid by consumers in well-nigh every category of trade and commerce" (Bernard Schwartz and H. W. R. Wade, *Legal Control of Government: Administrative Law in Britain and the United States* [Oxford, 1972], p. 28).

88. *Attorney General's Comm. Report*, p. 13.

89. See Schlesinger, *The Coming of the New Deal.* By 1941 there were nineteen separate law-making bureaus within executive departments and twenty-two independent agencies. See also *Attorney General's Comm. Report*, pp. 3–4.

90. See Natural Gas Act, ch. 556, 52 Stat. 821 (1938) (current version at 15 U.S.C. sec. 717–717a [1976]).

91. Ch. 90, 48 Stat. 195 (1933) (held unconstitutional in Schechter Poultry Corp. v. United States).

92. Ch. 25, sec. 1–19, 48 Stat. 31 (1933) (current version at 7 U.S.C. sec. 601–19 [1982]).

93. Federal Water Power Act, ch. 285, 41 Stat. 1063 (1920).

94. Federal Communications Act, ch. 652, 48 Stat. 1064 (1934) (codified in various sections of 47 U.S.C.).

95. Civil Aeronautics Act, ch. 601, 52 Stat. 973 (1938).

96. See Sanders, *The Regulation of Natural Gas*, pp. 17–45.

97. See Achbacker Radio Corp. v. FCC, 326 U.S. 327 (1945) (dealing with competing applicants for a single license); see also the cases discussed in Stewart, "The Reformation of American Administrative Law." These cases show the diverse economic interests among regulated entities as well as among potential beneficiaries of agency action, thus justifying their participation in these proceedings.

98. See Bernstein, *Regulatory Business by Independent Commission.* Of course, just where the emphasis should be between the regulated entities and other intended beneficiaries of the statutes has never been clear. A set of rulings favorable to industry is often said to indicate agency capture, but the statutes involved never fully resolved how the balance between the regulated and the beneficiary should be struck. See Hawley, *The New Deal and the Problem of Monopoly.*

99. This is not to argue that protecting consumers from monopolistic pricing was not important, but rather that the overall tone and orientation of New Deal regulatory statutes had a distinct producer orientation. This is perhaps highlighted best by comparing this legislation with the much more consumer-oriented legislation of the 1970s. This issue will be spoken to more extensively later in this chapter.

100. Stewart, "The Reformation of American Administrative Law," pp. 1671–76; P. R.

Verkuil, "The Emerging Concept of Administrative Procedure," *Colum. L. Rev.* 78 (1978): 258, 267.

101. Carol Harlow and Richard Rawlings, *Law and Administration* (London, 1984), p. 2.

102. Ibid., p. 35.

103. Such broad delegations were necessary both to provide the legislative flexibility to deal with issues that could not be anticipated, and because there was never any consensus on how best to accommodate the competing interests of consumers and industry. At best, these statutes were guaranteed to trigger a regulatory dialogue, but not to provide clear guidance, as to how the issues should ultimately be resolved. See Hawley, *The New Deal and the Problem of Monopoly*, pp. 35–36.

104. See Landis, *The Administrative Process*, pp. 14–16.

105. See Jackson, *The Struggle for Judicial Supremacy*, pp. 106–9.

106. For recent examples of this judicial viewpoint, see Office of Communication of the United Church of Christ v. FCC, 707 F.2d 1413, 1422–26 (D.C. Cir. 1983); Lead Indus. Ass'n, Inc. v. EPA, 647 F.2d 1130, 1145–48 (D.C. Cir.), cert. denied 449 U.S. 1042 (1980); Weyerhaeuser Co. v. Costle, 590 F.2d 1011, 1024–28 (D.C. Cir. 1978).

107. 5 U.S.C. sec. 706 (1982).

108. The courts took a deferential approach to legislation in the constitutional realm. See Williamson v. Lee Optical, Inc., 348 U.S. 483 (1955); Day-Brite Lighting, Inc. v. Missouri, 342 U.S. 421 (1952); Railway Express Agency, Inc. v. New York, 336 U.S. 106 (1949). Such cases adopted a rational-basis approach to judicial review rendering courts little more than lunacy commissions.

109. See *Pacific States Box & Basket Co.*, 296 U.S. 176, 185–86 (1935) ("Every exertion of the police power, either by the legislature or by an administrative body, is an exercise of delegated power. . . . [W]here the regulation is within the scope of authority legally delegated, the presumption of the existence of facts justifying its specific exercise attaches alike to statutes, to municipal ordinances, and to orders of administrative bodies") The APA did, however, seem to require that administrators themselves articulate their policies. See, for example, SEC v. Chenery Corp.

110. See *Hearst Publications*, 322 U.S. 111, 130 (1944); Gray v. Powell, 314 U.S. 402, 411 (1941). For a discussion of how the implicit questions of law in those cases were, in fact, theoretically preserved for court review, see Levin, "Identifying Questions of Law," pp. 1, 23.

111. Edward Shils, *Center and Periphery: Essays in Macrosociology* (Chicago, 1975), pp. 3–16.

112. See Theodore Lowi, *The Personal President* (Ithaca, N.Y., 1985), pp. 273–74.

113. This is particularly true if one includes in the definition of "capture" the neutralization of effective regulatory authority and the undermining of innovative ability in an agency. There is, however, no good theory of capture. Capture theories based in economics emphasize the laws of supply and demand. They imply that agencies inevitably supply the regulatory goods demanded by the regulated. See, for example, Richard Posner, "Theories of Economic Regulation," *Bell J. of Econ.* 5 (1974): 335; G. J. Stigler, "The Theory of Economic Regulation," *Bell J. of Econ.* 2 (1971): 3. Such capture theories, however, often imply a kind of consistency of results that the data do not support. For an excellent critique of capture theories to date, see W. H. Riker and R. P. Barke, "A Political Theory of Regulation with Some Observations on Railway Abandonments," *Pub. Choice* 39 (1982): 73. Moreover, such theories fail to consider seriously the effects of precedent or *stare decisis*. Legal reasoning, in and of itself, can be limiting, for once an agency makes certain choices, it is often precluded from making others. The regulated can manipulate agencies by forcing them to adhere to the logic of their previous positions. Without a clean slate to write on, an agency change can, at times, be prevented from changing. The agency may then *appear* to be captured, but the real problem is rather paralysis.

114. Ch. 324, 60 Stat. 237 (1946) (current version codified at 5 U.S.C. sec. 551–59, 701–06, 1305, 3105, 3344, 5372, 7521 [1982]).

115. Calvert Cliffs' Coordinating Comm. v. Atomic Energy Comm'n., 449 F.2d 1109, 1111 (D.C. Cir. 1971).

116. See, for example, Clean Air Act of 1970 and the Clean Water Act of 1977. See Shapiro, *Who Guards the Guardians?* pp. 79–87; Ackerman and Hassler, "Beyond the New Deal," pp. 1468–70, 1475.

117. S. P. Hays, "The Politics of Environmental Administration," in *The New American State*, ed. Louis Galambos (Baltimore, Md., 1987) pp. 22–25.

118. Ibid., p. 27. Contrast this consumer-oriented view with the producer-oriented view represented by the New Deal statutes.

119. A superb example is the Alaskan pipeline proceeding, 58 F.P.C. 810 (1977); 58 F.P.C. 1127 (1977) (Commission decision).

120. See, for example, Tanners' Council of America v. Train, 540 F.2d 1188, 1193 (4th Cir. 1976).

121. See, for example, Baltimore Gas & Elec. Co. v. NRDC, 462 U.S. 84 (1983) (Court upholds an NRC rule but only after a contextual approach that required an examination of a number of interrelated factors).

122. Calvert Cliffs' Coordinating Comm. v. Atomic Energy Comm'n. See also Ethyl Corp. v. EPA, 541 F.2d 1 (D.C. Cir.), cert. denied, 426 U.S. 941 (1976). The opinions in this Clean Air Act case highlight some important differences in the judicial role through the debate between Chief Judge Bazelon and Judge Leventhal. In separate concurring opinions, the Chief Judge argued for more procedural control of agency decision making and New Deal–style deference when it came to agency expertise involving substantive matters (id. at 66), while Judge Leventhal argued for more direct, substantive judicial review (id. at 68). Judge Leventhal's view eventually prevailed. For an example of the increased complexity of judicial review under the hard-look doctrine, see Sierra Club v. Costle, 657 F.2d 298 (D.C. Cir. 1981).

123. See W. F. West and Joseph Cooper, "The Rise of Administrative Clearance," in *The Presidency and Public Policymaking*, ed. G. C. Edwards III, S. A. Shull, and N. C. Thomas (Pittsburgh, 1985), pp. 192, 207–8). See also R. P. Nathan, *The Plot That Failed: Nixon and the Administrative Presidency* (New York, 1975).

124. See West and Cooper, "The Rise of Administrative Clearance," p. 208; Theodore Lowi, "The Constitution and Contemporary Political Discourse," p. 115 (unpublished paper on file with *Cornell Law Review*) (listing the new statutes passed from 1969 to 1976).

125. 347 U.S. 483 (1954).

126. See, for example, Shapiro v. Thompson, 394 U.S. 618, 634 (1969) (fundamental right to travel) ("[I]n moving from State to State . . . appellees were exercising a constitutional right, and any classification which serves to penalize the exercise of that right, unless shown to be necessary to promote a *compelling* governmental interest, is unconstitutional"); Hunter v. Erickson, 393 U.S. 385, 392 (1969) (fair housing law).

127. This is the second tier of the two-tiered approach to the judicial review of agency actions referred to earlier in this chapter.

128. See, for example, D. P. Currie, "Relaxation of Implementation Plans under the 1977 Clean Air Act Amendments," *Mich. L. Rev.* 78 (1979): 155: "[The] most striking feature of this scheme is its absoluteness"; see also W. H. Rodgers, *Environmental Law, Air and Water* (St. Paul, Minn., 1986), vol. 1, sec. 1.2. This is not to suggest that there were no examples of absolutist legislation in the past, see, for example, the Delaney amendment to the Food and Drug Act, mandating a no-risk approach to carcinogenic substances.

129. See National Environmental Policy Act of 1969, Pub. L. No. 91–190, 83 Stat. 852 (codified in various sections of 42 U.S.C. [1982]); Clean Water Act of 1977, Pub. L. No. 95–217, 91 Stat. 1566 (codified in various sections of 33 U.S.C. [1982]); Clean Air Amendments of 1970, Pub. L. No. 91–604, 84 Stat. 1676 (codified in various sections of 42 U.S.C. [1982]); Federal Water Pollution Act Amendments of 1972, Pub. L. No. 92–500, 86 Stat. 816 (codified at 12 U.S.C. sec. 24, 15 U.S.C. sec. 633, 636 [1982]); Water Quality Improvement Act of 1970, Pub. L. No. 91–224, 84 Stat. 91 (codified in various sections of 33 U.S.C. [1982]); Environmental Quality Improvement Act of 1970, Pub. L. No. 91–224, 84 Stat. 114 (codified at 42 U.S.C. sec. 4371–74 [1982]).

130. See Rodgers, *Environmental Law*, vol. 1, sec. 1.3(c).

131. See, for example, Industrial Union Department, AFL-CIO v. American Petroleum Institute, 448 U.S. 607 (1980) (benzene) and American Textile Manufacturers Institute v.

Donovan, 452 U.S. 490 (1981) (cotton dust). These cases are disputes surrounding the removal of benzene and cotton dust from the work place and litigation over just how risk-free an environment Congress had authorized.

132. See Sherbert v. Verner, 374 U.S. 398 (1963) (free exercise of religion); Brown v. Board of Educ. (school desegregation).

133. But see R. S. Melnick, *Regulation and the Courts: The Case of the Clean Air Act* (Washington, D.C., 1983), for an account of how the courts sometimes tempered these statutes through interpretation, allowing cost to be factored into the approach taken.

134. Clean Water Act of 1977, Pub. L. No. 95–217, 91 Stat. 1566 (codified in various sections of 33 U.S.C. [1982]).

135. Brown v. Board of Educ., 349 U.S. 294, 301 (1955) (Brown II).

136. See Rodgers, *Environmental Law*, vol. 1, sec. 1, p. 19: "Among the more salient examples of absolutism in environmental law are the goals in the Clean Water Act calling for fishable/swimming water everywhere by 1983 and no discharges anywhere by January 1, 1985. These two missions impossible . . . are among the most thoroughly denounced actions taken by any twentieth-century Congress."

137. See W. H. Rodgers, "Benefits, Costs, and Risks: Oversight of Health and Environmental Decisionmaking," *Harv. Envtl. L. Rev.* 4 (1980): 191.

138. 401 U.S. 402 (1971). Citizens to Preserve Overton Park, Inc. v. Volpe will be discussed further later in this chapter.

139. The statutory provision at issue was the Federal-Aid Highway Act of 1968, 23 U.S.C. sec. 138 (1982). It stated that the secretary of transportation should make a "special effort . . . to preserve . . . public park and recreation lands . . . [by] not approv[ing] any program or project which requires the use of any publicly owned land . . . unless (1) there is no feasible and prudent alternative." The Court interpreted this statute to mean that the Transportation Department was not merely to evaluate all prudent routes in terms of the cost to the public, but to give the protection of the parks "paramount importance" (401 U.S. at 412–13). Only if alternative routes presented problems of "extraordinary magnitude" could parks be sacrificed (id. at 411–13).

140. Id. at 420. This perspective is particularly common in cases dealing with the National Environmental Policy Act of 1969, Pub. L. No. 91–190, 83 Stat. 852 (1969) (codified as amended at 42 U.S.C. sec. 4321–709 [1977 and Supp. 1988]), and environmental cases in general.

141. 401 U.S. at 412–13.

142. See, for example, Environmental Defense Fund, Inc. v. Corps of Eng'r of the United States Army, 492 F.2d 1123 (5th Cir. 1974); Sierra Club v. Froehlke, 486 F.2d 946 (7th Cir. 1973); Conservation Council of N. Carolina v. Froehlke, 473 F.2d 664 (4th Cir. 1973); Environmental Defense Fund, Inc. v. Corps. of Eng'r of the United States Army, 470 F.2d 289 (8th Cir. 1972), cert. denied, 412 U.S. 931 (1973); Calvert Cliffs' Coordinating Comm. v. Atomic Energy Comm'n, 449 F.2d 1109 (D.C. Cir. 1971); Environmental Defense Fund, Inc. v. Tennessee Valley Auth., 371 F. Supp. 1004 (E.D. Tenn. 1973), aff'd on other grounds, 492 F.2d 466 (6th Cir. 1974).

143. See, for example, Environmental Defense Fund, Inc. v. EPA, 548 F.2d 998 (D.C. Cir. 1976) (supp. opinion 1977), cert. den. sub nom. Velsicol Chemical Corp. v. EPA, 431 U.S. 925 (1977). See E. F. Roberts, "The Right to a Decent Environment: Progress along a Constitutional Avenue," in *Law and the Environment*, ed. M. F. Baldwin and J. K. Page (New York, 1970), p. 134.

144. See, for example, *New York Times* v. United States, 403 U.S. 713, 714 (1971).

145. See, for example, the cases cited above at notes 142 and 143. See also R. B. Stewart, "The Development of Administrative and Quasi-Constitutional Law in Judicial Review of Environmental Decision Making: Lessons from the Clean Air Act," *Iowa L. Rev.* 62 (1977): 713, 750–54.

146. But see *New York Times*, August 12, 1987, p. 14 (discussing Secretary Hodel's recent proposal to complete construction of the Auburn Dam near Sacramento, California).

147. See Alfred Aman, "SEC v. Lowe: Professional Regulation and the First Amendment," *Sup. Ct. Rev.* 1985: 93.

148. See, for example, Environmental Defense Fund, Inc. v. Ruckelshaus, 439 F.2d 584, 597–98 (1980). A regulatory perspective is usually broad and is concerned largely with group rights. It tolerates a certain number of mistakes that result from good-faith estimates and best-guess probabilities. It is tailor-made for a rational-basis approach to judicial review. A constitutional perspective, however, is based on the individual. It demands more precision in reasoning, particularly if fundamental individual rights are at stake. In absolutist contexts, rational-basis reasoning and deference to good-faith guesses and probability inevitably give way to least restrictive alternative approaches and a higher demand for rationality and precision.

149. Hays, "The Politics of Environmental Administration," p. 23. See also Occupational Safety and Health Act of 1970, 29 U.S.C. sec. 651–78 (1985).

150. Judge Leventhal notes the similarity between administrative hard-look doctrines and constitutional strict scrutiny in Ethyl Corp. v. EPA, 541 F.2d 1, 68 (D.C. Cir. 1975) (Leventhal, J., concurring).

151. See Garrett Hardin, "The Tragedy of the Commons," Science 162 (1968): 1243. As one article of the era noted: "The fundamental cause of any common-pool problem is the difficulty of identifying, keeping track of, and asserting property rights over some part of the resource in question. As a consequence, each person with access to the resource has an incentive to exploit currently as much as he possibly can, thus neglecting the effects of his actions on recourse availability in the future, since he cannot hope to reap the future benefit that would result if he were to forgo some current profit" (R. J. Sweeney, R. D. Tollison, and T. D. Willett, "Market Failure, The Common-Pool Problem, and Ocean Resource Exploitation," Law J. & Econ. 17 [1979]: 179, 182–83).

152. Of course, the common-pool problem can also be conceptualized in market terms. It could be corrected by creating property rights in air or water so that individuals would maximize their individual interests in a way that internalized the external costs of their individual activities. This is not the approach that characterized the absolutist approaches of Congress in the early 1970s. See Shapiro, Who Guards the Guardians? pp. 80–87. See also R. S. Melnick, Regulation and the Courts: The Congress and the Clean Air Act (Washington, D.C., 1983), p. 369, for a discussion of how the courts sometimes read economics into the Clean Air Act.

153. Pub. L. No. 91–190, 83 Stat. 852 (1969) (codified as amended at 42 U.S.C. sec. 4321–70 [1977 and Supp. 1988]).

154. The National Environmental Policy Act of 1969 provides that "the Federal Government [is] to use all practicable means . . . " (42 U.S.C. sec. 4331[b] [1982]).

155. See Hays, "The Politics of Environmental Administration," pp. 25–27.

156. Ibid.

157. See, for example, Environmental Defense Fund, Inc. v. Corps of Eng'r of the United States Army, 470 F.2d 289 (8th Cir. 1972); Calvert Cliffs' Coordinating Comm. v. Atomic Energy Comm'n, 449 F.2d 1109 (D.C. Cir. 1971). Other relevant cases are cited at note 142.

158. In addition to the cases cited at note 157, see also, Jackson County v. Jones, 571 F.2d 1004, 1013 (8th Cir. 1978); County of Suffolk v. Secretary of the Interior, 562 F.2d 1368, 1384 (2d Cir. 1977); Environmental Defense Fund, Inc. v. Corps of Eng'r of the United States Army, 492 F.2d 1123, 1139–40 (5th Cir. 1974); Sierra Club v. Froehlke, 486 F.2d 946, 953 (7th Cir. 1973); Silva v. Lynn, 482 F.2d 1282, 1284 (1st Cir. 1973); Conservation Council of N. Carolina v. Froehlke, 473 F.2d 664, 665 (4th Cir. 1973).

For cases involving a judicial hard look independent of the National Environmental Policy Act of 1969, see National Lime Ass'n v. EPA, 627 F.2d 416, 453 (D.C. Cir. 1980); Columbia Gas Transmission Corp. v. Federal Energy Regulatory Comm'n, 628 F.2d 578, 593 (D.C. Cir. 1979); United States v. Nova Scotia Food Prods. Corp., 568 F.2d 240, 251–52 (2d Cir. 1977); H & H Tire Co. v. DOT., 471 F.2d 350, 355 (7th Cir. 1972).

See also W. H. Rodgers, "A Hard Look at Vermont Yankee: Environmental Law under Close Scrutiny," Geo. L. J. 67 (1979): 699, 704–8; H. J. Yarrington, "Judicial Review of Substantive Agency Decisions: A Second Generation of Cases under NEPA," San Diego L. Rev. 19 (1974): 279; Note, "The Least Adverse Alternative Approach to Substantive Review under NEPA," Harv. L. Rev. 88 (1975): 735.

159. 449 F.2d 1109 (D.C. Cir. 1971).

160. Pub. L. No. 91–190, 83 Stat. 852 (codified as amended at 42 U.S.C. sec. 4321–70q [1977 and Supp. 1988]).

161. The Nuclear Regulatory Commission was created in large part to correct this conflict of interest situation. See S. Rep. No. 980, 93d Cong., 2d sess., 1974, p. 14: "The Commission will have solely regulatory responsibilities, in keeping with a basic purpose of this act to separate the regulatory functions of the Atomic Energy Commission from its developmental and promotional functions." See also James Quirk and Katsuaki Terosawa, "Nuclear Regulation: An Historical Perspective," *Nat. Resources J.* 21 (1981): 833, 849.

162. See the cases cited at note 142. See also Hays, "The Politics of Environmental Administration."

163. 449 F.2d at 1111 (emphasis added).

164. For a critical assessment of the courts' role in environmental litigation, see J. L. Sax, "The (Unhappy) Truth about NEPA," *Okla. L. Rev.* 26 (1973): 239.

165. Ibid.

166. Old Colony Bondholders v. New York, N.H. & H.R. Co., 161 F.2d 413, 450 (2d Cir. 1947) (Frank, J., dissenting).

167. Id. at 451.

168. Id. 332 U.S. at 196.

169. 444 F.2d 841 (D.C. Cir. 1970), cert. denied, 403 U.S. 923 (1971).

170. See Sax, "The (Unhappy) Truth about NEPA," p. 247.

171. This approach is not unlike traditional approaches to evolution. See W. B. Provine, "Progress in Evolution and Meaning in Life" (unpublished manuscript on file at *Cornell Law Review*).

172. Initially, the commission had awarded the license to the station; however, "[w]hile the decision was on appeal in this court, it came to the court's attention that the Commission's award might be subject to an infirmity by virtue of improper *ex parte* contacts with the Chairman of the Commission" (444 F.2d. at 844). This possibility triggered another round of evidentiary hearings, at the end of which the commission again awarded the license to WHDH, but for only four months, instead of the customary three-year period. The commission was unsure about the extent of the *ex parte* contacts and whether and how they would affect the Commission's decision. When WHDH later filed for a renewal of its license, the commission began another round of comparative license hearings. Meanwhile, both WHDH and Greater Boston appealed the grant of the four-month license. During this appeal, Mr. Robert Choate of WHDH, who had initiated the improper *ex parte* contacts, died. The court then remanded the case to determine what effect, if any, his death should have on the licensing proceedings. The court also authorized the commission to combine the renewal proceedings with the remanded proceedings. The consolidated comparative proceeding began in May 1964. After further comparative hearings, the hearing examiner placed primary emphasis on the actual operating record of WHDH under its temporary authorizations of the preceding nine years and granted it a three-year license. The commission, however, reversed this decision in what turned out to be a very controversial opinion.

173. Id. at 848–49.

174. The commission explained that this case was unusual because WHDH's license had been granted only temporarily, because WHDH did not receive a license until 1962 and then only received a license for four months, and because of the commission's concern about "'inroads made by WHDH upon the rules governing fair and orderly adjudication'" (id. at 849).

175. Id. at 851.

176. Id. at 851–52.

177. Id. at 852–53.

178. Id.

179. Id. at 852.

180. Depending upon the complexity of the legislative history involved, however, the opportunities for the courts to decide what was a better as opposed to just a good reason might be considerable. See, for example, Judge Mikva's approach in State Farm Mut. Auto. Ins. Co. v. DOT., 680 F.2d 206 (D.C. Cir. 1982), which is discussed at notes 192 and 195.

181. 444 F.2d at 851. Judge Leventhal went on to note that "[t]he court is in a real sense part of the total administrative process, and not a hostile stranger to the office of first instance. This collaborative spirit does not undercut, it rather underlines the court's rigorous insistence on the need for conjunction of articulated standards and reflective findings" (444 F.2d at 851–52). See also Harold Leventhal, "Environmental Decision Making and the Role of the Courts," *U. Pa. L. Rev.* 122 (1974): 509, 511–12.

182. See L. J. Jaffe, "Administrative Law: Burden of Proof and Scope of Review," *Harv. L. Rev.* 79 (1966): 914.

183. See Environmental Defense Fund, Inc. v. Ruckelshaus, 439 F.2d 584, 597–98 (D.C. Cir. 1971). See also Scenic Hudson Preservation Conference v. FPC, 354 F.2d 608 (2d Cir. 1965) (the more important the rights involved, the sharper the scrutiny of the relevant facts and the broader the scope of court review). See Felix Frankfurter, "The Task of Administrative Law," *U. Pa. L. Rev.* 75 (1927): 614, 619–20: "Judicial review . . . derives significance from the nature of the subject matter under review as well as from the agency which is reviewed"; Jaffe, "Administrative Law," p. 79, who states that important rights asserted in environmental cases justify the imposition upon administrative agencies of greater burden of proof and the imposition on courts of the duty of more thorough judicial review.

184. See Jaffe, "Administrative Law," p. 920: "There is a special aspect of environmental rights which renders them more basic and more fundamental than most traditional civil rights. . . . That feature is the irrevocability of their breach"; Mark Sagoff, *The Economy of the Earth* (New York, 1988), pp. 24–49.

185. See Industrial Union Dep't, AFL-CIO v. American Petroleum Inst., 448 U.S. 607, 671–88 (1980).

186. Environmental Defense Fund, Inc. v. Ruckelshaus, 439 F.2d 584, 597–98 (D.C. Cir. 1971).

187. Id.

188. This approach was similar to that outlined in United States v. Carolene Products Co., 304 U.S. 144, 152 (1938): n. 4, which stated that courts would closely examine official actions that affect civil liberties, but would take, essentially, a hands-off approach in cases involving economic interests.

189. See Citizens to Preserve Overton Park, Inc. v. Volpe, 401 U.S. 402 (1971).

190. Administrative Procedure Act, 5 U.S.C. sec. 706 (1982).

191. 5 U.S.C. sec. 706(2)(A) (1982).

192. See State Farm Mut. Auto. Ins. Co. v. Department of Transp., 608 F.2d 206 (D.C. Cir. 1982). This clearly was a case where a variety of danger signals converged.

193. See Scenic Hudson Preservation Conf. v. FPC(I), 354 F.2d 608 (2d Cir. 1965) (agency must give adequate consideration to relevant factors and alternative solutions). See also Baton Rouge Marine Contractors, Inc. v. Federal Maritime Comm'n, 655 F.2d 1210, 1215–18 (D.C. Cir. 1981); National Lime Ass'n v. EPA, 627 F.2d 416, 451, n. 126 (D.C. Cir. 1980); International Union v. NLRB, 459 F.2d 1329, 1341–42, 1344 (D.C. Cir. 1972).

194. 5 U.S.C. sec. 706(2)(A) (1982).

195. See Association of Data Processing Serv. Orgs., Inc. v. Board of Governors of the Fed. Reserve Sys., 745 F.2d 677, 683–84 (D.C. Cir. 1984) (discussing *in dictum* the relationship of statutory substantial evidence and the Administrative Procedure Act's arbitrary and capricious standards); Motor Vehicle Mfrs. Ass'n v. State Farm Mut. Auto. Ins. Co., 463 U.S. 29 (1983) (White, J.). See M. J. McGrath, "Convergence of the Substantial Evidence and Arbitrary and Capricious Standards of Review during Informal Rulemaking," *Geo. Wash. L. Rev.* 54 (1986): 541.

196. For a collection of many of these statutes, see McGrath, "Convergence," p. 542 n. 6.

197. 5 U.S.C. sec. 553.

198. See *Motor Vehicle Mfrs. Ass'n*, 463 U.S. at 29.

199. See Vermont Yankee Nuclear Power Corp. v. NRDC, 435 U.S. 519 (1978) (construing Atomic Energy Commission jurisdiction).

200. 5 U.S.C. sec. 706(2)(A) (1982).

201. If, for example, an economic policy decision were under review and no "danger signals" were present, "arbitrary and capricious" could be interpreted to resemble the

rational-basis test commonly used by courts when reviewing the reasonableness of economic legislation under the due process clause. If, however, "fundamental interests" were involved and/or "danger signals" were present, the strict scrutiny or hard-look approach could be employed. As we shall see, just as in constitutional litigation, there were often more than two tiers of review available. The hard-look doctrine could apply with varying degrees of intensity, causing great doctrinal uncertainty, more litigation, and substantially greater control and power for reviewing courts.

202. See Administrative Procedure Act, 5 U.S.C. sec. 553(c).

CHAPTER 2 AGENCY DEREGULATION AND JUDICIAL REVIEW

1. See, for example, the following columns in the *New York Times* featuring the Howell Raines presidential radio address, August 19, 1984, p. A1; 1984 Republican party platform, August 22, 1984, p. A18; and Reagan's acceptance of the 1980 presidential nomination, July 18, 1980, p. A8.

2. See, for example, S. G. Breyer, *Regulation and Its Reform* (Cambridge, Mass., 1982), pp. 198–221, for a discussion of regulation and deregulation of the airline industry.

3. See E. W. Erickson, W. L. Peters, R. M. Spann, and P. J. Tese, "The Political Economy of Crude Oil Price Controls," *Nat. Resources J.* 18 (1978): 787; R. J. Pierce, "Reconsidering the Roles of Regulation and Competition in the Natural Gas Industry: Natural Gas Pipelines," *Harv. L. Rev.* 97 (1983): 345.

4. If welfare help is then necessary, a regulatory regime more consistent with market principles would provide that help directly by using energy stamps, for example, rather than a pricing structure that distorts the market and creates unnecessary demand for underpriced, regulated natural gas. For a discussion of various perspectives on energy and natural resources issues, to include a deregulatory, economic approach, see Alfred Aman, *Energy and Natural Law: The Regulatory Dialogue* (New York, 1984), chap. 1, pp. 1–49.

5. Milton Friedman, *Capitalism and Freedom* (Chicago, 1962), p. 3.

6. Ibid., p. 4.

7. Closely related to the goals of economic liberty and political freedom is the idea that "government power must be dispersed. If government is to exercise power, better in the county than in the state, better in the state than in Washington" (ibid., p. 3). As we shall see below, after the Department of Transportation's attempts to rescind the airbags rule failed, Secretary Dole took an alternative regulatory approach that sought to avoid federal regulation if a requisite number of states themselves initiated the use of airbags. That approach was an attempt to substitute local regulation for federal regulation and, as such, may or may not be viewed as ideologically, rather than pragmatically, motivated. For a case in which the United States Court of Appeals for the District of Columbia Circuit found an agency's use of federalism to be unauthorized by the statute involved and, in effect, motivated more by ideology rather than by the pragmatic use of discretion, see Farmworker Justice Fund, Inc. v. Brock, 811 F.2d 613 (D.C. Cir.), vacated as moot 817 F.2d 890 (D.C. Cir. 1987).

President Reagan also sought to encourage federalism at the agency level. For federalist principles raised when executive agencies engage in regulation, see Executive Order No. 12,612, 52 Fed. Reg. 41,685 (1987), reprinted in 5 U.S.C. sec. 601, at 298–300 (1987) (seeking "to restore the division of governmental responsibilities between the national government and the States . . . and to ensure that the principles of federalism . . . guide the Executive departments").

8. Airline deregulation certainly can be seen in this way. See Breyer, *Regulation and Its Reform*, pp. 317–40.

9. When the Carter administration first proposed deregulating the price of crude oil, it attempted to "sell" this approach by also advocating a politically popular windfall profits tax on oil companies, lest they reap the benefits of the higher decontrolled prices. See Aman, *Energy and Natural Resources Law*, chap. 1, sec. 5.04, pp. 81–85. See also *Windfall Profits Tax and Energy Trust Fund: Hearings Before the House Comm. on Ways and Means*, 96th Cong., 1st sess. 1979, pp. 6, 19 (statement of W. Michael Blumenthal); D. B. Drapkin and P.

K. Verleger, "The Windfall Profit Tax: Origins, Development, Implications," *B.C.L. Rev.* 22 (1981): 631, 665–66.

10. See Breyer, *Regulation and Its Reform*, pp. 317–40.

11. For an analysis of how market and regulatory values inevitably combine in various ways in the implementation of a regulatory program, see Alfred Aman, "Administrative Equity: An Analysis of Exceptions to Administrative Rules," *Duke L. J.* 1982, no. 3: 330–31: "On whatever end of the regulatory spectrum we begin—the free market or a complete regulation of the market—an examination of administrative equity suggests that an ongoing interplay of various market and regulatory values will occur and temper the dominant tendencies of whatever regulatory scheme is in effect. A regulatory regime based primarily on market principles will not be a static one. The regulatory dialogue will continue, and, given the basic values that pervade any regulatory scheme, the underlying structure of these new approaches will remain very much the same." For a case study examining how the fear of market regulatory approaches affected the legislative choices of the procedures and the ultimate structure of the Department of Energy, see Alfred Aman, "Institutionalizing the Energy Crisis: Some Structures and Procedural Lessons," *Cornell L. Rev.* 65 (1980): 491– 598.

12. See S. B. Foote, "Administrative Preemption: An Experiment In Regulatory Federalism," *Va. L. Rev.* 70 (1984): 1429, 1431, who notes that some federal agencies are exercising their preemptive powers to preclude state health and safety laws that would impose greater restrictions on industry. In this regard, some agencies have declared "that state laws on a given issue are preempted by the agency's decision not to regulate."

13. See, for example, Motor Vehicles Mfrs. Ass'n v. State Farm Mut. Auto. Ins. Co., 463 U.S. 29 (1983); International Bhd. of Teamsters v. United States, 735 F.2d 1525 (D.C. Cir. 1984).

14. See, for example, Public Citizen v. Steed, 733 F.2d 93 (D.C. Cir. 1984); Environmental Defense Fund, Inc. v. Gorsuch, 713 F.2d 802 (D.C. Cir. 1983). See also Peter Holmes, "Paradise Postponed: Suspensions of Agency Rules," *N.C.L. Rev.* 65 (1987): 645, who argues that judicial review should focus on agency suspensions that involve significant shifts in agency policy.

15. Public Citizen Health Research Group v. FDA, 740 F.2d 21 (D.C. Cir. 1984); Carpet, Linoleum & Resilient Tile Layers, Local 419 v. Brown, 656 F.2d 564 (10th Cir. 1981); Caswell v. Califano, 583 F.2d 9 (1st Cir. 1978); Sierra Club v. Gorsuch, 551 F. Supp. 785 (N.D. Cal. 1982).

16. See, for example, Heckler v. Chaney, 470 U.S. 821, 832 (1985) (FDA decision not to take investigatory and enforcement action regarding drugs used for lethal injections immune from judicial review). One can also petition an agency to make rules and then seek review of the agency's refusal to do so. The scope of this review is very narrow. For all practical purposes, an agency's refusal to promulgate new rules is virtually immune from judicial review. See WWHT v. FCC, 656 F.2d 807, 809 (D.C. Cir. 1981). Writs of mandamus might also be possible along with private causes of action. See also R. B. Stewart and C. R. Sunstein, "Public Programs and Private Rights," *Harv. L. Rev.* 95 (1982): 1193.

17. See WWHT v. FCC, 656 F.2d 807, 819–20 (D.C. Cir. 1981) (under narrow scope of judicial review, FCC's refusal to apply mandatory carriage requirements to scrambled signals of local subscription television seen as within agency's discretion).

18. See Marianne Smythe, "Judicial Review of Rule Rescissions," *Colum. L. Rev.* 84 (1984): 1928, 1930–31.

19. See 5 U.S.C. sec. 551(5).

20. See Motor Vehicle Mfrs. Ass'n v. State Farm Mut. Auto. Ins. Co., 463 U.S. 29, 41 (1983) ("We believe that the rescission . . . of an occupant-protection standard is subject to the [arbitrary and capricious] test").

21. Antonin Scalia, "Perspectives: Active Judges and Passive Restraints," *Reg.* 6 (July/ Aug. 1982): 13.

22. Ibid. (emphasis omitted).

23. Ibid.

24. See Motor Vehicle Mfrs. Ass'n, 436 U.S. at 41.

25. See Stewart and Sunstein, "Public Programs and Private Rights," p. 1195; C. R. Sunstein, "Deregulation and the Hard Look Doctrine," *Sup. Ct. Rev.* 1983: 177, 178.

26. See C. R. Sunstein, "Factions, Self-Interest, and the APA: Four Lessons since 1946," *Va. L. Rev.* 72 (1986): 271, 279: "[R]egulated class members are often well organized and may be better able to take advantage of the political process. Members of the beneficiary class, on the other hand, may be quite diffuse and thus unable to overcome transactions costs barriers to the exercise of political influence."

27. Ibid., pp. 279–80.

28. See R. B. Stewart, "The Reformation of American Administrative Law," *Harv. L. Rev.* 99 (1975): 1672: "The doctrine against delegation appears ultimately to be bottomed on contractarian political theory running back to Hobbes and Locke, under which consent is the only legitimate basis for the exercise of the coercive power of government."

29. See Sunstein, "Factions, Self-Interest, and the APA," p. 279. See also E. F. Roberts, "Natural Law Demythologized: A Functional Theory of Norms for a Revolutionary Epoch," *Cornell L.Q.* 51 (1966): 656, 667.

30. See, for example, Associated Gas Distrib. v. FERC, 824 F.2d. 981 (D.C. Cir. 1987).

31. See, for example, FCC v. WNCN Listeners' Guild, 450 U.S. 582, 593 (1981).

32. Sunstein, "Factions, Self-Interest, and the APA," pp. 279–80. This issue will be discussed more fully throughout this chapter.

33. See Vilhelm Aubert, "Competition and Descensus: Two Types of Conflict and Conflict Resolution," *J. of Conflict Resolution* 7 (1963): 26, 32–34, (who discusses how conflicts of interest that stem from the scarcity of resources are eliminated through the operation of the market); see also Mark Sagoff, *The Economy of the Earth* (New York, 1988), pp. 24–49.

34. See S. E. Rhoades, *The Economist's View of the World* (New York, 1985), pp. 201–3.

35. This, of course, assumes that both agencies and reviewing courts are substantially correct when they interpret the broad delegation clauses of New Deal statutes to allow the use of market means to achieve the various statutory ends. The statutory transformation that this economic discourse facilitates is ironic, particularly given the fact that Congress had concluded that regulation was necessary because unregulated markets did not work. Not all courts, of course, are willing to assume that the use of market means does not necessarily significantly change the statutory ends of a program that essentially rejected the market. See, for example, International Ladies' Garment Workers' Union v. Donovan, 722 F.2d 795, 827 (D.C. Cir. 1983), cert. denied, 469 U.S. 820 (1984); Farmers Union Cent. Exch. v. FERC, 734 F.2d 1486, 1518–20 (D.C. Cir. 1984). On balance, however, the open-ended nature of the delegation clauses, the economic conflicts of interest involved, and the implicit attempts to further the public interest make courts less suspicious of substantive interpretations of the statutes that allow the market to be used in this way.

36. 450 U.S. 582 (1981).

37. Id. at 584.

38. Id. at 585.

39. Id.

40. Id. at 590.

41. Id.

42. Id. at 585.

43. Id. at 600.

44. Id. at 590.

45. Id. at 595 (emphasis added).

46. Id. at 595–96 (emphasis added).

47. Id. at 595.

48. Id. at 597–99. The breadth of the FCC enabling act helped make this transformation possible. See M. S. Fowler and D. L. Brenner, "A Marketplace Approach to Broadcast Regulation," *Tex. L. Rev.* 60 (1982): 207, 233. See also R. E. Wiley, D. R. Patrick, L. A. Tisch, J. D. Blake, and M. J. Breger, "Broadcast Deregulation: The Reagan Years and Beyond," *Admin. L. Rev.* 40 (1988): 345. Not all statutes dealing with economic issues, however, so easily allow for a pure market discourse. See, for example, Farmers Union Cent. Exch., Inc. v. FERC, 734 F.2d 1486, 1500 (D.C. Cir.), cert. denied, 469 U.S. 1034 (1984) (FERC's

statute required that it "determine and prescribe what will be the just and reasonable rates" for oil pipelines. The court, quoting 49 U.S.C. sec. 15[1] [1976], rejected FERC's attempt to set rates solely on the basis of the market). See also Abner Mikva, "The Changing Role of Judicial Review," *Admin. L. Rev.* 38 (1986): 115, 132–33.

49. Mikva, "The Changing Role of Judicial Review, p. 595.

50. 682 F.2d 993 (D.C. Cir. 1982). See also Telocator Network of America v. FCC, 691 F.2d 525 (D.C. Cir. 1982).

51. 682 F.2d at 996–97.

52. Id.

53. Id. at 998.

54. Id. at 999 (quoting 47 U.S.C. sec. 151, 309[a], 310[b] [1976]).

55. Id.

56. Id. at 1003.

57. Id. ("The Top-Fifty Policy was not intended directly to promote those minority interests").

58. Id.

59. Id. at 1001.

60. Id.

61. Id. at 1002–3. Similarly, courts have looked with favor on the FCC's reversal of its regulatory policy regarding cable television. The Second Circuit, in upholding an FCC decision to rescind certain rules relating to syndicated program exclusivity and distant signal carriage, noted in Malrite T.V. of New York v. FCC, 652 F.2d 1140, 1147 (1981): "While the deregulation of the cable television industry raises serious policy questions, evidenced by the sharp division within the Commission . . . , these questions are best left to the agencies that were created, in large part, to resolve them."

These cases allow for an economic discourse that enables the courts to explain a resort to the market as an alternative regulatory approach. The openness of the statutes, the economic nature of the regulation, and the conflicts generated within the framework of the agency's enabling act allow an essentially economic discourse to take place—a discourse which courts have, by and large, been willing to recognize and approve. Such a discourse is less likely, however, in social regulation cases. In such cases, the statutes involved usually provide the agency with less leeway, and the nature of the regulation and the essentially value-oriented conflicts that emerge make resort to an economic discourse problematic. Courts should, and usually do, examine such cases with some care. For a similar judicial approach to deregulation, see, for example, Western Coal Traffic League v. United States, 719 F.2d 772 (5th Cir. 1983) (court deferred to an ICC decision not to set rates). But see also Global Van Lines v. ICC, 714 F.2d 1290 (5th Cir. 1983) (court rejected the ICC's extension of restriction removal rules to freight forwarders).

62. 682 F.2d at 1003.

63. 722 F.2d 795 (D.C. Cir. 1983).

64. Id. at 816.

65. Id. at 824–825.

66. Id. at 828.

67. See, for example, R. G. Noll, *Reforming Regulation* (Washington, D.C., 1971), pp. 33–46; Mark Green, "Uncle Sam the Monopoly Man," in *The Monopoly Makers* (New York, 1973), pp. 15–17.

68. S. P. Hays, "The Politics of Environmental Administration," in *The New American State*, ed. Louis Galambos (Baltimore, Md., 1987), p. 24.

69. See, for example, George Stigler, "The Theory of Economic Regulation," *Bell J. of Econ.* 2 (1971): 3–21; Richard Posner, "Theories of Economic Regulation," *Bell J. of Econ.* 5 (1974): 335–39. See also Sam Peltzman, "Toward a More General Theory of Regulation," *J. of Law & Econ.* 19 (1976): 211.

70. See Ralph Nader and Mark Green, "Economic Regulation vs. Competition: Uncle Sam the Monopoly Man," *Yale L. J.* 82 (1973): 871.

71. In fact, there does not appear to be a true theory of capture that can explain this level of behavior. For a critique of the economist's approach to this issue, see W. H. Riker and R. P.

Barke, "A Political Theory of Regulation with Some Observations on Railway Abandonments," *Pub. Choice* 39 (1982): 73–106.

72. A prime example of the combination of a court's pro-market leanings with an agency's attempt to instill competition into the interstate pipeline regulatory framework is Associated Gas Distrib. v. FERC, 824 F.2d 981 (D.C. Cir. 1987), where the court upheld FERC Order No. 436. This order began to transform the natural gas pipeline industry from individually regulated interstate pipelines into a competitive transportation system where pipelines play essentially the role of middlemen. Throughout the opinion the court emphasized the consumer perspective—one which stands to gain considerably at the expense of some interstate pipelines. Order No. 436 facilitates the sale of market-priced gas to a wide range of consumers. The linchpin of the opinion is the court's decision to treat interstate pipelines as if they were something akin to common carriers. On that issue the court simply deferred, citing, among other authorities, Chevron v. NRDC, 467 U.S. 837 (1984), though noting that *Chevron* is "not a wand by which the court can turn an unlawful frog into a legitimate prince" (id. at 1001).

In a partial dissent, however, Judge Mikva disagreed with the majority's extensions of these market-like approaches, particularly if they threatened the welfare of consumers. Specifically, he focused on the bypass problem, noting that the commission's decision will make it easier for "pipelines to 'bypass' . . . the local utilities with whom most consumers deal directly. . . . Thus, . . . the Commission has prevented the state commissions from protecting affordable rates for local customers" (id. at 1045).

73. There are, of course, limits to the deregulation that is possible under the economically oriented New Deal statutes. See, for example, International Ladies' Garment Workers' Union v. Donovan, 722 F.2d 795 (D.C. Cir. 1983), cert. denied, 469 U.S. 820 (1984) (preventing what the court believed to be the undermining of the minimum wage law). See also Farmworker Justice Fund v. Brock, 811 F.2d 613 (D.C. Cir.) (holding that OSHA had no basis to refuse to promulgate standards regulating farms), vacated as moot, 817 F.2d 890 (D.C. Cir. 1987).

74. See G. C. Eads and Michael Fix, ed., *The Reagan Regulatory Strategy* (Washington, D.C., 1984), p. 34.

75. 463 U.S. 29 (1983).

76. For a discussion of this program, see Robert A. Leone, "Regulatory Relief and the Automobile Industry," in Eads and Fix, *The Reagan Regulatory Strategy*, pp. 87–105.

77. Id. 463 U.S. at 49 (Justice White implied that the agency was too solicitous of industry's views on these issues). See also J. D. Graham and Patricia Gorman, "NHTSA and Passive Restraints: A Case of Arbitrary and Capricious Deregulation," *Admin. L. Rev.* 35 (1983): 193, 197 n. 35.

78. Congress perceived the problem of increasing highway deaths as having less to do with the conduct of individual drivers and more to do with the design of the car. Indeed, it treated these issues as public health concerns. The Motor Vehicle Act, in effect, adopts an epidemiological perspective. See J. L. Mashaw and D. L. Harfst, "Regulation and Legal Culture: The Case of Motor Vehicle Safety," *Yale J. on Reg.* 4 (1987): 258.

79. 463 U.S. at 43–44. Justice White's opinion noted that Congress required substantial-evidence review of cases like this and specifically required a record of the rulemaking proceedings to be compiled.

80. Presumably, the agency could have made a much stronger case than it did, but the rescission in this case may have been as symbolic as substantive, reflecting the Reagan administration's general policy of deregulation and Executive Order No. 12,291 in particular. See generally Holmes, "Paradise Postponed," p. 647.

Other resource constraints may also have influenced the agency's decision. For an excellent discussion of the effects that caseload, the nature of the record developed, the time an agency has to act, and other such factors have on the legal doctrine ultimately developed, see Peter Strauss, "One Hundred Fifty Cases Per Year: Some Implications of the Supreme Court's Limited Resources for Judicial Review of Agency Action," *Colum. L. Rev.* 87 (1987): 1093.

81. 15 U.S.C. sec. 1381–1481 (1982) (hereafter cited as the Safety Act).

82. See 15 U.S.C. sec. 1381 (1982) ("purpose of this chapter is to reduce traffic accidents and death and injuries to persons resulting from traffic accidents"); S. Rep. No. 1301, 89th

Cong., 2d sess., 1966, p. 1: "[T]his legislation reflects the faith that the restrained and responsible exercise of Federal authority can channel the creative energies and vast technology of the automobile industry into a vigorous and competitive effort to improve the safety of vehicles." See also Graham and Gorham, "MHTSA and Passive Restraints," p. 196.

83. See S. Rep. No. 1301, 89th Cong., 2d sess., 1966, p. 2: "[T]he committee met with disturbing evidence of the automobile industry's chronic subordination of safe design to promotional styling, and of an overriding stress on power, acceleration, speed, and 'ride' to the relative neglect of safe performance or collision protection. The committee cannot judge the truth of the conviction that 'safety doesn't sell,' but it is a conviction widely held in industry which has plainly resulted in the inadequate allocation of resources to safety engineering." The political reaction to Ralph Nader's book, *Unsafe at Any Speed: The Designed-In Dangers of the American Automobile* (New York, 1965), seemed to be to make automobile safety a consumer entitlement. Thus, for example, the act was seen by some of its proponents as an attempt to "equalize" automobile safety for everyone. See *Traffic Safety: Hearings on S. 3005 before the Senate Comm. on Commerce*, 89th Cong., 2d sess., 1966, p. 50. Senator Ribicoff remarked that a person driving a Plymouth, Ford, or Chevrolet is "entitled" to "certain basic things" "just as much as a person driving a Cadillac," including collapsible steering wheels and dual brakes. See also Mashaw and Harfst, "Regulation and Legal Culture," pp. 257–61.

84. Mashaw and Harfst, "Regulation and Legal Culture," p. 257.

85. Ibid.

86. Ibid., p. 258 n. 4.

87. For the latest judicial episode in this case, see State Farm Mut. Auto. Ins. Co. v. Dole, 802 F.2d. 474 (D.C. Cir. 1986). NHTSA's response to the Supreme Court's decision in *State Farm* was to suspend the rule for one year for reconsideration. In 1984, NHTSA issued a new rule concerning automatic occupant restraints (49 Fed. Reg. 28,962 [1984], codified at 49 C.F.R. sec. 571.208 [1987[). The most important provision of the new regulation states that the entire automatic restraint requirement would be rescinded if two-thirds of the population were covered by state imposed mandatory seatbelt use laws (MULs) by April 1, 1980. The agency reasoned that MULs are favored if enforced and airbags will offer the greatest amount of protection if development continues. See generally James Milstone, "Automatic Occupant Restraints and Judicial Review: How a Federal Agency Can Violate Congressional Will and Get Away with It," *Val. U.L. Rev.* 19 (1985): 693.

This new provision was challenged as contrary to the applicable statute and as arbitrary and capricious. The court found that the issue concerning deference to the states was not yet ripe. New York's challenge that the Department of Transportation should have adopted certain alternative standards was dismissed on the merits (State Farm Mut. Auto. Ins. Co. v. Dole, 802 F.2d 474 [D.C. Cir. 1986]). It is interesting to note that using federalism as a fallback to a more direct market-oriented approach is, to some extent, at odds with some of the legislative history on the role of the states in automobile safety concerns. See *Traffic Safety: Hearings on S. 3005 Before the Senate Comm. on Commerce*, 89th Cong., 2d sess., 1966, pp. 41–42. Senator Ribicoff remarked: "We have been sucked in with the propaganda that the Federal Government has no place in traffic safety; that we should leave this up to the States. There isn't a state in the country that has the facilities or the qualifications to go into the complexities of the automobile." Of course, the seatbelt option, if chosen by the states, would result in uniformity. As of August 1988, thirty-two states and the District of Columbia had enacted mandatory seatbelt laws. See "Seat-Belt Use Rising: Official's Credit Laws," *Chicago Tribune*, August 14, 1988, p. A32.

88. We now have our sixth president presiding over this issue. The matter is still pending awaiting the action of various states. See "Seat-Belt Use Rising." See also John Holusha, "Airbags on the Way as Chrysler Gives In," *New York Times*, May 26, 1988, p. A1.

89. See Graham and Gorman, "NHTSA and Passive Restraints," pp. 196–203. See also S. J. Tolchin, "Airbags and Regulatory Delay," *Issues in Sci. & Tech.* 1 (Fall 1984): 66.

90. 32 Fed. Reg. 2408, 2415 (1967).

91. Graham and Gorman, "NHTSA and Passive Restraints," p. 196 n. 26, citing L. J. White, *The Automobile Industry Since 1945* (Cambridge, Mass., 1971): pp. 241–42.

92. Graham and Gorman, "NHTSA and Passive Restraints," p. 197.
93. 34 Fed. Reg. 11,148 (1969).
94. 37 Fed. Reg. 3,911 (1972).
95. See Chrysler Corp. v. DOT, 472 F.2d. 659, 664–66 (6th Cir. 1972).
96. See 15 U.S.C. sec. 1410b(b)(1) (1982).
97. 15 U.S.C. sec. 1410b(d) (1982). Such provisions were subsequently declared unconstitutional in INS v. Chadha, 462 U.S. 919, 959 (1983).
98. 39 Fed. Reg. 10,271 (1974); 40 Fed. Reg. 16,217 (1975).
99. 42 Fed. Reg. 5,071 (1976).
100. See U.S. Department of Transportation, *The Secretary's Decision Concerning Motor Vehicle Occupant Crash Protection*, December 6, 1976.
101. Ibid. pp. 11–12, 52–57.
102. Ibid.
103. 42 Fed. Reg. 15,935 (1977).
104. 42 Fed. Reg. 34,289 (1977).
105. See Pacific Legal Foundation v. DOT, 593 F.2d 1338 (D.C. Cir. 1977), cert. denied, 444 U.S. 830 (1979).
106. See "President's Remarks to Annual Convention of United States Jaycees," *Weekly Compilation of Presidential Documents* 17 (June 24, 1981): 675, 676; "President's Remarks to Central City and California Taxpayers' Associations," *Weekly Compilation of Presidential Documents* 17 (June 25, 1981): 684, 685–86.
107. See Leone, "Regulating Relief and the Automobile Industry," in *The Reagan Regulatory Strategy*, pp. 87–105.
108. 46 Fed. Reg. 21,172 (1981).
109. 46 Fed. Reg. 53,419 (1981).
110. Id. See also 46 Fed. Reg. 21,172 (1981).
111. 46 Fed. Reg. 53,419 (1981).
112. Id.
113. Id.
114. Id.
115. Id.
116. See State Farm Mut. Auto. Ins. v. DOT, 680 F.2d. 206 (D.C. Cir. 1982).
117. See Presidential Task Force on Regulatory Relief, *Reagan Administration Regulatory Achievements* 67–68 (August 11, 1983).
118. Ibid. One of President Reagan's first acts in office was to order executive agencies to suspend for sixty days all regulations promulgated in final form that would otherwise become effective during that sixty-day period. See "Presidential Memorandum of January 29, 1981," 3 C.F.R. sec. 223 (1981). Shortly thereafter, the president issued Executive Order No. 12,291, 3 C.F.R. sec. 127 (1981), reprinted in 5 U.S.C. sec. 601 at 431–34 (1982), mandating the reassessment of existing regulations and directing the suspension of "major rules" that had not yet become effective, thereby permitting OMB reconsideration of their costs and benefits.
119. 680 F.2d. 206, 240 (D.C. Cir. 1982) ("NHTSA may not confuse its role with that of Congress").
120. Id. at 228–29.
121. Id. at 222–28. See Abner Mikva, "The Changing Role of Judicial Review," *Admin. L. Rev.* 38 (1986): 115. See also Mikva, "Foreword to Symposium on the Theory of Public Choice," *Va. L. Rev.* 74 (1988): 167.
122. 680 F.2d at 228–29.
123. Id. at 228 (quoting Pacific Legal Foundation v. DOT, 593 F.2d 1338, 1343 [D.C. Cir. 1979]).
124. Id. at 229.
125. Id. at 221.
126. Id.
127. Id.
128. Id. at 221.

129. Such an approach, as we shall see, is very much at odds with the judicial approach that mandates deference to the president when policy issues are involved.

130. 680 F.2d at 222–28.

131. Id.

132. See, for example, Graham and Gorman, "NHTSA and Passive Restraint," pp. 207–8. See also Justice White's majority opinion in *State Farm* interpreting these events negatively (463 U.S. 29, 44–96 [1983]).

133. 680 F.2d at 242.

134. Id.

135. Id. at 229.

136. Id. at 218.

137. Id. at 221.

138. Id. at 242.

139. In Vermont Yankee Nuclear Power Corp. v. NRDC, 435 U.S. 519 (1978), the Court instructed the appellate courts not to impose procedural requirements that were not found in the statutes themselves. Judge Mikva was, in a way, trying to instruct the executive on the parameters of its duty to "take care that the laws be faithfully executed" (U.S. Constitution, Art. 2, sec. 3).

140. These biases include an evolutionary notion of progress that is similar to the views held by early theorists in evolutionary biology. Normally, biological change was thought to occur gradually and incrementally and to be fully adaptable to preexisting intellectual and biological frameworks. All of this was thought to lead, inevitably, to a form of progress. See J. S. Huxley, *Evolution: The Modern Synthesis* (New York, 1942), pp. 556–79. But see William Provine, "Progress in Evolution and Meaning in Life" (unpublished manuscript on file with *Cornell Law Review*), who argues that "Huxley's idea of progress in evolution is merely the imposition of his cultural values upon evolution . . . and that the progress of evolution gives no meaning in life." The imposition of similar cultural values, however, is very much a part of the law governing agency change.

141. 680 F.2d at 241 ("NHTSA may yet conduct the reasoned decisionmaking that can support the rescission of the passive restraint standard, but it may not reject twelve years of preparation for such a standard until it does so").

142. Id. at 242 ("These changed factors—higher gasoline prices, smaller cars, an ailing automobile industry, and the methods of compliance being pursued by that industry—may fully justify reassessing, modifying, and even deferring date of the regulation. . . . There has been no showing, however, that these changes justify rescinding the standard outright").

143. Id. at 229 ("Judicial scrutiny of agency action—including the rescission of a rule-depends on the extent to which the agency has deviated from congressional expectations. An agency is seldom locked on course, but it must have increasingly clear and convincing reasons the more it departs from the path marked by Congress").

144. Id. at 220.

145. For an excellent treatment of the overall impact of judicial review on automobile safety, see Mashaw and Harfst, "Regulation and Legal Culture."

146. 463 U.S. 29, 40–46 (1983).

147. Id. at 45–46.

148. Id. at 45.

149. Id. at 42.

150. Id. at 41. In this regard, *State Farm* can be viewed not only as a case that implicitly reaffirms the hard-look doctrine but also one that loosened the grip of appellate courts on agencies. Indeed, the rhetoric of the opinion supports the conclusion that there is no sliding-scale approach to the interpretation and application of the arbitrary and capricious standard, but the fact of Justice White's close scrutiny suggests otherwise. For an argument why such a sliding scale is appropriate, see Peter Lehner, "Judicial Review of Administrative Inaction," *Colum. L. Rev.* 83 (1983): 627, 663–64.

151. 463 U.S. at 42.

152. Id. at 43 (quoting Bowman Transp., Inc. v. Arkansas-Best Freight System, Inc., 419 U.S. 281, 286 [1974]).

153. Id. at 42.

154. 463 U.S. at 43 n. 9. (distinguishing between rational-basis review appropriate for legislation and the standard appropriate for agency decisions).

155. Id. at 52–57.

156. Id. at 55.

157. Id. at 52–57.

158. Id. at 52.

159. Id. at 52–53.

160. Id. at 51 (quoting 46 Fed. Reg. 53423 [1981]).

161. Id. at 52.

162. Id. at 53.

163. Id. at 54.

164. Id. at 55.

165. Id. at 39.

166. Id. at 49.

167. 680 F.2d at 213.

168. 463 U.S. at 59.

169. Id.

170. Id.

171. Id. at 41.

172. Id. at 43–44.

173. Id. at 53–54.

174. See, for example, the Supreme Court's approach to sex discrimination in Craig v. Boren, 429 U.S. 190 (1976).

175. This doctrine has been hailed by some commentators. See, for example, R. J. Pierce, "*Chevron* and its Aftermath," *Vand. L. Rev.* 41 (1988): 301; Pierce, "The Role of Constitutional and Political Theory in Administrative Law," *Tex. L. Rev.* 64 (1985):469, 520–24; K. W. Starr, "Judicial Review in the Post-*Chevron* Era," *Yale J. on Reg.* 3 (1986): 283, 307–12. See generally K. W. Starr, C. R. Sunstein, R. K. Willard, A. B. Morrison, and R. M. Levin, "Judicial Review of Administrative Action in a Conservative Era," *Admin. L. Rev.* 39 (1987): 353–98. But see Stephen Breyer, "Judicial Review of Questions of Law and Policy," *Admin. L. Rev.* 38 (1986): 363; Cynthia Farina, "Statutory Interpretation and the Balance of Power in the Administrative State," *Col. L. Rev.* 88 (1988): 452–528. It has had, thus far, a somewhat checkered career in the lower courts and even in the Supreme Court. In some cases it has been applied with a vengeance. See, for example, Young v. Community Nutrition Inst., 106 S. Ct. 2360 (1986). In other cases, the Court seems to have moderated its view. See, for example, INS v. Cardozo-Forresca, 107 S. Ct. 1207 (1987); C. R. Sunstein, "Constitutionalism after the New Deal," *Harv. L. Rev.* 101 (1987): 421, 425–28; P. M. Wald, Paul Verkuil, Jeremy Rabkin, Lloyd Cutler, A. E. Bonfield, and T. M. Susman, "The Contribution of the D.C. Circuit to Administrative Law," *Admin. L. Rev.* 40 (1988): 507.

176. 467 U.S. 837 (1984).

CHAPTER 3 THE ADMINISTRATIVE PRESIDENCY AND GLOBAL COMPETITION

1. See, for example, G. R. Faulhaber, *Telecommunications in Turmoil: Technology and Public Policy* (Cambridge, Mass., 1987), pp. 23–37; A. E. Kahn, "Clip the Wings of the Mega-Airlines," *New York Times*, October 22, 1988, p. A27.

2. One can, of course, trace global trade and the comparative advantage that facilitates it far back in history. As Richard Rosecrance notes, "[T]rading city states existed in the late medieval period of European history and . . . they flourished down to the end of the fifteenth century" (*The Rise of the Trading State: Commerce and Conquest in the Modern World*, [New York, 1986], p. 72). But he also notes: "[W]hat is interesting and different about the world of international relations since 1945 is that a peaceful trading strategy is enjoying much greater efficacy than ever before. Through mechanisms of industrial-technological development and international trade, nations can transform their positions in international politics,

and they can do so while other states also benefit from the enhanced trade and growth that economic cooperation makes possible. International "openness," low tariffs, efficient means of transport, and abundant markets offer incentives to many nations that have only to find a niche in the structure of world commerce to win new rewards. The returns, as Japan, Korea, Taiwan, Hong Kong, the Association of Southeast Asian Nations . . . , Brazil, Mexico, China, India, and others have demonstrated, can be incredibly high. Small European nations, like Switzerland, Belgium, Holland, Austria, Denmark, Norway, and Sweden, have also grown dynamically as their foreign trade has risen as a fraction of the gross national product" (*The Rise of the Trading State*, p. ixx). For a discussion and analysis of various global perspectives on military and economic issues, see D. P. Calleo, *Beyond American Hegemony: Future of the Western Alliance* (New York, 1987), p. 3, who characterize the NATO alliance as "essentially an American protectorate for Europe"; R. O. Keohane, *After Hegemony: Cooperation and Discord in the World Political Economy* (Princeton, N.J., 1984); C. V. Prestowitz, *Trading Places: How We Allowed Japan to Take the Lead* (New York, 1988), who discusses problems with American business practices and governmental trade policies, particularly in light of Japanese practice and policies. See also Louis Uchitelle, "Trade Barriers and Dollar Swings Raise Appeal of Factories Abroad," *New York Times*, March 26, 1989, p. A1.

3. In addition, some industries grow, change, and evolve over time to the point that competition is possible where it once was unlikely. See, for example, R. J. Pierce, "Reconsidering the Roles of Regulation and Competition in the Natural Gas Industry," *Harv. L. Rev.* 97 (1987): 345. Pierce states (at pp. 346–47) the following: "Much has happened since 1935, however, to cast doubt on the continuing viability of FTC's recommendation [that the natural gas pipeline industry be regulated]. Three dramatic changes have taken place: (1) the pipeline industry's structure has changed—the size of the market has increased fifteen-fold . . . ; (2) our understanding of the effects of economic regulation has improved; and (3) our understanding of the operation of unregulated markets has improved. These changes warrant reconsidering the desirability of regulating gas pipelines. . . . Regulation of gas producers cannot be justified by a monopoly rationale. The industry is structurally competitive: no gas producer has significant market power, and barriers to entry are low."

4. The rise of new, innovative, flexible reconstructive approaches to regulation is part of the new global era of administrative law. For a discussion of the more flexible efficient regulatory approaches see R. B. Stewart, "Reconstitutive Law," *Md. L. Rev* 46 (1986): 86. See also C. R. Sunstein, "Constitutionalism after the New Deal," *Harv. L. Rev.* 101 (1987): 506–7.

5. See Duane Chapman, "Environmental Standards and International Trade in Automobiles and Copper: The Case for a Social Tariff," Cornell Agricultural Economics Working Paper no. 89–3 (on file with *Cornell Law Review*), who argues that regulatory costs are a key factor and that labor costs are, in fact, less of a factor in industries such as copper and silverware and automobile manufacturing.

6. Ibid.

7. For a general discussion of the unrealistic nature of these absolutist goals and the counterproductive role courts have played in enforcing them, see R. S. Melnick, *Regulation and the Courts: The Case of the Clean Air Act* (Washington, D.C., 1983).

8. State agencies could not regulate rates for natural gas and electricity sold in interstate commerce. The Supreme Court held that these matters involved interstate commerce and can only be regulated at the federal level. The 1938 Natural Gas Act and the Federal Power Act were passed in reaction to the Supreme Court's rulings in Public Utilities Comm'n v. Attleboro Steam & Elec. Co., 273 U.S. 83 (1927) and Missouri v. Kansas Natural Gas Col., 265 U.S. 298 (1924). See Alfred Aman, *Energy and Natural Resources Law* (New York, 1983), sec. 4–1 to 4–179.

9. See C. R. Sunstein, "Constitutionalism after the New Deal," p. 505: "Competition among the states would generate a 'race to the bottom' that would both harm the disadvantaged and prevent coordinated action."

10. Ibid.

11. Of course, globalism can be considered in a much broader, more interdependent way. Rather than decreasing domestic regulation, one can argue for increasing global regulation, as

182 NOTES TO CHAPTER 3

is occurring with the problem of ozone depletion. See, for example, United Nations, "Protocol on Substances That Deplete the Ozone Layer," *I.L.M.* 26 (September 16, 1987): 1541. The point here, however, is that, in the absence of international uniformity, the economic effects of the global perspective reinforce the actions taken by various administrative agencies that are pro-market and deregulatory.

12. It is interesting to note that even when a protectionist regulatory approach to global issues is taken, domestic manufacturers can suffer. For example, early in his administration, President Reagan sought to deal with Japanese competition in the auto industry by implementing quotas on the number of Japanese cars to be imported. Since these quotas were on relatively low-priced Japanese cars, they actually encouraged Japanese competitors to diversify their American offerings by competing for a share of the higher-priced, luxury car market. As one commentator concluded, "Any policy that encourages foreign producers to move away from their traditionally narrow product lines and seek greater fleet diversity, especially by shifting to higher-priced vehicles, works against the long-term competitive interests of U.S. producers" (Robert Leone, "Regulatory Relief and the Automobile Industry," in *The Reagan Regulatory Strategy*, ed. G. C. Eads and Michael Fix [Washington, D.C., 1984], p. 101).

13. Statement by Judge (now Justice) Antonin Scalia at 45th Judicial Conference of the D.C. Circuit, "Judicial Review of Administrative Action in an Era of Deregulation," 105 F.R.D. 321, 323 (1984).

14. As regulatory sophistication increases, however, it is, of course, also possible that some domestic regulatory choices will be made that will benefit domestic as opposed to foreign manufacturers of certain products. For a discussion of how various regulatory standards have resulted in something much less than a truly open market in the European Community, see Stanley Hoffman, "The European Community and 1992," *Foreign Aff. Q.* 68 (1989): 27.

15. Cf. Bruce Bagley, "Colombia and the War on Drugs," *Foreign Aff. Q.* 67 (1988): 70, 89–92, who sets forth the international dimensions of the drug problem, examines the pros and cons of decriminalizing certain drugs, and reviews various methods whereby the United States government can work with Latin American countries in the war on drugs.

16. 347 U.S. 672 (1954).

17. Of course, higher prices and a market approach would also encourage greater domestic production, lessen national security concerns, and encourage conservation. Thus, President Carter began the process of price decontrol as a part of his pro-conservation energy program. This approach not only moved toward deregulation, but it also helped extricate the government from a situation it really could not control.

Even in regulatory contexts with no international overtones, agencies have incentives to opt for the market rather than direct forms of regulation. For example, price controls often eventually contribute to shortages of the controlled commodity, necessitating agency allocation of that commodity. A political body may find it difficult to maintain its reputation if it must regularly deprive some groups of a commodity that others can have. When shortages arise, regulators may prefer to say that the market, rather than the regulators, requires these results. This approach makes such allocation decisions seem impersonal. On the other hand, in some instances, market prices are lower than regulated prices, and deregulation will, in fact, deliver a lower price to important constituent beneficiaries of the agency involved. In such cases, regulators want to achieve these results and take credit for them. See, for example, AGD v. FERC, 824 F.2d 981 (D.C. Cir. 1987).

18. For an interesting comparison of the adversarial character of the American with the more cooperative tone of the British regulatory system, see David Vogel, *National Styles of Regulation* (Ithaca, N.Y., 1986), pp. 146–92.

19. This phrase originates in Alfred Aman, "Administrative Equity: An Analysis of Exceptions To Administrative Rules," *Duke L. J.* 1982, no. X: 277.

20. See Aman, "Administrative Equity," p. 323, who notes how the making of exceptions provides a means of tempering regulatory regimes with market values and vice versa; P. H. Schuck, "When the Exeception Becomes the Rule: Regulatory Equity and the Formulation of Energy Policy through an Exceptions Process, Regulatory Equity," *Duke L. J.* 1984, no. X: 163. See also R. S. Melnick, *Regulation and the Courts*, pp. 64–70, who states that "the

courts have sought to moderate the zeal of agencies single-mindedly pursuing limited objectives and to bring greater balance to public policies"; T. J. Stukane, "EPA's Bubble Concept after Chevron v. NRDC: Who is to Guard the Guards Themselves?," *Nat. Resources Law.* 17 (1985): 647, 669–73: who argues that courts have a tendency to read economic reality into statutes even where the statutes do not explicitly allow it.

21. See Mark Sagoff, "At the Shrine of Our Lady of Fatima or Why Political Questions Are Not All Economic," *Ariz. L. Rev.* 23 (1981): 1283, 1285: "This essay concerns the economic decisions we make about the enviroment. It also concerns our political decisions about the environment. Some people have suggested that ideally these should be the same, that all environmental problems are problems in distribution. According to this view, there is an environmental problem only when some resource is not allocated in equitable and efficient ways." See also A. B. Morrison, "OMB Interference with Agency Rulemaking: The Wrong Way to Write a Regulation," *Harv. L. Rev.* 99 (1986): 1059, 1062: "[Executive Order 12,291] requires that agencies promulgate only those regulations that are the product of cost-benefit, least-cost analysis. . . . [T]he Order authorizes OMB to review virtually all proposed rules for consistency with the substantive aims of the Executive Order before an agency can even ask for public comment on the proposal." But see C. C. DeMuth and D. H. Ginsburg, "White House Review of Agency Rulemaking," *Harv. L. Rev.* 99 (1986): 1075, 1080–82.

22. See Morrison, "OMB Interference." See also E. D. Olson, "The Quiet Shift of Power: Office of Management & Budget Supervision of Environmental Protection Agency Rulemaking under Executive Order 12,291," *Va. J. Nat. Res. L.* 4 (1984): 1. For a detailed discussion of the legality of Executive Order 12,291, 3 C.F.R. 127 (1981) reprinted in 5 U.S.C. sec. 601 (1982), see C. R. Sunstein, "Cost-Benefit Analysis and the Separation of Powers," *Ariz. L. Rev.* 23 (1981): 1267. See also Morton Rosenberg, "Beyond the Limits of Executive Power: Presidential Control of Agency Rulemaking under Executive Order 12,291," *Mich. L. Rev.* 80 (1981): 193; P. L. Strauss and C. R. Sunstein, "The Role of the President and OMB in Informal Rulemaking," *Admin. L. Rev.* 38 (1986): 181, 187–88.

23. The extensive use of executive orders as a means of controlling administrative discretion has been a part of executive politics for some time. President Nixon's OMB instituted "Quality of Life" reviews. The EPA circulated proposed regulations among other agencies and responded to their comments. See Bureau of National Affairs, "Office of Management and Budget Plays Critical Part in Environmental Policymaking, Faces Little External Review," *Envir. Rep.* 7 (1976): 693; H. H. Bruff, "Presidential Power and Administrative Rulemaking," *Yale L. J.* 88 (1979): 451, 464–65: "The history of Quality of Life review reveals a tendency for 'procedural' techniques such as interagency review to pressure the subject agency toward substantive change, or to provide an opportunity for those opposed to statutory programs to delay their implementation. . . . Because agency comments were not made part of the public record and often occurred before notice of proposed rulemaking, Quality of Life review had low visibility."

24. In 1974, President Ford issued Executive Order No. 11,821, 3 C.F.R. 926, reprinted in 12 U.S.C. sec. 1904 (1976), amended by Executive Order No. 11,949, 3 C.F.R. 161 (1977). These orders required agencies to prepare "inflation-impact statements" for all major regulations. Major regulations were defined as those having an impact in excess of $100 million. Similarly, President Carter's attempts to control the bureaucracy led to the issuance of Executive Order No. 12,044, 3 C.F.R. 152 (1978), reprinted in 5 U.S.C. sec. 553 (1976 and Supp. II 1978).

25. Executive Order No. 12,291, 3 C.F.R. 127 (1981), reprinted in 5 U.S.C. sec. 601 (1982). See Peter Raven-Hansen, "Making Agencies Follow Orders: Judicial Review of Agency Violations of Executive Order 12,291," *Duke L. J.* 1983, no. 2: 285. The attempts by Nixon, Ford, and Carter to gain control of the regulatory agencies were, by no means, insignificant. They pale, however, in comparison to the extensive control that President Reagan sought, and largely achieved, in Executive Order No. 12,291.

26. See, for example, DeMuth and Ginsburg, "White House Review of Agency Rulemaking," pp. 1075, 1080–82; Strauss and Sunstein, "The Role of the President and OMB in Informal Rulemaking," pp. 181, 187–88. See J. V. DeLong, "Defending Cost-Benefit Analysis: Replies to Steven Kelman," *Reg.* 5 (March–April 1981): 39.

27. See, for example, T. O. McGarity, "Regulatory Analysis and Regulatory Reform," *Tex. L. Rev.* 65 (1987): 1243, 1273–1308; Morrison, "OMB Interference with Agency Rulemaking," pp. 1059, 1064–68.

28. See, for example, Environmental Defense Fund v. Thomas, 627 F.Supp. 566, 570–571 (D.D. 1986) (the Court noted the OMB delay problem extended beyond just the rule in this case, but often delayed other rules beyond the statutory deadlines for their issuance).

29. See OMB, *Regulatory Program of the United States Government: April 1, 1985– March 31, 1986.* See also, H. H. Bruff, "Presidential Management of Agency Rulemaking," *Geo. Wash. L. Rev.* 57 (1989): 533, 563.

30. 467 U.S. 837 (1984).

31. This is eloquently expressed in the concurring opinion of 343 U.S. 579, 653–54 (1952): "Executive power has the advantage of concentration in a single head in whose choice the whole Nation has a part, making him the focus of public hopes and expectations. In drama, magnitude and finality his decisions so far overshadow any others that almost alone he fills the public eye and ear. No other personality in public life can begin to compete with him in access to the public mind through modern methods of communications. By his prestige as head of state and his influence upon public opinion he exerts a leverage upon those who are supposed to check and balance his power which often cancels their effectiveness."

32. Edward W. Cowen, *The President: Office and Powers* (New York, 1957), p. 3.

33. S. P. Shane and H. H. Bruff, *The Law of Presidential Power* (Durham, N.C., 1988), p. 395.

34. Theodore Lowi, "The Constitution and the Regulation of Society" (unpublished paper on file with *Cornell Law Review*), pp. 18–19.

35. Ibid.

36. Pub. L. No. 67–13, cl. 18, 42 Stat. 20 (1921).

37. See Reorganization Plan No. 2 of 1970, 3 C.F.R. 197 (1970), reprinted in 5 U.S.C. app. at 824 (1976) and in 84 Stat. 2085 (1970), reprinted in 31 U.S.C. sec. 16 app. at 1177 (1976). See also Morton Rosenberg, "Presidential Control of Agency Rulemaking," *Ariz. L. Rev.* 23 (1981): 1199, 1218; Rosenberg, "Beyond the Limits of Executive Power," p. 222; DeMuth & Ginsberg, "White House Review of Agency Rulemaking," p. 1075.

38. "We all know that a government agency charged with the responsibility of defending the nation or constructing highways or promoting trade will invariably spend 'too much' on its goals. An agency succeeds by accomplishing the goals Congress set for it as thoroughly as possible—not by balancing its goals against other, equally worthy goals. This fact of agency life provides the justification for a countervailing administrative constraint in the form of a central budget office" (DeMuth and Ginsburg, "White House Review of Agency Rulemaking," p. 1081).

39. 31 U.S.C. sec. 16 (1976) (as amended by Pub. L. No. 93–250, sec. 1, 88 Stat. 11 [1974]).

40. Rosenberg, "Beyond the Limits of Executive Power," p. 223; Lowi, "The Personal President," p. 186.

41. Office of Management and Budget Circular A-95. Although not in the form of an executive order, it served much the same function as the later Ford, Carter, and Reagan executive orders. See *Federal Regulation & Regulatory Reform,* H.R. Doc. No. 134, 94th Cong., 2d sess., 1976.

42. Executive Order No. 11,821 (1974).

43. Executive Order No. 12,044, 3 C.F.R. 152 (1979).

44. Executive Order No. 12,291, sec. 3, 3 C.F.R. 128 (1981), reprinted in 5 U.S.C. sec. 601 at 432 (1982). For an excellent analysis and description of OMB in action, see Bruff, "Presidential Management of Agency Rulemaking," p. 533.

45. Executive Order No. 12,291 sec. 2(b), 3 C.F.R. 128 (1981), reprinted in 5 U.S.C. sec. 601 at 432 (1982).

46. Id., sec. 2(d).

47. Id., sec. 2(b).

48. Executive Order No. 12,498, 3 C.F.R. 323 (1985).

49. Id.

50. Sierra Club v. Costle, 657 F.2d 298, 406 (D.C. Cir. 1981).

51. National Academy of Public Administration, *Presidential Management of Rulemaking in Regulatory Agencies* (Washington, D.C., 1987), p. 16.

52. Executive Order No. 12,291, sec. 2, 3 C.F.R. 128 (1981), reprinted in 5 U.S.C. sec. 601 at 432 (1982).

53. Executive Order No. 12,291, sec. 1(d), 3 C.F.R. 128 (1981), reprinted in 5 U.S.C. sec. 601 at 432 (1982).

54. 627 F. Supp. 566, 571 (D.D.C. 1986).

55. Solid Waste Disposal Act, sec. 3004(w), 42 U.S.C. sec. 6924(w) (1982).

56. OMB review of regulations is undertaken by the Office of Information and Regulatory Affairs within OMB. This office has drawn intense criticism from Congress, especially in the early 1980s, when the House tried to "zero out" OMB's regulatory review office on the grounds that it was undermining Congressional legislation. See National Academy of Public Administration, *Presidential Management*, p. 6.

57. 627 F. Supp. at 569.

58. Id. at 570.

59. Id.

60. For a case history, see Public Citizen Health Research Group v. Brock, 823 F.2d 626, 627–28 (D.C. Cir. 1987).

61. See 47 Fed. Reg. 3566 (1982).

62. Public Citizen Health Research Croup v. Auchter, 702 F.2d 1150, 1154 n. 12 (D.C. Cir. 1983) (per curiam).

63. 48 Fed. Reg. 17283, 17294 (1983).

64. See National Academy of Public Administration, *Presidential Management*, p. 5.

65. Public Citizen Health Research Group v. Tyson, 796 F.2d 1479 (D.C. Cir. 1986).

66. Id. at 1507.

67. Public Citizen Health Research Group v. Brock, 823 F.2d 626, 629 (D.C. Cir. 1987).

68. This is particularly true if one includes, along with *Chevron*, recent developments in constitutional law taking a formalistic approach to separation-of-power issues and an expansive and protective view of executive power. There are, of course, exceptions to these trends. See, for example, Morrison v. Olson, 108 S. Ct. 2597 (1988) (appointment of independent counsel by federal court not violative of Appointments Clause or separation-of-powers concerns). Moreover, the Court's approach in *Chevron*, has not necessarily taken hold completely. In other contexts, the Court has shown some reluctance to defer to presidential power in quite the way *Chevron* would suggest. See, for example, Mississippi Power & Light Co. v. Mississippi, 108 S. Ct. 2428 (1987); INS v. Cardozo-Fonseca, 480 U.S. 421 (1987); Board of Governors of the Federal Reserve Sys. v. Dimension Fin. Corp., 474 U.S. 361 (1986). But see Young v. Community Nutrition Inst., 476 U.S. 974 (1986).

Nevertheless, the long-term trend seems very much in the direction of increasing executive power over the administrative process. This is very much of a piece with the general trend of increased presidential power and conforms to some of the reasons Justice Jackson noted for the inevitable increase in executive power in his concurrence in Youngstown Sheet & Tube Co. v. Sawyer, 343 U.S. 579, at 653–54 (1952). See also P. B. Kurland, "The Rise and Fall of the 'Doctrine' of Separation of Powers," *Mich. L. Rev.* 85 (1986): 592, 607–10. As far as the administrative process is concerned, the need for executive coordination has been increasing along with the increase in the policymaking power of the bureaucracy.

69. See Alfred Aman, "Symposium: How Separation of Powers Protects Individual Liberties," *Rutgers L. Rev.* 41 (1989): 796–805.

70. See Bowsher v. Synar, 478 U.S. 714 (1986). Though footnote 4 of *Bowsher* expressly states that this issue was not decided, the implications of this opinion were tested again in Morrison v. Olson, 108 S. Ct. 2597 (1988). Once again, the Court refused to rule in a manner that made the "headless fourth branch" unconstitutional. In fact, it seems to have put the issue to rest once again. But see 108 S. Ct. at 2622 (Scalia, J., dissenting).

For recent commentary criticizing the role of administrative agencies in our constitutional system, see G. P. Miller, "Independent Agencies," *Sup. Ct. Rev.* 1986:41–97; D. P. Currie, "The Distribution of Powers After Bowsher," *Sup. Ct. Rev.* 1986:19–40. For an overview of these important constitutional issues, see Peter Strauss, "The Place of Agencies in Government: Separation of Power and the Fourth Branch," *Colum. L. Rev.* 84 (1984): 573. For an application of this analysis to Bowsher v. Synar and other recent cases, see Strauss, "Formal and Functional Approaches to Separation-of-Powers Questions—A Foolish Inconsistency?" *Cornell L. Rev.* 72 (1987): 488.

71. 285 U.S. 22 (1932). For a recent use of this case, see Northern Pipeline Constr. Co. v. Marathon Pipe Line Co., 485 U.S. 50, 68 (1982).

72. 463 U.S. 29 (1983).

73. 108 S. Ct. 2597 (1988).

74. 109 S. Ct. 647 (1989).

75. See Strauss, "The Place of Agencies in Government." Strauss identified three distinct approaches to separation-of-powers issues—a separation-of-powers approach that "supposes that what government does can be characterized in terms of the kind of act performed" (p. 577), a separation-of-functions approach that is "grounded more in considerations of individual fairness in particular proceedings than in the need for structural protection against tyrannical government generally" (p. 577), and a more practically oriented checks-and-balances approach whose "focus is on relationships and interconnections" among governmental officials rather than "a radical division of government into three parts, with particular functions neatly parceled out among them" (p. 578). See also Sunstein, "Constitutionalism after the New Deal," pp. 495–96.

76. For a discussion of the Court's history of favoring the functional approach with separation-of-powers issues, see J. M. Burkoff, "Appointment and Removal under the Federal Constitution: The Impact of Buckley v. Valeo," *Wayne L. Rev.* 22 (1976): 1335, 1358 n. 108, who cites cases prior to *Buckley* that reflect the functional approach. See also Strauss, "Formal and Functional Approaches," pp. 616–22.

77. See Kurland, "The Rise and Fall," p. 593 who discusses Madison's perception of "checks and balances" as a result, in part, of the indeterminacy of governmental functions.

78. Increasing national power, whether through administrative agencies or congressional pronouncements, has been a continuing trend. As Kurland has noted, "limited government, or minimalist government, in Lockean or Harringtonian terms, is a matter of ancient history; its demise is probably coincident with the growth of the idea of implied powers" (Kurland, "The Rise and Fall," p. 604).

79. Ibid. This is not to say of course, that the Founding Fathers did not differ theoretically over the role that a federal government could play, with Hamilton usually taking an expansive view and Jefferson a much more limited one. At the time of the forming of the Constitution, however, the federal government, in fact, played so minimal a role that no one, including those who advocated a strong central government, could have truly foreseen how extensive a role in national affairs the federal government would one day play.

80. Ibid., p. 603.

81. Ibid., p. 604.

82. For an illuminating discussion of the difficulties involved in repealing old statutes, see Guido Calabresi, *A Common Law for the Age of Statutes* (Cambridge, Mass., 1982).

83. See, for example, Bowsher v. Synar, 478 U.S. 714, 749 (1986) ("One of the reasons that the exercise of legislative, executive, and judicial powers cannot be categorically distributed among three mutually exclusive branches of government is that governmental power cannot always be readily characterized with only one of those labels") (Stevens, J., concurring in part and dissenting in part).

84. See, for example, Federal Trade Comm'n v. American Nat'l Cellular, Inc., 810 F.2d 1511 (9th Cir. 1987) (formalistic arguments ultmately rejected in upholding FTC enforcement powers).

85. See Sunstein, "Constitutionalism after the New Deal," pp. 481–91 who argues for incorporation of a constitutional commitment to checks and balances into regulatory administration. For a discussion of positive and negative concepts of liberty, see Isaiah Berlin, *Four Essays on Liberty* (New York, 1969), pp. 118–72.

86. The Seventeenth Amendment was ratified in 1913, and it provides for direct popular election of U.S. Senators. Prior to the Seventeenth Amendment, they were elected by state legislatures.

87. The modern constitutional view of federal power is well stated in Garcia v. San Antonio Metropolitan Transit Authority, 469 U.S. 528 (1985).

88. 462 U.S. 919 (1983).

89. 478 U.S. 714 (1986).

90. For example, Executive Order No. 12,291, 3 C.F.R. 127 (1981), reprinted in 5 U.S.C. sec. 601 app. (1982), was promulgated shortly after the Reagan administration took office, but also after Congress had failed in its attempts to amend the APA to provide for similar regulatory analyses of proposed rules. See, for example, *Joint Report of the Senate Comm. on Governmental Affairs and the Comm. on the Judiciary on S. 262*, S. Rep. No. 1018, 96th Cong., 2d sess., 1980, part 1. For an argument that that order was, in fact, unconstitutional, see Rosenberg, "Beyond the Limits of Executive Power," p. 193. A formalistic approach makes the constitutional argument even stronger: if the legislature cannot influence or seek to control the executive, surely the executive cannot legislate.

Morrison v. Olson, 108 S. Ct. 2597 (1988), may, therefore, help to ensure, rather than undermine, an expansive executive role. The Court's flexible approach to the separation-of-powers issues in that case could also be used to uphold executive actions that are more legislative in nature.

91. See Peter Strauss, "Was There a Baby In the Bathwater? A Comment on the Supreme Court's Legislative Veto Decision," *Duke L. J.* 1983, no. 4: 789, who addresses the Court's inability in *Chadha* to distinguish the use of the veto in political and regulatory contexts. For a study of legislative vetoes in general and their effect on the administrative process, see H. H. Bruff and Ernest Gellhorn, "Congressional Control of Administrative Regulation: A Study of Legislative Vetoes," *Harv. L. Rev.* 90 (1977): 1369.

92. But see 462 U.S. at 968–74 (White, J., dissenting), noting the various kinds of legislative vetoes that have developed over time. See also Strauss, "Was There a Baby," pp. 804–12, who analyzes Justice White's "intellectual" approach to the legislative veto question.

93. Cf. Chevron v. NRDC, 467 U.S. 837 (1984), which demonstrates the rhetorical, all-or-nothing aspect of the formalistic approach. In that case, Justice Stevens set forth, as a condition of judicial intervention, the requirement that Congress speak *precisely* to the issue then before the Court. According to Stevens, courts should resolve all doubts in favor of agency discretion in the face of statutory silence or ambiguity.

94. 462 U.S. at 951 ("Although not 'hermetically' sealed from one another, . . . the powers delegated to the three Branches are functionally identifiable").

95. See Strauss, "Was There a Baby," pp. 794–801.

96. *Chadha*, 462 U.S. at 945–46.

97. James Landis, *The Administrative Process* (New Haven, Conn., 1938), p. 11.

98. This is not to say that the veto provision in *Chadha* was not, in fact, unconstitutional, but rather to emphasize that if unconstitutional, it was so for reasons more subtle and complicated than those articulated by the sweeping opinion of the majority. See, for example, 462 U.S. at 959 (Powell, J., concurring). See also Strauss, "Was There a Baby," p. 817; and Sunstein, "Constitutionalism after the New Deal," p. 496, who concludes that a functional approach to *Chadha* would yield the same result.

It is also important to note that, despite the impression of almost mechanical rigidity, formalism is also capable of flexibility and ambiguity. Judges have discretion when characterizing the nature or function of the official under review. The discretion involved in the labeling approach gives courts a great deal of power, not only because it makes legislation more vulnerable constitutionally, but because of confusion regarding the definitions of legislative, executive, and judicial functions. Once the court defines and applies these labels, the analysis appears very simple. But the process of judicial definition behind this approach is by no means clear-cut. See, for example, Bowsher v. Synar, 478 U.S. 714, 748–49 (1986) (Stevens, J., concurring). See Strauss, "Was There a Baby," pp. 797–98, discussing what is legislative; Kurland, "The Rise and Fall," p. 603, who comments on "the inefficacy of resorting to a general notion of separation of powers to resolve contests between two branches of government."

99. *Chadha*, 462 U.S. at 958–59.

100. Pub. L. 99–177, 99 Stat. 1038, 2 U.S.C. sec. 901–7, 921–22 (Supp. IV 1986).

101. For a similar problem that arises when the First Amendment is arguably overextended to certain kinds of commercial or regulatory speech, see T. H. Jackson and J. C. Jeffries, "Commercial Speech: Economic Due Process and the First Amendment," *Va. L. Rev.* 65 (1979): 1; see also, Alfred Aman, "SEC v. Lowe: Professional Regulation and the First Amendment," *Sup. Ct. Rev.* 1985:93–148.

102. Balanced Budget and Emergency Control (Gramm-Rudman-Hollings) Act of 1985, 2 U.S.C. sec. 901 (Supp. IV 1986).

103. Section 251(b), 2 U.S.C. sec. 901(b) (Supp. IV 1986), states:

(b) Report to President and Congress by Comptroller General
(1) Report to be Based on OMB-CBO Report—The Comptroller General shall review and consider the report issued by the Directors . . . and, with due regard for the data, assumptions, and methodologies used in reaching the conclusions set forth therein, shall issue a report to the President and the Congress . . . estimating the budget base levels of total revenues and total budget outlays, . . . identifying the amount of any deficit excess, . . . stating whether such deficit excess . . . will be greater than $10,000,000,000, . . . specifying the estimated rate of real economic growth, . . . and specifying . . . the base from which reductions are taken and the amounts and percentages by which such accounts must be reduced . . . in order to eliminate such deficit excess. . . . Such report shall be based on the estimates, determinations, and specifications of the Directors. . . .
(2) Contents of Report—The report of the Comptroller General under this subsection shall—
(A) provide for the determination of reductions . . . ; and
(B) contain estimates, determinations, and specifications for all of the items contained in the report submitted by the Directors. . . .
Such report shall explain fully any differences between the contents of such report and the report of the Directors.

104. Section 252(a), 2 U.S.C. sec. 902(a) (Supp. IV 1986), states:

(a) Issuance of Initial Order—
(1) In General—On September 1 following the submission of a report by the Comptroller General . . . the President . . . shall eliminate the full amount of the deficit excess . . . by issuing an order that . . .
(A) modifies or suspends the operation of each provision of Federal law that would (but for such order) require an automatic spending increase to take effect during such fiscal year, in such a manner as to prevent such increase from taking effect, or reduce such increase, in accordance with such report; and
(B) eliminates the remainder of such deficit excess . . . by sequestering new budget authority, unobligated balances, new loan guarantee commitments, new direct loan obligations, and spending authority, . . . and reducing obligation limitations, in accordance with such report.

105. 295 U.S. 602 (1935).
106. Synar v. United States, 626 F. Supp. 1374, 1398 (D.C. Cir. 1986).
107. Id.
108. Id.
109. *Synar*, 626 F. Supp. at 1399.
110. Id.
111. The lower court noted: "Under subsection 251(b)(1), the Comptroller General must specify levels of anticipated revenue and expenditure that determine the gross amount which must be sequestered; and he must specify which particular budget items are required to be reduced by the various provisions of the Act . . . and in what particular amounts. The first of these specifications requires the exercise of substantial judgment concerning present and future facts that affect the application of the law—the sort of power normally conferred upon the executive officer charged with implementing a statute. The second specification requires

an interpretation of the law enacted by Congress, similarly a power normally committed initially to the Executive under the Constitution's prescription that he "take Care that the Laws be faithfully executed" (Art. II, sec. 3). *And both of these specifications by the Comptroller General are, by the present law, made binding upon the President in the latter's application of the law.* In our view, these cannot be regarded as anything but executive powers in the constitutional sense" (*Synar*, 626 F. Supp. at 1400).

112. Id.

113. Id. at 1401 (quoting Buckley v. Valeo, 424 U.S. 1, 129 [1976]).

114. Bowsher v. Synar, 478 U.S. 714 (1985).

115. The Court gave short shrift to the various standing arguments that were advanced and, given its disposition of the separation-of-powers arguments, the majority did not have to reach the delegation questions raised by the act. See 478 U.S. at 736 n. 10.

116. See Strauss, "Formal and Functional Approaches," p. 489, who discusses the formalism on which seven justices ruled in Bowsher v. Synar.

117. 424 U.S. 1 (1976).

118. 478 U.S. at 727 (quoting *Buckley,* 424 U.S. at 129; and *Chadha,* 462 U.S. at 951).

119. 478 U.S. at 726.

120. Justice Stevens rejected this approach, which, in his view, was too dependent on "a labeling of the functions assigned to the Comptroller General as 'executive powers'" (id. at 737 [Stevens, J., concurring]). Indeed, "[o]ne reason that the exercise of legislative, executive, and judicial powers cannot be categorically distributed among three mutually exclusive branches of government is that governmental power cannot always be readily characterized with only one of those three labels" (id. at 749). Justice White, in his dissent, also rejected the majority's "distressingly formalistic view of separation of powers" (id. at 759 [White, J., dissenting]). He saw this case as one that was decided on a triviality. There was no evidence whatsoever that the comptroller general was, in fact, subservient to Congress. Moreover, the official could not be removed at will, but only for certain stated causes. As White pointed out, the majority did *not* take the position that the comptroller general must be removable at the will of president. Rather, the majority objected to the fact that the president seemingly played no role. But this too, according to Justice White, was inaccurate. Not only must Congress remove the comptroller general for cause, but by a joint resolution. A joint resolution requires passage by both houses of Congress *and* presentment to the president. This not only satisfies the *Chadha* case upon which the majority relies so heavily, but ensures that the president *does* have a role to play in the removal process.

Justice White's alternative approach to the separation-of-powers issues forms the most important aspect of his dissent, however. He takes a pragmatic, power-balancing approach, recognizing the complexity of modern government and the fact that Congress and the president can, for the most part, sort out allocation of power problems for themselves. His dissent advocates a practical, deferential approach: "The wisdom of vesting 'executive' powers in an officer removable may indeed be debatable—as may be the wisdom of the entire scheme of permitting an unelected official to revise the budget enacted by Congress—but such matters are for the most part to be worked out between the Congress and the President through the legislative process, which affords each branch ample opportunity to defend its interests" (id. at 776).

Justice White was thus willing to defer to political realities. Indeed, "[u]nder such circumstances, the role of this Court should be limited to determining whether the Act so alters the balance of authority among the branches of government as to pose a genuine threat to the basic division between the lawmaking power and the power to execute the law" (id.). Justice White saw no such threat in this case and viewed the majority's concern with removal as being "of minimal practical significance and . . . no substantial threat to the basic scheme of separation of powers" (id. at 759).

Justice Blackmun also dissented, agreeing with Justice White that it was unrealistic to assume that the comptroller general was subservient to Congress. On the other hand, he agreed with the majority to the extent that he believed "an attempt by Congress to participate *directly* in the removal of an executive officer . . . might well violate the principle of separation of powers by assuming for Congress part of the President's constitutional responsibility to carry out the laws" (id. at 777). Justice Blackmun, however, concluded that the court need not decide that question because the plaintiffs were not entitled to the relief they sought.

121. See Strauss, "Formal and Functional Approaches," p. 489.

122. As the majority noted: "The statutes establishing independent agencies typically specify either that the agency members are removable by the President for specified causes, . . . or else do not specify a removal procedure. . . . This case involves nothing like these statutes, but rather a statute that provides for direct Congressional involvement over the decision to remove the Comptroller General" (478 U.S. at 725 n. 4).

123. Pub. L. No. 95–521, tit. VI, 92 Stat. 1867–75 (codified as amended at 28 U.S.C. sec. 591–98 [Supp. 1987]).

124. The act directs the Chief Justice to assign three judges to a special division of the United State Court of Appeals for the District of Columbia Circuit ("Special Court") created for the purpose of appointing an independent counsel (28 U.S.C. sec. 49). When the attorney general receives information that persons subject to the act have violated a federal criminal law other than a petty offense, he or she must investigate the matter within ninety days (28 U.S.C. sec. 592[a][1]). If the attorney general finds that reasonable grounds exist for further investigation or prosecution, he or she must then apply to the Special Court for the appointment of an independent counsel and must provide sufficient information to assist in selecting the independent counsel and in defining the independent counsel's prosecutorial jurisdiction (28 U.S.C. sec. 592[c][1], 592[d]). The Special Court must then appoint the independent counsel and define his or her jurisdiction.

125. Upon removal, the attorney general must report the reasons for the decision to the Special Court and to Congress 28 U.S.C. sec. 596[a][1], [2]). The independent counsel may seek judicial review of this decision (28 U.S.C. sec. 596[a][3]).

126. 108 S. Ct. at 2626 (Scalia, J., dissenting).

127. 108 S. Ct. at 2616.

128. Id. (quoting 28 U.S.C. sec. 596[a][3]).

129. Id. at 2627 (Scalia, J., dissenting).

130. Id. at 2619.

131. Id. at 2629 (Scalia, J., dissenting).

132. As Justice Scalia vigorously argued in dissent: "What are the standards to determine how the balance is to be struck, that is, how much removal of presidential power is too much? . . . The most amazing feature of the Court's opinion is that it does not even purport to give an answer. It simply *announces*, with no analysis, that the ability to control the decision whether to investigate and prosecute the President's closest advisors, and indeed the President himself, is not "so central to the functioning of the Executive Branch" as to be constitutionally required to be within the President's control. Apparently this is so because we say it is so. Having abandoned as the basis for our decision-making the text of Article II that "the executive Power" must be vested in the President, the Court does not even attempt to craft a *substitute* criterion. . . . Evidently the governing standard is to be what might be called the unfettered wisdom of a majority of this Court, revealed to an obedient people on a case-by-case basis" (id. at 2629–30).

133. Id. at 2620.

134. See id. at 2620–21.

135. Only Justice Scalia dissented. Justice Kennedy did not sit.

136. See A. E. Kahn, "The Special-Prosecutor Stakes," *New York Times*, May 9, 1988, p. A19. See also Stuart Taylor, "Rehnquist's Court: Tuning Out the White House," *New York Times Magazine*, September 11, 1988, p. 38.

137. But see Bowsher v. Synar, 478 U.S. 714, 771 (1986) (White, J., dissenting) (noting that the executive had a role to play when it came to possibly vetoing Congress's joint resolution to remove).

138. U.S. Constitution, Art. 2, sec. 2, cl. 2, specifically provides for the appointment of inferior officers by "Courts of law."

139. Pub. L. No. 95–521, tit. VI, 92 Stat. 1872 (codified at 28 U.S.C. sec. 596 [1982]).

140. Of course, a decision to remove by the executive branch could be appealed in court, but the executive made the primary decision to propose removal of an individual.

141. Morrison v. Olson, 108 S. Ct. 2597, 2625 (1988) (Scalia, J., dissenting).

142. As Justice Scalia noted: "That is what this suit is about. Power. The allocation of power among Congress, the President and the courts in such fashion as to preserve the equilibrium the Constitution sought to establish—so that 'a gradual concentration of the several powers in the same department,' can effectively be resisted" (id. at 2623 [Scalia, J., dissenting] [citation omitted]).

143. 109 S. Ct. at 659.

144. See, for example, DeMuth and Ginsburg, "White House Review of Agency Rule-making," pp. 1080–86. For a less enthusiastic view, see T. O. McGarity, "Presidential Control of Regulatory Agency Decisionmaking," Am. U.L. Rev. 36 (1987): 443.

145. 295 U.S. 495 (1935).

146. 448 U.S. 607, 671 (1980).

147. 452 U.S. 490, 543 (1981).

148. For a recent discussion of the delegation doctrine where a number of scholars conclude that it is not a particularly realistic doctrine, see "A Symposium on Administrative Law," The Uneasy Constitutional Status of Administrative Agencies, Am. U.L. Rev. 36 (1987): 276.

149. 29 U.S.C. sec. 651–67 (1983).

150. 452 U.S. at 547.

151. Id. at 548.

152. See David Lyons, "Constitutional Interpretation and Original Meaning," Soc. Phil. and Pol. 4 (1986): 75, 93. See also William Rehnquist, "The Notion of a Living Constitution," Tex. L. Rev. 54 (1976): 693.

Tracking this originalist theme and approach, the Chevron Court also, in effect, concluded that political value choices were best supervised by the president, rather than a court.

153. Occupational Safety and Health Act of 1970, 5 U.S.C. sec. 5108, 5134, 5135, 7902; 15 U.S.C. sec. 633, 636; 18 U.S.C. sec. 1114; 29 U.S.C. sec. 553, 651–78; 42 U.S.C. sec. 3142–51; 49 U.S.C. sec. 1421 (1983).

154. The statutory language "to the extent feasible" could, for example, mean economic feasibility, technological feasibility, or administrative or political feasibility. As Justice Rehnquist notes: "We are presented with a remarkable range of interpretations of that language" (452 U.S. at 544).

155. See, for example, Lichter v. United States, 334 U.S. 742 (1948); Yakus v. United States, 321 U.S. 414 (1944); United States v. Rock Royal Co-operatives, 307 U.S. 533 (1939); Amalgamated Meat Cutters v. Connally, 337 F. Supp. 737 (D.D.C. 1971).

156. See, for example, Industrial Union Dep't, AFL-CIO v. Hodgson, 499 F.2d 467, 474 (D.C. Cir. 1974); Administrative Procedure Act, 5 U.S.C. sec. 553(c) (1983).

157. But see George Bunn, Kathleen Irwin, and F. K. Sido, "No Regulation without Representation: Would Judicial Enforcement of a Stricter Nondelegation Doctrine Limit Administrative Lawmaking?" Wis. L. Rev. 1983, no. 2: 341, 368, who argues that in Illinois and Wisconsin a strong judicial approach to delegation issues has little or no effect on legislators.

158. 462 U.S. at 959 (emphasis added).

159. 463 U.S. 29, 57 (1983).

160. But see Sierra Club v. Costle, 657 F.2d 298 (D.C. Cir. 1981). Judge Wald's opinion in that case skillfully separates that which is appropriate for agency expertise from that which is more political in nature. It is important to maintain this analytic perspective in order to keep in focus the proper roles of the agency and the court. Nevertheless, given the political momentum of a new regulatory age, the line between expert judgment and political choice can easily blur. The underlying substantive basis for an agency's action may thus elude review altogether. The technocratic rationales a court might come to expect and demand from an agency can easily give way to an acceptance of more political rationalizations of an agency's position, premised largely on the agency's power. This deference to agency power may be particularly appropriate when Congress has staked out a new area or new approach and an agency is doing its best to carry out its mandates. See also Jerry Mashaw, "Conflict and Compromise among Models of Administrative Justice," Duke L. J. 1981, no. 2: 181, who

argues among other things, that judicial rationality is very different from agency or bureaucratic rationality and may, in fact, focus on the wrong issues. But such deference to agency power can create particularly difficult problems in a deregulatory context. In a deregulatory context an agency may believe it has license to equate market means with ends in a manner arguably at odds with congressional intent. In such cases, a judicial requirement that agencies articulate their rationales clearly can protect Congress from a form of executive legislation that goes far beyond the executive's duty to take care that the laws are faithfully executed.

161. For a general discussion of some of the perspectives that come into play in a regulatory setting, particularly agency or bureaucratic rationality as contrasted with judicial rationality, see Mashaw, "Conflict and Compromise," pp. 181, 185. See also H. H. Bruff, "Legislative Formality, Administrative Rationality," *Tex. L. Rev.* 63 (1984): 207.

162. See Bruff, "Legislative Formality," pp. 233–35, who argues that the executive branch is well suited for this supervisory role.

163. Pub. L. No. 91–604, 84 Stat. 1676 (1970) (current version at 42 U.S.C. sec. 7401–7642 [1982]).

164. Clean Air Act Amendments, Pub. L. No. 95–95, 91 Stat. 685 (codified at 42 U.S.C. sec. 7401–7642 [1982]).

165. See 42 U.S.C. sec. 7502(b)(6) (requiring permits for "new or modified major stationary sources" of air pollution).

166. Id.

167. Id.

168. As the Court noted in *Chevron*, "the House Committee Report [to the 1977 Amendments] identified the economic interest as one of the 'two main purposes' of this section of the bill" (467 U.S. at 851, citing H.R. Rep. No. 294, 95th Cong., 1st sess., 1977, p. 211). However, commentators and courts have argued that Congress intended cost to be a significant factor only if the economic viability of plants would be endangered. See Stukane, "EPA's Bubble Concept," pp. 663–64, who describes the strictness of Congress's standards; Melnick, *Regulation and the Court*, pp. 96–103, who notes Congress's emphasis on the prevention of significant deterioration. See also Alabama Power Co. v. Costle, 636 F.2d 323 (D.C. Cir. 1979) (amended 1980); ASARCO, Inc. v. EPA, 578 F.2d 319 (D.C. Cir. 1978). But see J. L. Landau, "Chevron, U.S.A. v. NRDC: The Supreme Court Declines to Burst EPA's Bubble Concept," *Envtl. L.* 15 (1985): 285, 292 and n. 31: The government's use of the economic perspective in its arguments in *Chevron* thus arguably went far beyond Congress's intent.

169. 42 U.S.C. sec. 7501(3).

170. 46 Fed. Reg. 16,280, 16,281 (1981) (notice of proposed rulemaking).

171. 46 Fed. Reg. 50, 766 (1981). The United States Court of Appeals for the District of Columbia Circuit dealt with the bubble concept on various occasions. See NRDC v. Gorsuch, 685 F.2d 718 (D.C. Cir. 1982), rev'd sub nom. Chevron v. NRDC, 467 U.S. 837 (1984); Alabama Power Co. v. Costler, 636 F.2d 323 (D.C. Cir. 1982); ASARCO, Inc. v. EPA, 578 F.2d 319 (D.C. Cir. 1978).

172. 46 Fed. Reg. 50,766 (1981).

173. See S. D. Hays, "The Politics of Environmental Administration," in *The New American State*, ed. Louis Galambos (Baltimore, Md., 1987), pp. 32–33; Stukane, "EPA's Bubble Concept," p. 648.

174. See Stukane, "EPA's Bubble Concept," pp. 653–68; see also "The Supreme Court, 1983 Term—Leading Cases," *Harv. L. Rev.* 98 (1984): 87, 247. But see Landau, "Chevron U.S.A. v. NRDC," p. 285.

175. See Stukane, "EPA's Bubble Concept," p. 666, who quotes from the government briefs in Chevron v. NRDC, 467 U.S. 837 (1983).

176. Ibid. at 666–67.

177. See Alabama Power Co. v. Costle, 636 F.2d 323 (D.C. Cir. 1979) (amended 1980); ASARCO, Inc. v. EPA, 518 F.2d 319 (D.C. Cir. 1978). See also, Landau, "Chevron U.S.A. v. NRDC," pp. 307–8.

178. People disagree about this substantive point, and the Supreme Court and some commentators believe that the legislative history of the act easily accommodates the new reading the EPA has given it. The significant point here, however, is whether there was

enough ambiguity to justify closer judicial scrutiny of the agency's rule. In other words, the very difficulty that this issue presented and the ambiguity that surrounded Congress's desires on this issue should not have been reasons to defer, but reasons to look more closely at what the agency wished to do. This scrutiny was particularly necessary because of the agency's new emphasis on an economic, cost-conscious view of issues previously treated in terms of environmental values. The Court had a duty to examine these issues more fully, regardless of the wisdom of the agency's approach.

179. Stukane, "EPA's Bubble Concept," p. 669. See Melnick, *Regulation and the Court*, who discusses the absolutist qualities of the Clean Air Act at pp. 369–70.

180. See Mark Sagoff, "Economic Theory and Environmental Law," *Mich. L. Rev.* 79 (1981): 1393, 1397–98. See also Sagoff, *The Economy of the Earth* (New York, 1988), pp. 200–205; M. M. Shapiro, *Who Guards the Guardians?: Judicial Control of Administration* (Athens, Ga., 1988), pp. 91–94.

181. 450 U.S. 582 (1981).

182. 467 U.S. 837 (1984). Justices Rehnquist, Marshall, and O'Connor did not sit on this case

183. Id. at 842–43.

184. Id. at 843 n. 11.

185. Motor Vehicles Mfrs. Ass'n v. State Farm Mut. Auto. Ins. Co., 463 U.S. 29, 57 (1983) (Rehnquist, J., concurring in part and dissenting in part).

186. 467 U.S. 865–66.

187. Id. at 843.

188. See 293 U.S. 388 (1935).

189. Id. at 433–48 (Cardozo, J., dissenting).

190. See Patricia Wald, "The Sizzling Sleeper: The Use of Legislative History in Construing Statutes in the 1988–89 Term of the United States Supreme Court," *Amer. Univ. L. Rev.* 39 (1990): 277.

191. 109 S. Ct. 939 (1989).

192. Id. at 941.

193. See, for example, Green v. Bock Laundry Mach. Co., 109 S. Ct. 1981, 1994 (1989) (Scalia, J. concurring).

194. See, for example, Antonin Scalia, "Judicial Deference to Administrative Interpretations of Law," *Duke L. J.* 1989, no. 3: 511, 516.

195. Ibid., p. 517.

196. Wald, "The Sizzling Sleeper," p. 301.

197. For another critique of the reasoning in *Chevron* and its separation-of-powers implications, see Cynthia Farina, "Statutory Interpretation and the Balance of Power in the Administrative State," *Col. L. Rev.* 88 (1988): 452–528. See also 42 U.S.C. sec. 7502–8 (provisions dealing with nonattainment areas). See W. H. Rodgers, *Handbook on Environmental Law* (St. Paul, Minn., 1977), p. 273 n. 37: "Surely section 111 does not mean to tolerate a horrendously controlled new facility because of a fortuity that has led to the coincidental shutdown of 90 percent of the other capacity at a given source"; Stukane, "EPA Bubble Concept," p. 650, who explains that Congress envisioned that "every time new sources of pollution were constructed, pollution controls would be installed."

198. See, for example, UAW v. General Dynamics Land Sys. Div., 815 F.2d 1570, 1575 (D.C. Cir. 1987) ("some will find amabiguity even in a No Smoking sign").

199. 107 S. Ct. 1207 (1987); see also, NLRB v. United Food & Com'l Workers Union, 108 S. Ct. 413 (1987).

200. 107 S. Ct. at 1225.

201. The Court continues to waffle between approaches that broadly embrace *Chevron* and those that undercut it. Compare Dole v. United Steelworkers of America, 110 S. Ct. 929 (1990) (broadening *Chevron*) with Sullivan v. Everhart, 110 S. Ct. 960 (1990) (applying a stricter *Chevron* approach).

202. For a critical discussion of this phase of the Court's opinion, see Robert Anthony, "Which Agency Interpretations Should Bind Citizens and the Courts," *Yale J. Reg.* 7 (1990): 1, 31–36.

203. The ambiguities in *Chevron's* approach have begun to surface with some regularity in Supreme Court opinions.

204. See Jonathon Bloomberg, "The Chevron Legacy: Young v. Community Nutrition Institute Compounds the Confusion," *Cornell L. Rev.* 73 (1987): 113, 121, who argues that the Court carefully considered but failed to resolve the competing policy goals, one environmental and the other economic.

205. 467 U.S. at 851, citing H.R. Rep. No. 294, 95th Cong., 1st sess., 1977.

206. Id. at 851–52. The Court's discussion of the Senate Committee report was inconclusive. Noting that the Senate intended a case-by-case approach to plant additions and that its emphasis on "the net consequences of the construction or modification of a new source, as well as its impact on the overall achievement of the national standards, was not . . . addressed to the *precise* issue raised by these cases" (id. at 853). This seems to be an unduly narrow reading of the Senate's intent, aimed at authorizing the EPA's action in this case. See Stukane, "EPA Bubble Concept," p. 673, for a discussion of the Court's methods for narrowing its scope of review. See Rodgers, *Handbook*, p. 273, who questions the validity of the bubble concept under the statutory definition of "modification" and the general purpose of the statute. But see Landau, "Chevron U.S.A. v. NRDC," p. 320: "*Chevron*, taken with several other recent decisions, confirms the Court's intention to broaden systematically the deference due agency interpretations of statutes and regulations."

207. 467 U.S. at 858 (citations omitted).

208. 467 U.S. at 863.

209. Id.

210. See Thedore Lowi, *The Personal President* (Ithaca, N.Y., 1985), pp. 52–58, who discusses both the demise of the theory that politics should be separate from administration and the growth of presidential power; R. P. Nathan, *The Plot That Failed: Nixon and the Administrative Presidency* (New York, 1975), pp. 7–10, who discusses Nixon's plans to concentrate on administrative, rather than legislative, approaches to domestic policy change; J. E. Anderson, "Presidential Management of Wage-Price Policies: The Johnson and Carter Experiences," in *The Presidency and Public Policymaking*, pp. 173–214, who notes that the president has more responsibility than authority to manage the economy. Cf. American Bar Association, Commission on Law and the Economy, *Federal Regulation: Roads to Reform* (Washington, D.C., 1979), pp. 1–4, which recommends greater executive involvement.

211. See Anderson, "Presidential Management," p. 192.

212. During the environmental era Congress created some new independent commissions, such as the Occupational Health and Safety Commission within the Department of Labor and the reconstituted Federal Energy Regulatory Commission within the Department of Energy, but many of its new creations were more executive in character than the New Deal model of an independent commission. For example, the Environmental Protection Agency, established by the Reorg. Plan No. 3 of 1970, 3 C.F.R. 1072 (1966–70), reprinted in 5 U.S.C. app. at 1132 (1982), and in 84 Stat. 2086 (1970), is headed by a single administrator appointed by the president with the advice and counsel of the Senate, but who is not protected by any formal removal provisions. Similarly, the Council on Environmental Quality (CEQ), a significant source of rules and regulations, functions largely as an arm of the executive. See National Environmental Policy Act of 1969, 42 U.S.C. sec. 4342 (1982) (creating the CEQ). Moreover, much health and safety regulation is administered by the secretary of labor, a cabinet-level executive office. See, for example, the Occupational Safety and Health Act of 1970, 29 U.S.C. sec. 651–78 (1982). The Department of Energy was created in 1977 to pull together a variety of energy-related regulatory activities scattered throughout the bureaucracy. It too was primarily an executive agency, headed by a cabinet-level secretary. For a case study of how and why the agency took the form it did, see Alfred Aman, "Institutionalizing the Energy Crisis: Some Structural and Procedural Lessons," *Cornell L. Rev.* 65 (1980): 516–26.

213. That such supervisory control is generally within the Article II powers of the president is well documented. See, for example, Strauss, "The Place of Agencies in Government," p. 597, who argues that the United States Constitution conceived "the President as the unitary, politically accountable head of all law-administration"; R. J. Pierce, "The Role of Constitutional and Political Theory in Administrative Law," *Tex. L. Rev.* 64 (1985): 469, 522,

who agrees with Strauss that "the President has effective control over policymaking by independent agencies"; Strauss and Sunstein, "The Role of the President and OMB in Informal Rulemaking," pp. 206–7; DeMuth and Ginsburg, "White House Review of Agency Rulemaking," pp. 1080–88. There have also been bills proposing greater presidential control in Congress. See, for example, S. 1080, 97th Cong., 2d sess., *Cong. Rec.* 128 (1982): 5,297–5,305; ABA resolutions in *The Roads to Reform*, pp. 1–4. See ABA Report, Administrative Law Section, agenda item F (1986). See also the following in "A Symposium on Administrative Law, The Uneasy Constitutional Status of the Administrative Agencies," *Am. U.L. Rev.* 36 (1987): 276–601; Bruff, "On the Constitutional Status of the Administrative Agencies," pp. 491, 514; Diver, "Presidential Powers," pp. 519–33; and McGarity, "Presidential Control of Regulatory Decisionmaking," p. 443.

214. Some commentators argue that independent agencies should not be exempt from greater executive control. See, for example, Miller, "Independent Agencies," pp. 65–67.

215. For a discussion of the theoretical breadth of the presidential perspective, see Bruff, "Legislative Formality, Administrative Rationality."

216. See Sunstein, "Constitutionalism after the New Deal," p. 453, who argues that "[t]he President's institutional position is useful for coordinating the wide range of sometimes inconsistent legislation of the modern regulatory state . . . [because] the President is able not only to coordinate, but also to energize and to direct regulatory policy in a way that would be difficult or impossible if that policy were set individually by agency officials."

217. See Civil Aeronautics Board Sunset Act of 1984, Pub. L. No. 98–443, 98 Stat. 1703 (codified as amended in various sections of 49 U.S.C.). See also, Bus Regulating Reform Act of 1982, Pub. L. 97–861, which reduces entry restrictions in the passenger-bus industry; the Garm–St. Germain Depository Institutions Act of 1982, providing new and expanded powers for banks and other depository institutions. See generally, M. L. Weidenbaum, "Regulatory Reform under the Reagan Administration," in *The Reagan Regulatory Strategy*, ed. G. C. Eads and Michael Fix (Washington, D.C., 1984), pp. 19–21.

218. See Charles Lindblom, "The Science of 'Muddling Through,'" *Pub. Admin. Rev.* 19 (1959): 79.

219. See D. R. Mayhew, *Congress: The Electoral Connection* (New Haven, Conn., 1974), p. 17, who characterizes members of Congress as "single-minded reelection seekers"; R. H. Davidson, "Subcommittee Government: New Channels for Policy Making," in *The New Congress*, ed. T. E. Mann and N. J. Ornstein (Washington, D.C., 1981), p. 105. Davidson asserts that careerism in both houses, marked by low turnover, had a "tendency that accentuated certain committees' membership bias and perpetuated their decision-making premises and norms"; See also M. P. Fiorina, *Congress: Keystone of the Washington Establishment* (New Haven, Conn., 1977), pp. 5–14, who writes "the only reliable way to achieve policy change in Congress is to change Congressman." As Senator Saxbee has noted: "Congress has declined into a battle for individual survival. Each of the Congressmen and each of the Senators has the attitude: 'I've got to look out for myself.' If you remember the old best advice you ever had in the army, it wound up with: 'Never volunteer.' This applies to Congress, and so we have very few volunteers. Most of them are willing only to follow those things that will protect them and give them the coloration which allows them to blend into their respective districts or their respective states. If you don't stick your neck out, you don't get it chopped off." (Quoted in Mayhew, *Congress: The Electoral Connection*, p. 81.)

220. Mayhew, *Congress: The Electoral Connection*, p. 81.

221. For an interesting, journalistic account of the life of a congressman, see Fred Barnes, "The Unbearable Lightness of Being a Congressman," *The New Republic*, February 15, 1988, p. 18. It highlights the difficulty of being substantive and surviving in Congress. Of course, given the time constraints of legislators, their ability to take a broader, more public-interest view of issues is a far more complex problem. For a classic and rich study, see R. F. Fenno, Jr., *Home Style: House Members in Their Districts* (Boston, 1978). See also Fenno, *Congressmen in Committees* (Boston, 1973).

It is also interesting to note the increasing fragmentation in the House that results from the proliferation of subcommittees and subcommittee chairmen. See R. H. Davidson and W. J. Oleszek, *Congress and Its Members*, 2d ed. (Washington, D.C., 1985), p. 232, who maintain that "proliferating committees and fragmented jurisdictions inhibit Congress's ability to advance comprehensive responses to problems"; T. R. Dye and L. H. Zeigler, *The Irony of Democracy*, 6th ed. (Monterey, Calif., 1984), p. 363, who theorize that the committee system places effective control over legislation in the hands of a few; Davidson, "Subcommittee Government," p. 105, who describes in detail the historical proliferation of committee assignments and asserting that the factionalism in Congress buttresses the committee system.

222. See Louis Galambos, "By Way of Introduction," in his *The New American State: Bureaucracies and Policies Since World War II* (Baltimore, Md., 1987), pp. 19–20: "Stasis, not hegemony, is the central problem of the modern administrative state in this country."

An excellent example of an area in which comprehensive change is needed but Congress seems unable or unwilling to effect that change is banking. See A. F. Burns, *The Ongoing Revolution in American Banking* (Washington, D.C., 1988), pp. 22–23, who suggests that continuing the trend of deregulation in the banking industry that began in 1970 may not be satisfactory today because of rapid technology and financial innovation. See also Donald Langevoort, "Statutory Obsolescence and the Judicial Process: The Revisionist Roles of the Courts in Federal Banking Regulation," *Mich. L. Rev.* 85 (1987): 672.

223. See, for example, J. M. Buchanan and Gordon Tullock, *The Calculus of Consent* (Ann Arbor, Mich., 1962). The insights of this approach have become increasingly useful for a number of modern theorists. See M. T. Hayes, *Lobbyists and Legislators: A Theory of Political Markets* (New Brunswick, N.J., 1981), who posits a transactional theory to explain how interest-group system works); J. Q. Wilson, *The Politics of Regulation* (New York, 1980); Gary Becker, "A Theory of Competition among Pressure Groups for Political Influence," *Q. J.Econ.* 98 (1983): 371. For a critique of the application of public-choice insights to the legislative process, see D. A. Farber and P. P. Frickey, "The Jurisprudence of Public Choice," *Tex. L. Rev.* 65 (1987): 873; Mark Kelman, "On Democracy-Bashing: A Skeptical Look at the Theoretical and 'Empirical' Practice of the Public Choice Movement," *Va. L. Rev.* 74 (1988): 199. See also R. B. Ripley, *Congress: Process and Policy*, 3d ed. (New York, 1983).

224. See, for example, Farber and Frickey, "The Jurisprudence of Public Choice," pp. 926–27, who criticizes public choice proponents as cynics who greatly exaggerate the decline of the public interest. The authors assert "[a]lthough beleaguered, the public interest remains a significant factor in politics," and they argue that courts can foster the legislature's ability to make policy and thereby strengthen the democratic process; Kelman, "On Democracy Bashing," p. 270, who criticizes public choice scholars as cynics preoccupied with economic considerations and argues that political action "is the creation of communities, shared references, commonsensical stories that help shape and order an amorphous world."

225. For a republican conceptualization of the legislative process, see C. R. Sunstein, "Interest Groups in American Public Law," *Stan. L. Rev.* 38 (1985): 29; see also Bruce Ackerman, "The Storrs Lecture: Discovering the Constitution," *Yale L. J.* 93 (1984): 1013–72; F. I. Michelman, "The Supreme Court, 1985 Term—Forward: Traces of Self-Government," *Harv. L. Rev.* 100 (1986): 4.

226. See Ripley, *Congress*, who argues *inter alia*, that while there may be a great deal of fragmentation in Congress, policy making is only possible when these fragmented views are integrated. See also B. A. Ackerman, *Reconstructing American Law* (Cambridge, Mass., 1984), pp. 39–40; Hayes, *Lobbyists and Legislators*; K. A. Shepsle and B. R. Weingast, "Political Solutions to Market Problems," *Am. Pol. Sci. Rev.* 78 (1984): 417.

227. See Hedrick Smith, *The Power Game* (New York, 1988), p. 711. For a case study of the role that crisis plays in congressional legislation, see Alfred Aman, "Institutionalizing the Energy Crisis: Some Structural and Procedural Lessons," *Cornell L. Rev.* 65 (1980): 491. But see J. H. Birnbaum and A. S. Murray, *Showdown at Gucci Gulf* (New York, 1987), who relate the saga of congressional adoption of the Tax Reform Act of 1986).

228. The unicameral legislative veto, a means by which this could have occurred, was struck down in *INS v. Chadha*, 462 U.S. 919 (1983).

229. See, for example, Executive Order No. 12,291, 3 C.F.R. 127 (1981), reprinted in 5 U.S.C. sec. 601 (1982) (imposing cost benefit analysis); Executive Order No. 12,248 (mandating regulatory planning). For a more current example see Executive Order No. 12,630, 53 Fed. Reg. 8859 (1988). Entitled *Governmental Actions and Interference with Constitu-*

tionally Protected Rights, this order suggests a constitutional approach to regulatory takings that arguably is more stringent than what current case law would allow. It is another means of encouraging agencies to be very wary of extending their regulatory authority. Indeed, it is interesting to note that before this order was issued, Congress tried but failed to pass a reformed Administrative Procedure Act that would have added similar cost-benefit analysis provisions. Though Congress failed to pass these reforms, they nevertheless became the centerpiece of the Reagan administration through the issuance of Executive Order No. 12,291.

230. See, for example, Heckler v. Chaney, 470 U.S. 821 (1985); UAW v. Brock, 783 F.2d 237 (D.C. Cir. 1986). See C. R. Sunstein, "Reviewing Agency Inaction after Heckler v. Chaney," *U. Chi. L. Rev.* 52 (1985): 653, who advocates judicial review of agency inaction; P. M. Wald, "Contributions of the D.C. Circuit to Administrative Law," *Admin. L. Rev.* 40 (1988): 507, 522, who describes recent years as an era of "nonregulation" in which agencies have failed to enforce existing rules or to promulgate rules where the statute appears to contemplate rules.

231. See, for example, Chevron v. NRDC, 467 U.S. 837 (1984) (bubble approach).

232. See, for example, Budget Reconciliation Act, Pub. L. No. 99–272, 100 Stat. 82 (codified as amended in scattered sections of 7 U.S.C.).

233. See, for example, Tax Reform Act of 1986, 26 U.S.C. sec. 1 (Supp. IV 1986).

234. See Motor Vehicles Mfrs. Ass'n v. State Farm Mut. Auto. Ins. Co., 463 U.S. 29 (1983).

235. From the song in the musical *Chess*, entitled "The American and Florence/Nobody's Side." See also E. F. Roberts, "Re-Regulation, The Global Environment and Ignorance Equals Pessimism: A Tory Perspective," *Wash. & Lee L. Rev.* 45 (1988): 1345, 1354: "With luck, this being an [*sic*] universe governed by chance, a new faith compatible with the global environment and consonant with democratic values will emerge. More likely, somewhere in the sands of the desert, the rough beast will have found its hour come round at last."

236. For an analysis of "thin" and "strong" democracy in modern politics, see B. R. Barber, *Strong Democracy* (Berkeley and Los Angeles, 1984).

CHAPTER 4 GLOBAL REGULATION

1. See Richard Rosecrance, *The Rise of the Trading State: Commerce and Conquest in the Modern World* (New York, 1986).

2. See World Commission on Environment and Development (WCED), *Our Common Future* (New York, 1987), pp. 1–23.

3. See Jutta Brunnee, *Acid Rain and Ozone Layer Depletion: International Law and Regulation* (Dobbs Ferry, N.Y., 1988), pp. 112–21, who discusses a variety of liability questions.

4. See Philippe Sands, ed., *Chernobyl: Law and Communication; Transboundary Nuclear Air Pollution—The Legal Materials* (Cambridge, 1988); Peter Cameron, Leigh Hancher, and Wolfgang Kuhn, ed., *Nuclear Energy Law after Chernobyl* (Boston, 1988).

5. See, for example, Convention on Long-Range Transboundary Air Pollution, No. 13, 1979, T.I.A.S. No. 10541, reprinted in *I.L.M.* 18 (1979): 1442 (hereafter called the 1979 Convention); Protocol to the 1979 Convention on the Reduction of Sulphur Emissions or Their Transboundary Fluxes by at Least 30 Per Cent, July 8, 1985, reprinted in *I.L.M.* 27 (1988): 698; Protocol to the 1979 Convention on the Control of Emissions of Nitrogen Oxides or Their Transboundary Fluxes, reprinted in *I.L.M.* 28 (1989): 212.

6. For an excellent history of this term, see Carl Fleischer, "The International Concern for the Environment: The Concept of Common Heritage," in *Trends in Environmental Policy and Law*, ed. Michael Bothe (Gland, Switzerland, 1980), pp. 321–39.

7. Montreal Protocol on Substances That Deplete the Ozone Layer, opened for signature September 16, 1987, reprinted in *I.L.M.* 26 (1987): 1550. As of 1990, fifty-eight nations plus the European Community had ratified or acceded to the protocol.

8. U.N. Doc. UNEP/1 G.53/5/Rev. 1, reprinted in *I.L.M.* 26 (1987): 1529.

9. Ibid.

10. Montreal Protocol, Article 2.

11. Ibid.

12. Annex 1 to Montreal Protocol, "Adjustments to the Montreal Protocol on Substances That Deplete the Ozone Layer," Art. 2A (CFCs).

13. See Proceedings of a Joint Symposium by the Board on Atmospheric Sciences and Climate and the Committee on Global Change, and Resources Natural Council, *Ozone Depletion, Greenhouse Gases, and Climate Change* (Washington, D.C., 1989) (hereafter cited as Joint Symposium); see Daniel Albritton, "Stratospheric Ozone Depletion: Global Processes," in Joint Symposium, pp. 10–18.

14. Ibid.

15. R. T. Watson, "Stratospheric Ozone Depletion: Antarctic Processes," in Joint Symposium, pp. 19–32.

16. Irving Mintzer, "Cooling Down a Warming World," *International Environmental Affairs* 1 (1989): 12, 13.

17. See, for example, D. H. Ogden, "The Montreal Protocol: Confronting the Threat to Earth's Ozone Layer," *Washington L. Rev.* 63 (1988): 997, 1017.

18. Mintzer, "Cooling Down a Warming World," p. 24.

19. See "United Nations Environment Programme, Report of the Second Meeting of the Parties to the Montreal Protocol on Substances That Deplete the Ozone Layer," London, June 27–29, 1990 (hereafter cited as "Report of the Second Meeting").

20. See V. P. Nanda, *Stratospheric Ozone Depletion: A Challenge for International Environmental Law and Policy, Michigan Journal of International Law* 10 (1989): 482, 484.

21. Ibid., pp. 488–90.

22. See Richard Benedick, *Ozone Diplomacy—New Directions in Safeguarding the Planet* (Cambridge, Mass., 1991), p. 10. This book provides an excellent, comprehensive, and insightful account of the origins and development of the Montreal Protocol and the negotiating positions of the various parties involved. This chapter relies considerably on the descriptive accounts of the negotiations leading up to the actual protocol and its 1990 amendments.

23. Ibid.

24. M. J. Molina and F. S. Rowland, "Stratospheric Sink for Chlorofluoromethanes: Chlorine Atomic Catalyzed Destruction of Ozone," *Nature* 249 (June 28, 1974): 810–812.

25. Benedick, *Ozone Diplomacy*, pp. 11-12.

26. World Meteorological Organization, "Atmospheric Ozone 1985: Assessment of Our Understanding of the Processes Controlling Its Present Distribution and Change" (Geneva, 1986).

27. Benedick, *Ozone Diplomacy*, p. 14.

28. Ibid., pp. 23–24.

29. Clean Air Act, 42 U.S.C. sec. 7457(b).

30. See Duane Chapman, "Environmental Standards and International Trade in Automobiles and Copper: The Case for a Social Tariff," working paper in Agricultural Economics, Cornell University (1989), pp. 1–3.

31. See John Holusha, "The Next Refrigerator May Take a Step Back," *New York Times*, March 4, 1989, p. 37.

32. Benedick, *Ozone Diplomacy*, p. 31.

33. Ibid., p. 33.

34. Ibid.

35. See David Doniger, "Politics of the Ozone Layer," *Issues in Science and Technology* 4 (1988): 86, 87.

36. Frederick Kirgis, "The United States Commitment to the Norms of the United Nations and Its Related Agencies," *Transnational Law and Contemporary Problems* 1 (1991): 125, 136.

37. Military and Paramilitary Activities in and against Nicaragua (Nicar. v. U.S.), 1986 I.C.J. 14 (Merits Judgment of June 27), discussed in Kirgis, "The United States Commitment to the United Nations," pp. 139–40.

38. Frederick Kirgis, "The United States Approach To Public Law," paper delivered on British Lecture Tour, April-May 1991, pp. 3–4.

39. Ibid. p. 6.
40. See NRDC v. Thomas and Alliance for Responsible CFC Policy, Civ. Action No. 84–3587 (D.C.D.C.), filed May 17, 1988.
41. See David Doniger, "Politics of the Ozone Layer," p. 87.
42. Montreal Protocol, Art. 2(1).
43. Ibid., Art. 5(2).
44. See "Report of the Second Meeting," pp. 12–15. The goal of the 1990 amendments, to ban all CFCs by the year 2000, results in the removal of a key inequity between developing and developed signatories that existed in the initial version despite its attempt to include a developing country perspective. For example, the Montreal Protocol placed a permanent cap of 0.3 kg per capita as the maximum developing country usage level of the controlled substances identified. This would have permanently locked developing countries into a usage level well below that of the developed world. In addition, the 1990 amendments are somewhat more specific regarding technology transfers. They state that the parties must establish a means of providing financial and technical cooperation to developing countries and that this mechanism will "meet all agreed incremental costs of such Parties in order to enable their compliance with the control measures of the Protocol" ("Report of the Second Meeting," Art. 10, par. 1, June 1990). To achieve this goal a multilateral fund was created to be funded by developed nations. The development of an environmental fund to help with these costs is particularly significant ("Report of the Second Meeting," Annex 3).
45. Art. 6, p. 1556. This reassessment provision had a good deal to do with many of the new amendments that were proposed and adopted in June 1990.
46. Benedick, *Ozone Diplomacy*, pp. 124–25.
47. Annex 1 to Montreal Protocol, "Adjustments to the Montreal Protocol on Substances That Deplete the Ozone Layer," Art. 2A (CFCs), Art. 2B (Halons); Annex 2 to Montreal Protocol, "Amendment to the Montreal Protocol on Substances That Deplete the Ozone Layer," Art. 2D (carbon tetrachloride), Art. 2E (methyl chloroform).
48. Ibid., Art. 2C (other fully halogenated CFCs).
49. Benedick, *Ozone Diplomacy*, pp. 90–91.
50. Art. 9(2) and (3).
51. The London Amendments extend this ban to parties that fail to comply with Art. 4.
52. Montreal Protocol, Art. 4, *I.L.M.* 26, p. 1554.
53. Art. 4(4), p. 1555.
54. Ibid., p. 1555.
55. Benedick, *Ozone Diplomacy*, pp. 104–5.
56. Annex 2 to Montreal Protocol, "Amendment to the Montreal Protocol on Substances That Deplete the Ozone Layer," Art. 4 (trade with nonparties).
57. Art. 5(1).
58. Ibid.
59. Annex 2 to Montreal Protocol, "Amendment to the Montreal Protocol on Substances That Deplete the Ozone Layer," Art. 10 (financial mechanism).
60. Ibid., Art. 10A(a) (transfer of technology).
61. Benedick, *Ozone Diplomacy*, pp. 188–96.

Table of Cases

Index

Library of Congress Cataloging-in-Publication Data
Aman, Alfred C., Jr.
    Administrative law in a global era / Alfred C. Aman, Jr.
        p.   cm.
    Includes bibliographical references (p.   ) and index.
    ISBN 0-8014-2372-4 (cloth : alkaline paper)
    1. Administrative law—United States.   2. Administrative agencies—
United States. 3. Deregulation—United States.   4. Judicial
review—United States.   5. Executive power—United States.
6. United States—Politics and government—1981–1989.   I. Title.
KF5407.A84   1992
342.73'06—dc20
[347.3026]   91-33216